THE
ROAD
TO PEARL
HARBOR

THE
ROAD
TO PEARL
HARBOR

GREAT POWER WAR IN
ASIA AND THE PACIFIC

EDITED BY JOHN H. MAURER AND ERIK GOLDSTEIN

NAVAL INSTITUTE PRESS

ANNAPOLIS, MARYLAND

Naval Institute Press
291 Wood Road
Annapolis, MD 21402

Library of Congress Cataloging-in-Publication Data

Names: Maurer, John H., editor. | Goldstein, Erik, editor.
Title: The road to Pearl Harbor : great power war in Asia and the Pacific / edited by John H Maurer, and Erik Goldstein.
Other titles: Great power war in Asia and the Pacific
Description: Annapolis, Maryland : Naval Institute Press, [2022] | Includes bibliographical references and index.
Identifiers: LCCN 2022014654 (print) | LCCN 2022014655 (ebook) | ISBN 9781682477700 (hardback) | ISBN 9781682477694 (ebook)
Subjects: LCSH: World War, 1939-1945--Causes. | Great powers--Foreign relations--20th century. | Pacific Area--Foreign relations--20th century. | Japan--Foreign relations--1912-1945. | China--Foreign relations--1912-1949. | United States--Foreign relations--1913-1921. | United States--Foreign relations--1933-1945. | Great Britain--Foreign relations--1910-1936. | Conference on the Limitation of Armament (1921-1922 : Washington, D.C.) | BISAC: HISTORY / Wars & Conflicts / World War II / General | HISTORY / Military / United States
Classification: LCC D741 .R528 2022 (print) | LCC D741 (ebook) | DDC 940.53/11--dc23/eng/20220408
LC record available at https://lccn.loc.gov/2022014654
LC ebook record available at https://lccn.loc.gov/2022014655

30 29 28 27 26 25 24 23 22   9 8 7 6 5 4 3 2 1
First printing

CONTENTS

ACKNOWLEDGMENTS

WE ARE DEEPLY GRATEFUL TO THE FOREIGN POLICY RESEARCH Institute for sponsoring and supporting this book. Since the Institute's founding, it has stood for open discussion and for a principled realism in foreign policy and grand strategy. When serving as the Institute's president, Alan Luxenberg was an enthusiastic backer of the project. His firm belief about the importance of studying history to gain perspective on today's foreign policy and strategy dilemmas drove the project forward. The Institute's current President Carol "Rollie" Flynn also shared our enthusiasm for publishing this book. Her advice and support brought the book to completion. Roger Hertog gave his support to this project and got it off the ground. Roger is a longstanding friend of those who value history as a guiding light that provides clarity in understanding the pressing domestic and international problems of our times. Alan, Rollie, and Roger know that mature study and reflection on the past serves as a sure guide to a better future. At the Naval Institute Press, we want to thank Adam Kane, Glenn Griffith, Jack Russell, Robin Noonan, and Ashley Baird for taking on the book and shepherding it through to publication. We appreciate the careful editing given the manuscript by Drew Bryan. Finally, to Grant, Peter, Rich, Walter, and Toshi, we appreciate the outstanding contribution that you made in writing chapters for the book.

INTRODUCTION

GREAT POWER WAR in ASIA

Why Pearl Harbor?

John H. Maurer and Erik Goldstein

"REMEMBER PEARL HARBOR!" THAT WAS THE RALLYING CRY FOR the American people during the Second World War. It has been eighty years since imperial Japan attacked the United States on December 7, 1941, "a date which will live in infamy," in the words of President Franklin D. Roosevelt in his famous speech to the Congress asking for a declaration of war. The American people, government, and armed forces found themselves caught up in a desperate global struggle from which there could be no turning back. The ordeal of waging a world war transformed the United States into a global superpower. From that day to the present, American power and purpose have played a leading role in shaping the international order.

This volume of essays looks back on the period between the two world wars and examines why the struggle for mastery in Asia resulted in a horrific conflict that cost the lives of millions. Our approach to examining why war occurred has been to underscore the contingent nature of history by

1

highlighting the decisions made by leaders who directed the actions of the great powers. These leaders include David Lloyd George, Chiang Kai-shek, Franklin D. Roosevelt, Winston Churchill, and the uniformed leadership of the Japanese navy. We analyze the menu of foreign policy and strategy choices open to these leaders and explain why the steps they took led to war. In highlighting the role played by these central figures in examining the path to war, we pay close attention to the domestic political and international settings in which they operated. Their internal and external surroundings both provided opportunities for action as well as constrained their policy menu of choice to act creatively.

The outcome of their actions, a great power hegemonic war ranging across Asia and the Pacific, was not inevitable. An alternative prospect existed when in November 1921, statesmen from around the world gathered in Washington to arrest an arms race in naval weaponry and to settle outstanding disputes threatening the peace of Asia. The Washington Conference proved dramatic. The American secretary of state, Charles Evan Hughes, stunned the conference and captured the attention of public opinion around the world in his opening speech, which called for an immediate stop to the naval arms race in the construction of capital ships—that is, large surface warships, battleships, and battle cruisers—that emerged after the First World War. Hughes' highly publicized diplomatic initiative spurred the statesmen in Washington to achieve what had seemed impossible: an arms control agreement that halted construction of the latest, most powerful generation of capital ships. This outcome required that political leaders in Britain, Japan, and the United States agree to overrule their naval advisors, who deemed the acquisition of capital ships to be an urgent strategic necessity. In addition, the negotiations established a treaty framework that promoted the security of the great powers in Asia and the Pacific. At the time, the treaties hammered out in Washington were heralded as a triumph of diplomacy and enlightened statecraft. It is difficult to disagree with that judgment. At the Washington Conference, Britain and the United States took the lead in building a system for international cooperation and security in Asia. Japan's leaders, too, partnered with this American and British initiative that promised the prospect of enduring peace.

The success in Washington, in bringing about an arms control agreement and constructing a framework for international cooperation in Asia, owed much to the actions of Prime Minister David Lloyd George of Great Britain. The first chapter of this volume, by Erik Goldstein, examines Lloyd George's statecraft. At the end of the First World War, great power rivalries threatened Britain's standing as the leading power in Asia. The war to end all wars had spawned new struggles for power. Lloyd George wanted to avert these rivalries and promote the security of the British Empire. He worked hard to bring about an arms control agreement to prevent the construction of capital ships. Not only did he see the naval arms race as economically wasteful, but he also feared that a dramatic buildup of the world's navies might prove a precursor to another great war, much as the competition in warship construction between Britain and Germany had preceded the First World War. Lloyd George also wanted a settlement in the Pacific so he could work to pacify the region and bring about recovery from war in Europe. Britain's global empire required that Lloyd George connect and promote British security east of the Suez as well as closer to home.

Goldstein explains how Lloyd George paved the way for the successful conclusion of the Washington Conference by his persistence in advocating diplomatic arrangements with Japan and the United States to curb the naval arms race and to settle problems that heralded conflict in Asia. It is ironic that despite Lloyd George's efforts to bring about these negotiations, he did not attend the conference in Washington. Instead, Britain's elder statesman Arthur Balfour led the British delegation in Washington and won accolades for working with Charles Evans Hughes to achieve a signal success of constructing a security framework for peace in the Pacific. The treaty system erected in Washington provided an alternative to arms races and territorial disputes that threatened a return to war as a way to determine Asia's future. Goldstein shows that cooperation between Britain and the United States was key to building a liberal international order in the aftermath of the Great War, with the object of preventing another great power war.

Alas, the treaties signed at Washington did not endure. Within a decade, a return to great power competition mocked the hopes for peace and security in Asia that had motivated the statesmen who had assembled in

Washington. Japan's rulers, intent upon expanding and imposing their imperial domination on East Asia, overturned the treaties. The aggression of the
Japanese army on the mainland of Asia showed the scant regard with which
Japan's warlords held the sanctity of international treaties designed to avoid
confrontation. Japan's drive for hegemony in Asia would provoke a life-
and-death struggle with Nationalist China. Meanwhile, American protests
of Japanese treaty violations proved unavailing because the United States
lacked the will and the naval power to confront Japan's aggression during
the 1930s. In overthrowing the Washington treaty system, Japan's military
put their country on a collision course with Britain and the United States.

The arms control regime established at Washington also collapsed as
the leaders of the Imperial Japanese Navy raced to build the latest generation of capital ships and naval weaponry to wage war against the United
States. Japan's admirals sought nothing less than to win naval mastery in
the Pacific and, hence, stand as Asia's hegemon. In the ensuing arms race,
Britain and the United States fell behind Japan in recapitalizing their navies,
thereby ceding command of the western Pacific to the Japanese navy at the
outbreak of fighting in December 1941. A mere twenty years had elapsed
between the opening fanfare inaugurating the Washington Conference and
the opening shots fired by Japanese aircraft attacking forward-deployed
American and British naval forces in the Pacific. What an irony that the
capital ships, regulated by the arms control regime negotiated at the Washington Conference, would become the main targets sunk in Pearl Harbor
and the South China Sea by Japanese aircraft at the war's beginning.

In this volume's second chapter, Peter Mauch examines the political
and strategic calculations and actions of Japanese naval leaders. The Washington Conference had provided Japan with a dominant strategic position
in the western Pacific. At Washington, Britain and the United States agreed
not to build up fortified bases in the western Pacific. The closest major
bases from which the American and British navies could securely operate
were Pearl Harbor and Singapore. Hong Kong and the Philippines were vulnerable to capture by Japan. In addition, the ratios in fleet strength established by treaty at Washington limited the American and British navies in
relation to Japan's. While the arms control treaty fashioned at Washington
limited Japan's capital ship strength to 60 percent of that of Britain and the

United States, this ratio actually gave the Japanese navy command of the waters of East Asia. Neither Britain nor the United States possessed the naval strength—even with a superior ratio in warships—to project their power across the Pacific without first building much more powerful navies. As the Second World War would show, only in 1944—four years after the United States embarked on a major buildup in warship strength—would American naval power prove able to wrest control of the western Pacific from the Imperial Japanese Navy.

Mauch's examination of Japanese naval thinking points up the hostility displayed by some of Japan's leading admirals toward the provisions of the Washington Conference. These opponents of arms control wanted a much stronger navy to fight the United States in the coming clash of civilizations they viewed as inevitable. The demands of the admirals for a much larger navy meant a repudiation of the Washington Conference. To carry out their plans to acquire the forces to fight the United States, the Japanese navy's leadership undertook a public relations campaign to condition the Japanese people to prepare for a coming trial of strength. Building a larger navy meant rejecting a foreign policy of cooperation with Britain and the United States. The Japanese navy's leaders portrayed Britain and the United States as arrogant overlords determined to deny Japan's ambition to become Asia's hegemon.

In addition to the breakdown of arms control, the Washington treaties failed in their endeavor to prevent conflict between China and Japan. During the 1920s, the rise of Chinese nationalism augured a revival of China's power and standing in Asia. The third chapter of this volume, by Grant Rhode, explores the rise of Chiang Kai-shek and his efforts to impose order in a failed state that resulted from revolution and the end of imperial rule. Chiang's successes in consolidating power in China over rival claimants, although far from complete, frightened Japan's leaders. In particular, the Japanese army's leadership, already fearful of the growing military power of the Soviet Union in the Far East, saw a renewal of Chinese power as threatening Japan's position on the Asian mainland. In earlier wars, Japan had defeated imperial China in 1894–1895 and Russia in 1904–1905 to wrest a foothold on the mainland in northeast Asia. What Japan had won in war now appeared jeopardized by the growth of Chinese and Soviet Russian power. In 1931, the Japanese army sought to expand and secure Japan's position on the mainland by occupying Manchuria. The Japanese leaders' resort to force in confronting China brought on a brutal war between the two giants of Asia that would escalate into war with Britain and the United States. In his chapter, Richard Frank rightly observes that Japan's rapacious treatment of China made a mockery of Japanese claims of fighting to liberate Asia from Western dominance. Japan was fighting to impose its hegemony on the peoples of Asia.

Rhode examines the difficult political and strategic position that confronted Chiang. Even as conflict with Japan loomed before him, Chiang needed to secure his position within China against internal enemies, the most dangerous of which was the communist movement led by Mao Zedong. Chiang might well have finished off Mao as an opponent if war with Japan had not occurred. As leader of a newly assertive nationalist movement, Chiang refused to back down from confrontation and a major war with Japan, even though Mao and the communists remained a danger to win out in an internal contest to rule within China. Japan's war on China tilted the balance of forces within China and contributed to Mao's victory over Chiang in the Chinese civil war. Rhode examines Chiang's strategic predicament of having to face these internal and external adversaries who were determined to defeat his bid to rule China. Chiang's legacy in today's China is also explored by Rhode. Chiang is nowadays recognized as an ardent Chinese nationalist on both sides of the Taiwan Straits.

Japan's rulers found in Chiang's China a much more formidable adversary than what they had anticipated. Rhode examines Chiang's political aims, strategy, and conduct of the war with Japan. Chiang's will to fight against the invader and his refusal to negotiate led to a protracted war on the Asian mainland that would impose an immense drain on Japanese lives and resources. By the time of Pearl Harbor, China and Japan had been engaged in gruesome fighting for more than four years. Rhode and Richard Frank, in their chapters, highlight the savagery and immense losses suffered by China in fighting Japan. By the end of 1941, Chiang's forces were in grave danger of defeat if Britain and the United States could not pressure Japan's leaders to accept a negotiated settlement to cease fighting and withdraw from China. Fearful of a collapse of Chinese resistance, Britain and the United States increased the economic pressure on Japan and undertook a buildup of their armed forces in the Pacific. This increased pressure did not induce Japan's rulers to withdraw from the war against Chiang. To Japanese leaders, a negotiated end to the fighting in China meant to admit defeat and concede victory to the power of Chinese nationalist resistance. Chiang's war thus provided impetus to the confrontation that would lead Japan to attack Britain and the United States. Richard Frank underscores the importance of China in the breakdown of the final negotiations and the Japanese attack on the British Empire and the United States.

In addition to the contest with China, Japan's international alignment with Nazi Germany pointed toward war with Britain and the United States. The three chapters by John Maurer, Walter McDougall, and Richard Frank underscore the close connection between the fighting taking place in Asia and Europe during the Second World War. The Pacific War formed part of a larger struggle for world power involving Britain and the United States against Hitler's Germany. The Axis between Nazi Germany and imperial Japan threatened the global balance of power. Germany's military successes in Europe provided an opportunity for Japan to pursue an expansionist foreign policy agenda in Asia. The crushing defeat of France in 1940 was pivotal in weakening the strategic position of the European empires in Southeast Asia. The British, Dutch, and French colonial empires, unable to mount an effective defense, were vulnerable to seizure by Japan. By taking the highly coveted resources of the region, Japan would be strengthened in fighting its wars to achieve hegemony in Asia. The German invasion of the Soviet Union in 1941 also provided Japan with a favorable moment to strike south to conquer Southeast Asia. Hitler's war against Stalin's Russia reduced the fears among Japan's leaders of the Soviet Red Army in Northeast Asia. Soviet forces in Northeast Asia were desperately needed to defend Moscow from the surge of the German army. Stalin feared that Japan would gang up with Germany to defeat the Soviet Union. Richard Frank points out that Stalin wanted Mao's forces to act against Japan to help shield the Soviet Union from a Japanese onslaught. Again, the fighting in China loomed large and shaped the strategic views of the Allied and Axis leaders about the interconnection between the wars in Europe and Asia. Not having to fear Soviet military power, Japan's leaders could exploit

Germany's early victories in the European war to attack Britain and the United States in the Pacific at a time when they were tied down fighting in the Atlantic.

Maurer and McDougall track the changing views of Churchill and Roosevelt about Japan. During the 1920s, both Churchill and Roosevelt saw Japan as a responsible stakeholder in the international system, adhering to the treaties hammered out in Washington. Both dismissed the warnings given by American and British naval planners about the Japanese navy's rising strength. They urged restraint in American and British naval spending as a way to reduce the urge to engage in a renewed arms race in the Pacific. They also discounted signs that the civilian control of Japan's parliamentary system might erode and be replaced by governments dominated by militarists determined to expand the Japanese empire. Japan's move into Manchuria in 1931 signaled the beginning of the end of the Washington treaty system. The Japanese navy, not wanting to be outdone by the army, wanted to tear up the arms control regime that limited their naval ambitions. Throughout the 1930s, Japan's naval buildup dashed the hopes of Churchill and Roosevelt that a return to a great power arms competition could be avoided in the Pacific. In response to Japan's decision to walk away from the Washington arms control regime, Churchill and Roosevelt changed their stance and advocated building up the American and British navies.

Maurer's chapter examines the political and strategic dilemmas confronting Churchill when he became prime minister, as Britain fought a desperate struggle against Nazi Germany in Europe, in the Atlantic, and in the Middle East while at the same time providing for the security of the British Empire against Japan. Churchill's story is an extreme example of imperial overstretch: Britain lacked the resources to fight against two great power adversaries in Germany and Japan on opposite ends of the globe. Germany's defeat of France put Britain in grave strategic danger. While Britain inflicted setbacks on Hitler's march of conquest, preserving the British army by the evacuation at Dunkirk and beating back the German air offensive in the Battle of Britain, Germany's domination of western and central Europe was beyond British power to reverse. Britain had avoided complete defeat in 1940, but it had not come close to eliminating the Nazi regime. Further, Churchill feared that a German victory in Russia and a

Japanese win in China would put the Eurasian landmass under Axis control. The British Empire would then be overwhelmed. He wanted to keep Stalin's Russia and Chiang's China in the field fighting against Germany and Japan.

Churchill fully knew that Britain's survival, rolling back the Nazi conquests, and overthrowing Hitler's regime could only be achieved by an alliance with the United States. Maurer shows that Churchill had long recognized that Britain's ability to win a war against either Germany or Japan, or both in combination, depended on the United States joining the conflict as an ally. In the crisis year of 1940, the British military chiefs underscored for Churchill that American assistance was necessary if Britain was to remain in the war. Churchill sought to get as much support from the United States as American public opinion would allow. He knew that in Roosevelt he had a hawk who also wanted to defeat the menace posed by Hitler's Germany. Maurer emphasizes that Churchill wanted Roosevelt to remain as president in the 1940 election because it increased the likelihood of American intervention in the war against Germany and a strong American stance to deter Japan from attacking either the British Empire or the Soviet Union. Churchill followed the lead of Washington in the confrontation with Japan that led to war. His worst nightmare was that Japan would attack the British Empire in Southeast Asia but avoid fighting the United States. When Churchill heard the news of Japan's attack on Pearl Harbor, his worst nightmare ended, and he was confident of ultimate victory despite the initial defeats suffered in the Pacific.

McDougall provides a fresh assessment of Roosevelt's foreign policy and strategic outlook during the period between the world wars. While Roosevelt's views about conflict in the Pacific evolved over time, his words and actions reflected a deep understanding of American interests in the kaleidoscopic changes taking place in the politics among nations. As the strategic environment changed, Roosevelt altered his views about American foreign policy. During the 1920s, he supported naval arms control. His views, however, shifted when the Japanese navy took Japan's foreign policy away from the arms control regime put in place at the Washington Conference. Faced by Japan's naval challenge, Roosevelt pushed for a buildup of the American navy. He used Japan's refusal to remain bound by arms control treaties as justification for building up the U.S. Navy. In response to Japan's aggression against China, he moved step-by-step to disengage the American and Japanese economies. After the defeat of France, Roosevelt saw that American military power was required to roll back Nazi aggression in Europe and Japan's expansion in Asia. At the summit conference in August 1941 off the coast of Newfoundland, Roosevelt and Churchill prepared and then proclaimed the Atlantic Charter, which called for nothing less than the destruction of Nazi tyranny, what a later generation would call regime change.

In supporting Britain, China, and the Soviet Union, Roosevelt faced the problem of entering into a war fighting on two fronts against Germany and Japan. His priority was the defeat of Germany, which he believed was the greater danger. McDougall shows how Roosevelt consciously worked to keep Japanese actions against Britain or the Soviet Union from shifting the European war in Germany's favor, even if that increased the risk of coming to blows with Japan. Roosevelt stationed the main American battle fleet at Pearl Harbor to act as a deterrent against a Japanese drive to exploit the weakness of the European powers in Asia and widen the war. To rectify the weakness of the American armed forces, Roosevelt's administration mobilized the economy to make the United States into a military superpower, and to employ the resources of the New World to gain decisive victories in the Old World.

In directing the foreign policy and strategy of the United States, Roosevelt could not ignore the hurly-burly of American domestic politics. Deep partisan divides hobbled Roosevelt's attempts to bring American power to bear in the world war. His efforts to take more active measures to confront the rising dangers of Nazi Germany and a belligerent, expansionist Japan were countered by vocal opposition. His vision of what steps to take to provide for American security was very different from the views of his opponents. Even after the fall of France, when the danger to the United States increased dramatically, Roosevelt's political opponents pushed to keep the country from getting engaged in the unrelenting struggle ripping apart Europe and Asia. While his political opponents saw a need to increase American defense efforts, their aim was to secure the Western Hemisphere from attack and not prepare expeditionary forces to fight across the wide seas. McDougall examines Roosevelt's efforts to overcome the domestic political opposition to projecting American military power across the Atlantic and the Pacific. The Japanese attack on Pearl Harbor broke the domestic political logjam. With grim determination, the American people followed Roosevelt's lead into the war.

While the fighting between Japan and the United States began with a surprise attack on battleship row at Pearl Harbor, the war continued with ferocious intensity for almost four more years. The wartime escalation in violence provides a sober warning about the dangers that come when great powers wage war against one another. Not only were armed forces fighting in the front lines, but civilian populations came under assault. In invading China, Japan's army leaders sought to terrorize the Chinese population into capitulating. We must also never forget that the war came to a horrific end with the use of nuclear weapons. In the crisis year of 1941, when it looked as if the German invaders might take Moscow, Roosevelt and Churchill took the decision to collaborate in undertaking urgent research to develop nuclear weapons. Even before Pearl Harbor, the American and British leaders considered nuclear weapons as potentially decisive to terminate the war and to uphold the peace in a postwar international order led by Britain and the United States.

The history of the war can still inflame popular passions among the peoples of Asia. Bitter memories of the past continue to project themselves onto the present. History is not over but remains a driving force behind conflict in today's world. What happened in the past can help to inform policy guidance for addressing problems of the present. The historical example of the interwar era—the twenty-year period from the 1921 Washington Conference to the attack on Pearl Harbor—offers much-needed perspective and insight into the great power competition that was unfolding in Asia. Promoting mutual security among the great powers of Asia and the Pacific, deterring aggression, and constructing an international framework that advances the prosperity and well-being of the peoples in the region remain supreme goals of American foreign policy, just as they did one hundred years ago.

American aims in Asia now stand threatened by the foreign policy ambitions of China's communist rulers, the heirs of Mao. These ambitions to make China great again are backed up by the growing strength of the Chinese armed forces. China's sustained military buildup has already triggered an arms competition, as other countries strive to uphold the balance of power throughout the region. Advances in the sophistication of Chinese military technology—enhancing China's nuclear arsenal, naval and long-range missile strike forces, cyber, space, and artificial intelligence capabilities—also raise the haunting specter of twenty-first-century weaponry being used to carry out a future shock attack like Pearl Harbor to defeat the United States in the Pacific during the initial round of fighting.

In the volume's concluding chapter, Toshi Yoshihara offers a sobering examination of the outlook held by naval officers in today's China who study the strategic contours and imagine how to fight a future war in the Pacific against Japan and the United States. It is haunting to note the similarities between the views held by China's naval leaders with those of imperial Japan's admirals between the wars. Yoshihara sees in the writings of Chinese naval officers an imperative to launch crushing opening strikes on bases and forward-deployed naval forces in an attempt to win quickly against Japan and the United States. The views of Chinese naval leaders indicate that China might escalate a confrontation in the western Pacific by striking first. Of course, the Pacific War shows the side that struck first did not win.

The breakdown of the Washington network of treaties is a story that deserves to be retold for our own troubled times. This history highlights the clashing ambitions of the great powers in Asia. The breakdown of an arms control regime also resonates with changes taking place in today's international strategic environment. Shining a light on the history of great power competition in Asia—a light that shows the quest for strategic advantage in developing advanced weaponry and how war came to the United States—can illuminate the dangers that currently confront American leaders. As Japan's shock attack underscores, heightened nationalism, coupled with an escalating competition in the latest technology and generation of weaponry, can confound the best efforts of policy makers and strategists to deter war.

At a time when American power and purpose in the world is increasingly questioned, looking back on the record of history to study what ignited the explosion of war among the great powers of Asia and the Pacific can surely provide insight into current-day dangers. To grapple with today's problems, we should endeavor to know more about what went wrong in the past. It is our hope that this book will contribute informed history to understand current policy debates about America's role in building a framework for international security, comity, and prosperity in Asia.

CHAPTER ONE

CONSTRUCTING a LIBERAL INTERNATIONAL ORDER

*David Lloyd George
and Peacemaking*

Erik Goldstein

THE GREAT WAR ALTERED THE GLOBAL MAP OF POWER, AS OLD empires crumbled and were replaced with a new constellation of great powers. During the conflict both the British and American leaders, David Lloyd George and Woodrow Wilson, eloquently articulated the need to seize this opportunity to reshape international relations. What they envisaged was a liberal international order, a rules-based system, underpinned by the new dominance of democratic states. At the 1919 Paris Peace Conference the League of Nations, the key piece of the new machinery, was developed, but on the eve of its birth the United States, to Britain's chagrin, absconded from its parental responsibilities. Wilson's health collapsed in October 1919, causing American foreign policy to enter an eerie twilight phase for the remainder of his presidency. As the British foreign secretary, Lord Curzon, observed, "Official relations with the American Government almost ceased to exist, and for ten months we practically did no business with America at all."[1] Lloyd George was left as the only global champion of these ideals, but he sat at the apex of a weakened and overstretched empire. Despite the malfunction in the planned partnership with the United States, it remained a British objective to have the United States as an active participant in international affairs. The United States, despite some areas of difference, was the great power most compatible with Great Britain, sharing values, a commitment to the rule of law, and governance through democratic institutions. The possibility of reengaging the United States came from an unexpected direction in early 1921 over the linked issues of East Asian stability and naval armaments.

In March 1921 a new administration took office in Washington, and Lloyd George saw an opportunity.[2] A decision was looming on the renewal of the twenty-year-old Anglo-Japanese alliance, while simultaneously there was the specter of a financially crippling naval arms race with the United States. While the new Harding administration opposed membership in the League of Nations, it sent early signals that it was not isolationist. Pressures for budgetary restraint were as current in America as in Britain, and, given the less active foreign policy being espoused by Harding, there was a reasonable hope that the new American government would be less enamored of the navalism of the Wilson years. Lloyd George recalibrated how to approach Anglo-American collaboration, and the result would be the Washington Conference of 1921–22. While not providing the ideological glitter of the 1919 Paris Peace Conference, the Washington Conference resulted in a breakthrough arms limitation treaty, with a substantive and mechanically detailed arms control regime, combined with an effort to constrain great power tension in East Asia. The objective at both Paris and Washington for Britain was the same, to provide the basis for a more stable international order.

Britain emerged from the war as the one truly global power, but well aware that its capabilities were overstretched. During 1919 alone it faced simmering unrest on the Indian subcontinent with the Amritsar massacre, a war with Afghanistan, a revolt in Egypt, and, close to home, rebellion in Ireland. Although Germany and Russia no longer threatened British interests, the United States and Japan had emerged from the war as the newest great powers. They did not, however, easily conform to the patterns of the old Concert of Europe, the prewar functional clubhouse of the European great powers. The American president, Woodrow Wilson, an inveterate writer of constitutions, had wanted to write a new rule book for the international order. One of the initial challenges of postwar British policy had been to keep Wilson from departing too far from the norms of prewar international relations. The settlement reached at the 1919 Paris Peace Conference seemed to have produced a new international order that was acceptable to the key victor states. Then in November 1919, to the bafflement of the British government, the United States proceeded to repudiate both the settlement and, in effect, the foreign policy of its president. By 1921 Lloyd George was the only one of the Big Four who had met at Paris who was still in office. That the essence of the 1919 design was partially rescued after the implosion of Wilson's visionary moment was due to the efforts of the British government through Lloyd George's support for a liberal international order.

Many of the advocates of this new order had been deeply influenced by the ideals of the late Liberal prime minister William Gladstone, and his ghost hovered over the thinking of the new diplomacy. Although Gladstone's views on foreign policy, stretching over a long career, are hard to categorize, there was a commitment to a rules-based international system. The adherents of Gladstonian liberalism in foreign affairs supported his ideal of "the enthronement of this idea of Public Right, as the governing idea of European policy."[3] "[T]here was no hint of pacifism in his principles, but only a resolute attempt to promote peace and regulate the use of force by subjecting it to international authority."[4] The chief architects of this new era in international relations—the leaders of Britain, France, and the United States—had all encountered Gladstonian thinking. The teenage Woodrow Wilson kept a picture of Gladstone above his desk.[5] Lloyd George, while never personally comfortable with Gladstone, shared many of the policy concerns he had seen Gladstone advocate while he was one of the Grand Old Man's backbenchers. The French premier Georges Clemenceau met Gladstone in 1883 and reportedly later observed that Gladstone was "quite simply the most amazing politician of modern times."[6] Gladstone, who had also served as chancellor of the exchequer, was a notable opponent of unnecessary expenditure, which included armaments if ways could be found for an international agreement on limiting them. During his first government an effort to achieve this was blocked by Bismarck, the Prussian chancellor. The British people did not always share Gladstone's enthusiasm for reducing defense expenditure, and he resigned for the fourth and last time in 1894 over his opposition to increasing naval appropriations.[7] By the time the Great War was nearing its end, views had evolved and the Gladstonian legacy came into its own.

Lloyd George's ideas on the postwar order were publicly expressed in his Caxton Hall speech of January 5, 1918, which foreshadowed by three days Woodrow Wilson's Fourteen Points speech.[8] Lloyd George's postwar agenda was expressed in less idealistic rhetoric, but it nonetheless proposed a new international framework. In good Gladstonian language he spoke of the war as being one "to defend the violated public law of Europe," and he called for a new international organization that would provide "an alternative to war as a means of settling disputes." He saw as the foremost task of this organization "to limit the burden of armaments and diminish the possibility of war."[9] Wilson would likewise call for "Adequate guarantees given and taken that national armaments will be reduced to the lowest point consistent with national safety." Provision was made in the peace treaties concluded at the Paris Peace Conference to begin this process by restricting the military establishments of the defeated Central Powers, with the intention to eventually address arms control more generally.

In evolving a postwar strategy, the Lloyd George government focused on one region of the world after another, commencing with Europe, then the Middle East, and finishing with East Asia. Starting in 1919 with western Europe, the focus was on restoring a continental balance of power that would prevent any country from posing an invasion threat, a policy entirely in line with traditional British foreign policy. In eastern Europe, where the prewar borders had disappeared, the objective was to assist in the creation of a new, stable set of states with enough critical mass to be unlikely to fail. This would in turn help keep western Europe stable.[10] Once the European questions were settled, mostly at the 1919 Paris Peace Conference, London turned its attention to the Middle East, which occupied a great deal of the government's time during 1920 and into early 1921. During the last phase of the war Britain had begun to imagine a reconstructed region, one that would largely fall under British control, either directly or indirectly.[11] Eventually the aspiration of a British imperium replacing the Ottoman Empire had to be seriously trimmed due to the evolving regional situation. In March 1921 final shape was given to Britain's Middle Eastern policy at the Cairo Conference, chaired by the new colonial secretary, Winston Churchill. Two key results of the conference were to consolidate British territorial control on both sides of the Suez Canal and to assure British control of the potentially rich oil fields around Mosul for the benefit of the navy. Both these objectives were linked to British imperial maritime necessity and the ability to securely link Britain with its Asian empire. With this matter settled, the final region of the world to receive attention from London was East Asia, from early 1921. Questions relating to East Asia, in complex ways, were tied to Britain's postwar relations with the United States and the dangers of a naval arms race, which brought the strategic considerations of the British Empire almost full circle back to the Atlantic world.

It had been expected that one of the first big tasks of the League of Nations would be to handle the global issue of armaments, but the nonadherence of the United States to the organization made that impractical. As a result, during the next decade, while the league would attempt with limited success to fulfill this remit, substantive negotiations on arms control were conducted in a parallel diplomatic world, directly by the key states. Interwar diplomacy became an era where smaller, more technical issues and those more amenable to unproblematic resolution were often handled by the league, while issues of potential tension between the great powers were dealt with by direct negotiation in ad hoc conferences. The Washington Conference of 1921–22 would be the first of these. The British cabinet secretary, Sir Maurice Hankey, would dub this an era of "diplomacy by conference."[12]

Given the scale of the British imperial footprint, there were many stakeholders in the decisions to be made. Lloyd George's task in piloting postwar foreign policy was a delicate one. At home Lloyd George led an uneasy coalition government. Some of the old Liberal Party members had not supported the idea of a coalition government, certainly not one that would continue after the end of the war. Many Liberals remained loyal to the former party leader and prime minister, H. H. Asquith. This split crystalized in the November–December 1918 general election, with seats being contested by coalition-supporting Liberals, as well as Asquithian independent Liberals, splitting the traditional Liberal vote. The result was that while the coalition was reelected, the Conservatives held the most seats. This electoral arithmetic may have constrained some of Lloyd George's earlier inclinations for more radical policies.[13] The new Lloyd George government formed after the 1918 general election was able to face the world with supreme assurance, as one of the victors of the Great War, with a vast empire, and its forces globally deployed. It was likewise well aware of the terrifying vulnerabilities that needed to be confronted. Britain's economic position had been eroded by four years of total war. With the end of the war and general demobilization came domestic labor unrest, while always hovering in the background were not only the large domestic wartime debt the government had accrued but also the loans from the United States that needed to be repaid. This called into question what the postwar force structure should be, and what could be afforded.[14]

One by-product of being a coalition was the necessity of finding posts for a number of senior figures from both parties, which provided an unusually strong bench of individuals engaged in external policy. Arthur Balfour, a Conservative, had previously served as first lord of the admiralty and then as prime minister, and was the coalition government's foreign secretary until October 1919, in which role he helped guide Britain at the Paris Peace Conference. He then swapped posts with Lord Curzon to become lord president of the council, which left him free of day-to-day departmental responsibilities, in order to chair a number of key committees, including the Committee of Imperial Defence (CID). During the Boer War he and Lloyd George had been the fiercest of opponents, but the prime minister had shown his remarkable nonpartisan skill during the Great War in forging a good working relationship with his onetime rival. Lord Curzon, also a Conservative, had already taken over the day-to-day running of foreign affairs while Balfour attended the peace conference in Paris. Curzon had previously served as viceroy of India and was deeply interested in the Middle East. Winston Churchill had started his political career as a Conservative before defecting to the Liberals. He had been a notable first lord of the admiralty until resigning over the failed campaign at Gallipoli. He returned to government, first as minister of munitions during the closing stages of the war, then secretary of state for war and air in January 1919, before being moved to the Colonial Office in February 1921. The role of Lloyd George in orchestrating overall strategy in accord with his own ideas of international relations should not be underestimated. His success as minister of munitions had helped propel him to the premiership. In the course of his work, he became well aware of the industrial capacity of the United States, especially when he tried to acquire sufficient metal and shells for Britain's war effort.[15] It was while Lloyd George was in this post that President Wilson launched a program to build a navy second to none.[16] For Lloyd George the specter of a naval arms race with the United States was disquieting, while a renewed cooperative relationship was enticing.

Just as the administration in Washington was changing, there were also changes in London. In February and April Lloyd George restructured the government in preparation for dealing with the next set of issues. This included moving Churchill to the Colonial Office, where he, in addition to focusing on the Middle East, was also responsible for day-to-day relations with the dominions as well as the Irish negotiations. In March 1921 the sudden resignation of the Conservative leader Andrew Bonar Law, for health reasons, gave Lloyd George further opportunity to reshuffle the government. With Austen Chamberlain, the chancellor of the exchequer, now replacing Bonar Law, Lloyd George was able to appoint one of his most loyal supporters, Sir Robert Horne, to the finance post. This would enable a fresh approach on the war debts issue. Walter Long, the first lord of the admiralty, was given a peerage and sent to the House of Lords, to be replaced by Lloyd George's good friend Arthur Lee. The result was a cabinet reasonably supportive of the next set of Lloyd George's objectives for the next stage of the postwar settlements.

Two important international actors Britain had to consider in its global calculations were Japan and the United States. With Japan, Britain had had historically warm relations, stretching back to the Meiji transformation of the country. The increasingly powerful Imperial Japanese Navy was modeled on the Royal Navy, and many of its officers had trained in Britain. The two countries had been allies since 1902, and in 1911 the Anglo-Japanese alliance was renewed for a further decade. Balfour had been a key member of the government that had made the initial alliance. For Britain the alliance had, in part, been motivated by the rise of German naval power, and it allowed Britain to concentrate its fleet in the North Sea. During the Great War, Japan, as Britain's ally, sent ships to the Mediterranean to relieve strains on the British navy there. The treaty of alliance was due for renewal in 1922. The public optics for renewal looked positive, with the Japanese crown prince, soon to become regent, the future Emperor Hirohito, making a successful and highly publicized official visit to Britain in May 1921. Behind the scenes, however, there were many difficulties in Anglo-Japanese relations. "On the nitty-gritty elements of international relations like trade, the financial consortium, territorial acquisitions, there were hardly any issues on which there was cordial agreement between Britain and Japan."[17] To add to British concerns about renewing the alliance, when the new American Secretary of State Charles Evans Hughes was asked by the British ambassador about the Anglo-Japanese alliance, he replied bluntly, if diplomatically, that the United States would look upon renewal of the alliance "in any form" with "disquietude."[18] The comment encapsulated a long-running American view of the alliance.[19]

Regarding British aspirations for Anglo-American collaboration, the issues of the Anglo-Japanese alliance, naval armaments competition, and the war debts were all intertwined. For some time, relations between the United States and Japan had been increasingly strained, as both vied for regional power. Britain's alliance with Japan was seen as potentially aligning it against the United States, to which it was heavily indebted financially. The Wilson administration, to its end, had been insisting on British repayment. On the eve of the Washington Conference the cabinet noted that "the financial position between Great Britain and the United States (which though not part of the Agenda of the Conference) has an important bearing."[20] Given the need for financial austerity, as well as a long-term aim of establishing a better working relationship with the United States, Lloyd George's government was desperate to avoid an Anglo-American naval arms race.

While Lloyd George and Woodrow Wilson shared similar ideas, their personal chemistry was poor, and the increasingly irascible and then bedridden American president proved a difficult partner to work with in crafting a postwar settlement. It was no doubt a relief when Wilson was replaced by the new administration of Warren Harding in March 1921, with the well-respected figure of Charles Evans Hughes as secretary of state. Lloyd George, once viewed as a radical, had demonstrated a remarkable ability to work with more conservative politicians. London noted that the new administration in Washington was signaling that the United States, although it had rejected membership of the League of Nations, as currently formulated, still desired international cooperation. Lloyd George was well aware that there was a progressive, pragmatic, and even Anglophile element in the new Republican government. Harding had floated the idea of an "Association of Nations" in his 1920 presidential campaign, and soon after entering the White House he delivered two speeches that made clear that the United States still sought to engage actively with world affairs. One Foreign Office official commented, "Both addresses seem to point to a realization by President Harding that the U.S.A. cannot settle down to a policy of isolation and leave Europe to shift for itself. He seems to be inclining towards the 'Moderate 30' of the Republican Party."[21] In the late nineteenth and early twentieth centuries there had been close ties and a commonality of views on the part of British Liberals and the progressive wing of the Republican Party. There was hope in London that although for reasons of American domestic politics the United States would not be directly involved with the nascent League of Nations, it was open to active participation in shaping the postwar order. In terms of functional diplomacy, it was a question of finding a palatable mechanism.

The genesis of the Washington Conference lies in the immediate budgetary tribulations of Britain in 1921. Lloyd George well understood the problems of the budget from his time as one of Britain's most dynamic chancellors of the exchequer from 1908 to 1915. There was political pressure to reduce the war-induced high tax rates, which in turn would require significant budgetary restraint. The powerful newspaper proprietor Lord Rothermere was funding an Anti-Waste League, which in the first half of 1921 supported three successful candidates in by-elections to the House of Commons. The Treasury advised in May 1921 that significant reductions in expenditure would be needed if there was a reduction in government revenues, which would obviously entail severe cuts in the defense budget.

Britain had traditionally relied on the navy for its essential protection and had long adhered to a planning formula that called for maintaining a two-power standard, meaning that the navy must be at least as large as the next two largest navies combined. In 1913 the then foreign secretary, Sir Edward Grey, made it clear that "the Navy is our one and only means of defence, and our life depends upon it and upon it alone."[22] The difficulties with trimming the naval budget were the building plans of the other major naval powers. Both the United States and Japan had ambitious naval building programs, and with memories of the expense of the prewar Anglo-German naval arms race still fresh, there was little appetite for another such competition, especially if it was with states that were either allies or not viewed as likely threats. The immediate necessity of budgetary stringency, combined with the longer trend to find solutions to the expense of armaments, triggered British efforts toward promoting an international effort to reduce and control naval armaments in a way compatible with the needs of British homeland defense. These domestic pressures were not unique to Britain. In May 1921 the U.S. Senate unanimously adopted the Borah Resolution, as an amendment to the navy bill, which called for a 50 percent reduction in naval building programs by Britain, Japan, and the United States.[23]

The aspiration to control armaments had deep roots in the British liberal political traditions that Lloyd George came from. Jeremy Bentham had proclaimed that "whatsoever nation should get the start of the other in making the proposal to reduce and fix the amount of its armed force, would crown itself with everlasting glory."[24] Such views were not confined to the political fringe. Sir Robert Peel in 1841, on the eve of becoming prime minister, posed the question to the House of Commons, "What is the advantage of one Power greatly increasing its army or navy? Does it not see, that if it possesses such increase for self-protection and defence, the other powers would follow its example? The consequence of this state of things must be that no increase of relative strength will accrue to any one power, but there must be a universal consumption of the resources of every country, in military preparations."[25] Gladstone liked to cite the precedent of Peel's efforts when discussing arms control. Arthur Link, Wilson's biographer, has observed that "all international liberals were convinced that the existence of large armies and navies was a prime cause of conflict."[26]

They therefore advocated sweeping reductions in armaments. The postwar world seemed to provide an opportunity for voluntary arms reduction.

Gladstone and Lloyd George, and indeed Woodrow Wilson, came from a liberal political tradition that was neither liberal imperialist nor pacifist. Lloyd George had been derided as a pacifist during the Boer War, which in 1901 led to him almost being lynched by a mob. Yet it was his 1911 Mansion House speech that sent to the European powers a stark, if lightly coded, warning that Britain would use force to protect its interests. This removed any thoughts that he was a pacifist, uninterested in Britain's global status.[27] As his most comprehensive biographer, John Grigg, observed, "If the Boers had been threatening Britain's maritime supremacy, Lloyd George would have been a whole-hearted supporter of the Boer War."[28] For Lloyd George, a liberal international order was one that was rules-based, with a venue to discuss matters of concern, initially intended to be provided by the League of Nations. He was also a fan of ad hoc solutions and made full use of special purpose conferences.

There had long been an aspiration in Britain, especially among liberals, for Anglo-American collaboration in maintaining world peace. This was a view with deep roots and an extensive network of support on both sides of the Atlantic. The concept of an "English-speaking peoples" that had been advanced by Gladstone, and later taken up by Winston Churchill and others, was basically "a liberal view of the possibility of understanding through a common language, and a hopeful projection of future growth . . . [that] presumed that shared moral purposes justified special personal relationships."[29] These earlier developments all helped shape the trajectory of British policy in 1921, when it was confronted with critical strategic decisions, to give primacy to continuing these efforts at working closely with the United States.

Britain, as a global power, was concerned with both regional equilibriums as well as the wider international requirements for stability. The anchor of British diplomacy in East Asia since 1902 had been its alliance with Japan, a combination the United States assessed as a potential threat to its interests. An overextended Britain was now being forced to reassess how essential East Asia was to its global concerns and how best to assure that position with the lowest possible expenditure. On the eve of the Washington Conference, the Committee of Imperial Defence advised that "The United States of America and Japan, which already possess the second and third strongest navies in the world and undoubtedly will in the next few years, unless further construction is undertaken in the British Empire, become the first and second naval Powers in the world."[30] Any British naval building, though, would also require substantial infrastructure developments in Asia to adapt to much larger capital ships and to store oil. This led the CID to advise renewal of the alliance to avoid such immediate expenses. This, however, ran counter to the needs of Britain's global concerns.

Renewal of the alliance would cause the United States to calculate the potential threat posed by the combined Imperial Japanese and Royal Navies. This assessment would likely impel the United States to continue naval construction. Winston Churchill, who had been in the midst of decision making during the Anglo-German naval arms race, warned the cabinet that if the United States decided "to put up the money and persevere, [it would] have a good chance of becoming the strongest Naval Power in the world and thus obtaining the complete mastery of the Pacific." Any competition with the United States would involve Britain in ruinous expense. Churchill, with great clarity, observed that "in all this business the United States have a great deal to give and a great deal more to withhold."[31]

Beyond the concerns of the government in London, Lloyd George had to consider the views of the self-governing dominions, now virtually fully sovereign states. To maintain imperial cohesion, it was imperative to consult them, so Lloyd George summoned a conference of imperial premiers to meet in London from June through August 1921. The challenge of how to retain the coherence of the British Empire, as its dominions were achieving increasing levels of self-government, was one of the many challenges that had been escalated by the war. Lloyd George's ingenuity elevated the earlier occasional gatherings of colonial premiers to a mechanism of imperial coordination, starting during the war with the creation of an Imperial War Cabinet, to include the dominions in coordinating the war effort.[32] Naval expenditure was a domestic British issue, but the renewal of the Anglo-Japanese alliance was an imperial one. The Australian and New Zealand premiers were concerned not to alienate Japan and wanted renewal, while Canada did not want to cause problems with its powerful neighbor. For Lloyd George, considering both wider imperial and more local British concerns, the issue hinged on the impact it would have on relations with the United States. As events two decades later would demonstrate, this was a moment of seminal decision for Britain, one that would later help determine its fate in the Second World War. Lloyd George in his opening remarks to the conference made his own views clear, "Friendly co-operation with the United States is for us a cardinal principle, dictated by what seems to us the proper nature of things, dictated by instinct quite as much as by reason and common sense."[33]

One of the more unlikely and colorful characters in shaping a liberal international order was the South African premier, Jan Smuts. A brilliant lawyer, he was educated at Cambridge and was an effective guerrilla leader against British forces during the Boer War. Reconciled to Britain and at the center of events during the First World War, he was one of the architects of the League of Nations. In later years he would go on to become a British field marshal and was the only signatory of the 1919 Treaty of Versailles to also sign the Charter of the United Nations, the preamble of which he drafted. He and Lloyd George had forged a strong working relationship during the war, when Lloyd George made Smuts one of the four members of his War Cabinet. They shared similar views on the wider postwar world, and as a South African Smuts could take a detached view of the current issues in a way his fellow dominion prime ministers could not. Smuts came to Lloyd George's aid and helped guide the debate by advising that "To my mind it seems clear that the only path of safety for the British Empire is a path on which she can walk together with America"[34] and "I am strongly for union with America and for coming to some general settlement with America as the basis for our foreign policy."[35] The conference tilted in the direction of exploring cooperation with the United States, though given the experience of the Wilson presidency there were justifiable reservations this could be realized. The rejection of the Treaty of Versailles, and with it the League of Nations, had caused incalculable damage to America's standing and would continue to haunt it for years to come. Smuts, though he had been one of the strongest advocates for the creation of the League of Nations, advised his fellow dominion premiers that they had to move past this irritant. "If we could get America once more to work with us, even if she were not in the League of Nations, it might alter the whole situation."[36] The United States was well aware of the thinking in London. In September 1921 U.S. Naval Intelligence advised that "It is frequently apparent that the British have at the back of their heads an idea that some sort of an alliance, agreement or understanding may be obtained from the United States" and as a consequence might give up the Anglo-Japanese alliance.[37] This may have helped shape the course of America's own plans.

While the Imperial Cabinet deliberated, a series of communications, and sometimes miscommunications, between London and Washington were exchanged about the possibility of holding a conference. Given the legacy of Wilson's foray to attend a conference abroad, it was understood that the venue for any conference involving the United States would have to be domestic. It was equally important for both domestic and international political reasons that the United States be the country to publicly propose a conference, which Secretary of State Hughes duly did. Initially what was envisaged was a gathering of the wartime five great powers, plus China. Once the initiative became known, the European countries with a presence in East Asia clamored to be included, and so the conference grew to nine participants with the addition of Belgium, the Netherlands, and Portugal.[38]

Lloyd George decided that the duration and distance of this conference were too great for him to attend in person.[39] The motivations for this decision have been debated, but at the time he was deeply engaged in the final, critical stages of the Irish negotiations. Many of his colleagues, however, thought that Britain's position would benefit from the prime minister's presence. Churchill, who understood the importance of personal relations in dealing with America, unsuccessfully attempted to change Lloyd George's mind, arguing that "I feel you ought to establish friendly personal relations with Harding and Hughes, that you ought to make them conscious of the loyalty and friendliness of our motives and at the same time of our strong determination not to be ousted from our world position."[40] Churchill also hoped to be able to attend if the Irish negotiations were concluded in time, no doubt relishing the prospect of discussing battleships.[41] It poses the intriguing question of what the consequences would have been for the outcome and future policies if Churchill had attended. It is possible that Lloyd George had become pessimistic about the potential of achieving anything at Washington. British diplomats had been unable to gain any insight into American plans, and, more worryingly, British intelligence had been unable to detect any evidence that the Americans had even made any preparations. Lloyd George told one of his inner circle a fortnight before the conference that "He thought the Washington Conference would open with a great blare of trumpets, that the papers would be full of reports for a week or so, and that then the proceedings would begin to lose interest."[42] Perhaps he saw the conference only as providing for the gentle re-entry of the United States to the international arena. In the end it was left open that Lloyd George would attend, if circumstances permitted, perhaps making a dramatic last-minute appearance as the savior of the negotiations.[43] As events transpired, the Americans stole the limelight with dramatic effect from the very first moment.

If Lloyd George could not attend, it was agreed that Balfour would be the most influential representative. Given his career, he was well-known and familiar with naval issues and East Asian affairs.[44] As the second British delegate, Lloyd George chose Lord Lee. Although a Conservative, Lee was close to Lloyd George and is now best remembered for donating Chequers to serve as a prime ministerial country residence.[45] His experience of East Asia was limited to a brief tour there while a junior army officer and on naval affairs from two years as civil lord of the admiralty, where he dealt mostly with civilian staffing issues and maintenance. In February 1921 Lloyd George had made him first lord of the admiralty, clearly in preparation for what was to follow. His utility was his broad American network; his wife was American, and he had been a close friend of Theodore Roosevelt, whose son Theodore Jr. was now Assistant Secretary of the Navy.

The American delegation was to be led by Secretary of State Charles Evans Hughes, who came from the nineteenth-century liberal strand that ran through the Republican Party. He was another of the admirers of Gladstone, whose portrait hung in his study.[46] The son of an English immigrant Baptist preacher, Hughes was a lawyer who had already served as governor of New York, served as a Supreme Court justice, and had been the 1916 Republican candidate for president, against Woodrow Wilson. Hughes had been a supporter of a modified League of Nations covenant, and as secretary of state began American reengagement with the league by send-ing unofficial observers.[47] He also made an effort to have the United States join the new Permanent Court of International Justice. Hughes would later go on the serve as chief justice of the United States. Under Hughes' stewardship American foreign policy returned to supporting many of the objectives of the new international world order, albeit more often as a fly-ing buttress from without than as a pillar within. As governor, "His pre-ferred political technique was to build popular pressures for the measures he backed."[48] He used the same approach to the Washington negotiations, both to quell any domestic opposition as well as to encourage international popular support. Hughes choreographed the opening of the conference with a sense of drama and timing, which helped to propel the negotiations to the desired result.

The Washington Conference opened with great solemnity on Novem-ber 12, 1921, the day previous being given over to attending the dedication of the American Tomb of the Unknown Soldier. After anodyne opening remarks by President Harding, who otherwise did not participate in the conference, Hughes sprung his surprise with great tactical skill. Operating with a tight circle of advisors in maximum secrecy, he developed a detailed plan of action that blindsided all the other delegations. His very public pro-posal was a detailed scheme for naval arms limitation and arms reduction, within the framework of set ratios between the navies of the great maritime power, and a ten-year hiatus in new naval construction. It took the assem-bled delegates by surprise and captured the public imagination. Hughes, as his earlier political career demonstrated, understood the modern necessity of having public opinion assist in propelling policy in the desired direction. Hughes proved more adept than his old rival Wilson in going over the heads of government to public opinion. The outpouring of support for his proposals in America was mirrored in Europe.[49]

The British failure to anticipate America's proposals did not mean they were uncongenial. At the following sitting of the conference, Balfour, after receiving the concurrence of Lloyd George and the cabinet, publicly aligned Britain with the Hughes plan. The usually skeptical Maurice Hankey, the cabinet secretary who also attended the CID, and was in Washington as secretary to the British delegation, wrote to his wife of Hughes' proposal,

"It is really magnificent and stunning. None but a great nation would have conceived it. So far as I can judge it is a superb offer."[50] There was general relief at not having to pursue a financially draining naval arms race with the United States, and as a consequence clearing the way for improved Anglo-American relations.

The Hughes plan, however, implicitly in public and explicitly in the negotiations, assumed the nonrenewal of the Anglo-Japanese alliance. To do otherwise would be to nullify the ratio scheme and its underlying principle of parity, as a combined Anglo-Japanese Allied fleet would clearly be dominant. Britain accepted the reality, and a face-saving mechanism was found in the Four-Power Treaty, by which Britain, Japan, the United States, and France agreed to maintain the status quo in the Pacific. As Hankey noted, there was "strong feeling in America against the Anglo-Japanese Alliance. In order to create an atmosphere in which a lasting settlement could be achieved on disarmament we had to find some substitute for the alliance, which would conciliate both parties. This we have succeeded in doing."[51] This solution has been criticized as believing in a chimera, that Britain had opted to replace the reality of a proven alliance with Japan with hope for a better future with the United States.[52] The participants at the time, however, were generally optimistic. The British ambassador in Washington, Sir Auckland Geddes, wrote to Lord Irwin (later British foreign secretary and better known as Lord Halifax), then undersecretary for the colonies, his belief that the Four-Power Treaty "ends for a long time the chance of a Europe v. Asia line up. Japan takes her place now as one of the great powers with all the obligations & restraints that place imposes."[53] This was therefore seen as more fully integrating Japan into the postwar international framework.

Not everyone on the British side was happy with the naval terms, especially Admiral Beatty, the first sea lord, who warned of the long-term impact on skills and capacity of a ten-year capital ship building holiday.[54] London understood the risk, but it placed improved relations with the United States as the higher priority. Beatty's views were, however, in a minority, and upon his return Balfour was showered with honors in the euphoria of what was seen as another step toward a more peaceful world. The view that the Washington Conference opened a new era in Anglo-American relations and for cooperation in East Asia was shared in Washington. Admiral

Sims, who had commanded U.S. naval forces in European waters during the war, commented, "I believe this is the beginning of a thorough understanding between the English-Speaking peoples as to the development of the Far East."[55]

Although Britain and the United States did not form an alliance for another twenty years, with the biggest impediments removed at the Washington Conference their relations continued to grow closer on multiple levels, albeit with occasional, usually financial, bumps along the way. The Washington system inaugurated a new era in arms control, and the 1930 London Naval Conference attempted a further advance by closing the gaps in the Washington system. Shifts in East Asia, however, prevented the further evolution of the Washington Conference efforts for multilateral, rules-based arms control. In Japan's government circles the Washington treaties received a mixed reaction, and as Ian Nish has observed, "It was only accepted in the teeth of great opposition" though "in the course of time, some of the rancour was dissolved."[56] The growing economic crisis from late 1929 onward, and the consequent instability, led Japan to adopt a new course. Japan's prime minister, Hamaguchi, who supported the efforts to control naval armaments, fell victim to an assassin in 1930 and soon after Japan tacked to a more militant course.

As Japan began to aggressively challenge the status quo in East Asia, it encountered Anglo-American opposition. Even without the formality of an alliance these two powers had formed a sort of common-law marriage in international relations. When in 1931 the League of Nations sent a commission under Lord Lytton to report on Japan's occupation of Manchuria, one of its members was the American major general Frank McCoy, which was evidence of how the United States had come functionally, if quietly, to work with the league. The report, and the related Stimson Doctrine of the United States, which affirmed the nonrecognition of territorial changes by force, were all part of the continuum of thought in support of a liberal international order. In this instance, among many international commitments, Japan had violated its commitments made in the Four-Power Treaty of 1922. When Japan decided in 1941 on an all-out bid for mastery in East Asia, it was initiated by simultaneous attacks on Britain and the United States. They were the roadblocks to Japan's ambitions of expansion by force and the violation of the principles of international order enshrined after the Great War, and their ultimate victory in 1945 ensured the continuation of that international order.

Britain and the United States cohabited the same space in their broader thinking on the nature of the international system. The Washington Conference of 1921–22 clearly had technical successes, and perhaps some failures, but it opened the way for future Anglo-American collaboration. As the British ambassador commented at the end of the conference, "Anglo-American relations are undoubtedly on a better footing than they have been, certainly since colonial days probably, possibly even in the history of England & America."[57] From every analytical standpoint, good relations with the United States lay at the foundation of British foreign policy and were essential for the success of any new, stable, rules-based international order. With the signing of the bundle of treaties and agreements concluded at Washington in early 1922, Britain accomplished what it hoped was the first step toward resolving many of the critical issues between the two countries and building a closer working relationship with the United States. On balance Lloyd George opted to continue to pursue stronger Anglo-American cooperation, even at the expense of the established Anglo-Japanese relationship, as in the best long-term interests of Britain. Although a political and military alliance with Japan had existed since 1902, efforts at creating an Anglo-American pairing had been a recurrent effort of Britain, both at diplomatic and subdiplomatic levels, since a least the 1890s, with even earlier roots.[58] Lloyd George and his government attempted to construct a global architecture for the security necessities of the postwar world, though he may not have articulated it as a single vision in the way Wilson did. This was probably politically astute since he did not suffer the same resistance Wilson did.

By the time Lloyd George's government fell in October 1922 the scheme was not fully completed, and key aspects were awaiting further work. This was a task left to his successors in office, some of whom were perhaps less creative about how to achieve these objectives. To cite just one example, the Washington Treaty allowed Britain to develop Singapore as a forward naval base, which subsequent governments failed adequately to do, and likewise in the crises of the 1930s failed to deploy a fleet to Singapore.[59] This, however, should not negate the solid accomplishments of Lloyd George, who in a world exhausted by a cataclysmic war had led a consistent effort over four years to construct a better world order. As Lloyd George told the House of Commons in reporting on the Washington treaties, "The arithmetic of peace therefore means reducing the dynamics of war, and this is done."[60] He went on to observe the diplomatic reality of conference diplomacy. "You can only carry things forward step by step, but their great achievement is preventing conflict from developing into war, and that in itself is an achievement of value."[61] After the fall of the Lloyd George government, one of his Liberal cabinet colleagues, the historian H. A. L. Fisher, observed, in a retrospective of Lloyd George's foreign policy, that Britain's paramount interest was "the preservation of peace throughout the world."[62] The immediate issues of concern to Britain in 1921–22 were the avoidance of further military expenditure and to complete the cycle of postwar geographical settlements with the consideration of East Asia, which was made increasingly pressing by the looming decision on whether or not to renew the Anglo-Japanese alliance. The solutions reached at Washington provided a viable basis for the envisaged new world order, but it would be for succeeding governments to maintain that postwar aspiration for a new world order. In this task some would seek to continue the grand strategy, while others would falter. Come the Second World War it would be one of the veterans of this earlier era, Winston Churchill, who would inherit the legacy of the Lloyd George era and the need to think in both regional and global terms.

Notes

1. CAB 32/2, Imperial Conference, 5th Meeting, June 22, 1921. Minutes of the Imperial Conference, Cabinet Office Papers, The National Archives, London.
2. Lloyd George's inner motivations and thoughts are notoriously difficult to pin down, an issue discussed by Bentley B. Gilbert, "Lloyd George and the Historians," *Albion* 11, no. 1 (1979): 74–86.
3. W. Gladstone, "Germany, France, and England," *Edinburgh Review* (Oct. 1870): 554–93.
4. E. F. Biagini, "Gladstone's Midlothian Campaign of 1879: The Realpolitik of Christian Humanitarianism," *Journal of Liberal History* 42 (Spring 2004): 6–12.
5. Ray Stannard Baker, *Woodrow Wilson: Life and Letters* (New York: Doubleday, Page & Co., 1927), 1:57.

6. David R. Watson, "Clemenceau's Contacts with England," *Diplomacy & Statecraft* 17 (2006): 715–30, "tout bonnement l'homme politique le plus épatant des temps modern."

7. Paul Knaplund, *Gladstone's Foreign Policy* (New York: Archon, 1935), 11–12. See also F. R. Flournoy, "British Liberal Theories of International Relations (1848–1898)," *Journal of the History of Ideas* 7, no. 2 (April 1946): 195–217.

8. David R. Woodward, "The Origins and Intent of David Lloyd George's January 5 War Aims Speech," *The Historian*, Nov. 1971.

9. David Lloyd George, *War Memoirs*, vol. II (London: Odhams Press Limited, 1938), 1492–93.

10. On Lloyd George and the European settlement, see Alan Sharp, "From Caxton Hall to Genoa via Fontainebleau and Cannes: David Lloyd George's Vision of Post War Europe," *Diplomacy & Statecraft* 30, no. 2 (2019): 314–35.

11. Erik Goldstein, "British Peace Aims and the Eastern Question: The Political Intelligence Department and the Eastern Committee, 1918," *Middle Eastern Studies* 23, no. 4 (1987): 419–36.

12. Maurice Hankey, *Diplomacy by Conference* (London: Ernest Benn, 1946).

13. John Grigg, *Lloyd George: The People's Champion, 1902–1911* (London: Eyre Methuen, 1978), provides a good account of the more radical Lloyd George.

14. On the new government and implications for foreign and naval policy, see G. H. Bennett, *The Royal Navy on the Age of Austerity: Naval and Foreign Policy under Lloyd George* (London: Bloomsbury Academic, 2016), especially 47–66.

15. R. J. Q. Adams, *Arms and the Wizard: Lloyd George and the Ministry of Munitions, 1915–1916* (College Station: Texas A&M University Press, 1986).

16. Since 1901 the generally accepted standard for U.S. naval power had been a navy second only to Britain's. In 1915 the General Board recommended that the United States build a navy "equal to the most powerful maintained by any nation of the world" and to do so by 1925. The request for a massive building program was sent to Congress in December 1915, and passed, slightly modified, in June 1916. See Harold and Margaret Sprout, *The Rise of American Naval Power, 1776–1918* (Princeton, N.J.: Princeton University Press, 1939), 335–38.

17. Ian Nish, "Lord Curzon," in *British Foreign Secretaries and Japan, 1850–1990*, ed. Antony Best and Hugh Cortazzi (Folkestone: Renaissance Books, 2018), 139. This comment was in the context of relations during 1920. On the legacy of the Anglo-Japanese alliance, see Antony Best, "The 'Ghost' of the Anglo-Japanese Alliance: An Examination into Historical Myth-Making," *Historical Journal* 49, no. 3 (2006): 811–31.

18. FO 410/70, Geddes to Curzon, June 23, 1921. Foreign Office Papers, The National Archives, London.

19. See Ira Klein, "Whitehall, Washington, and the Anglo-Japanese Alliance, 1919–1921," *Pacific Historical Review* 41, no. 4 (Nov. 1972): 460–83.

20. CAB 23/27/77(21) conclusion 5, Oct. 7, 1921.

21. Minute by R. Hadow, July 4, 1921, FO 371/5704/A4716/4715/45. Harding's speeches were given on Memorial Day at Arlington National Cemetery and at the commencement of American University on June 8.

22. Sir Edward Grey to Sir Rennell Rodd (British ambassador to Italy), Jan. 19, 1913, FO 800/64, with original in box 15, Rennell of Rodd Papers, Bodleian Library, Oxford.

23. The Senate adopted the amendment on May 26, 1921, by a vote of 74-0, and the House of Representative on June 29, 1921, by a vote of 330-4. See Thomas Buckley, *The United States and the Washington Conference, 1921–1922* (Knoxville: University of Tennessee Press, 1970), 11–19. Also FO 371/5616/A918/18/45, Craigie (Washington) to Curzon, Jan. 28, 1921. Dayer has noted that, "Ironically, the Anglophobic senator little suspected that, in launching an enormous campaign for disarmament, he actually was helping British strategy." Roberta Allbert Dayer, "The British War Debts to the United States and the Anglo-Japanese Alliance, 1920–1923," *Pacific Historical Review* 45, no. 4 (Nov. 1976): 569–95. Also Robert James Maddox, *William E. Borah and American Foreign Policy* (Baton Rouge: Louisiana State University Press, 1969), 97–117.

24. In his *Plan for a Universal and Perpetual Peace*, in John Bowring, ed., *The Works of Jeremy Bentham*, vol. 2 (New York: Russell & Russell, 1962), 551.

25. W. Cooke Taylor, *Life and Times of Sir Robert Peel*, vol. III (London: Peter Jackson, Late Fisher, Son, & Co., 1851), 149.

26. Arthur Link, *Wilson the Diplomatist* (Baltimore, Md.: Johns Hopkins University Press, 1957), 92–93.

27. The Mansion House speech is traditionally delivered annually by the chancellor of the exchequer to the financial community, and it usually focuses on economic issues. The speech has been much analyzed. Timothy Boyle, "New Light on Lloyd George's Mansion House Speech," *Historical Journal* 23, no. 2 (June 1980): 431–33; Richard Cosgrove, "A Note on Lloyd George's Speech at the Mansion House," *Historical Journal* 12, no. 4 (Dec. 1969): 698–701; Bentley Gilbert, "Pacifist to Interventionist: David Lloyd George in 1911 and 1914. Was Belgium an Issue?" *Historical Journal* 28, no. 4 (Dec. 1985): 863–85.

28. Grigg, *Lloyd George: The People's Champion*, 309.

29. F. H. Herrick, "Gladstone and the Concept of the 'English-Speaking Peoples,'" *Journal of British Studies* 12, no. 1 (Nov. 1972): 150–51.

30. CAB 34/1/6, "Strategic Situation in the Event of the Anglo-Japanese Alliance Being Determined," June 15, 1921.

31. Memorandum by Churchill, July 23, 1921, Martin Gilbert, ed., *Winston S. Churchill, 1874–1965*, vol. 4, Companion part 3 (London: Heinemann, 1977) (hereinafter cited as Churchill Companion vol. 4:3), 1563–66.

32. Colonial Conferences had originally been held from 1887 to coincide with royal jubilees and the coronation of Edward VII, to take advantage of the presence of

the colonial premiers in London. In 1907 it was agreed to change the name to Imperial Conference and to make it a more regular event. During the war Lloyd George had created an Imperial War Cabinet.

33.   CAB 32/2, Imperial Conference, 1st Meeting. Minutes of the Imperial Conference, June 20, 1921.

34.   CAB 32/2, Imperial Conference, 2nd meeting, June 21, 1921.

35.   CAB 32/2, Imperial Conference, 6th meeting, June 24, 1921.

36.   CAB 32/2, Imperial Conference, 6th meeting.

37.   From X, a report issued by U.S. Navy Office of Naval Intelligence, Sept. 29, 1921. Library of Congress, file no. 101-100.

38.   Soviet Russia also wanted to be included, but at the time it was unrecognized by any other state, and its request was refused. Sun-Yat-sen's Canton government likewise made a unsuccessful bid for participation, hoping to appear together with the internationally recognized Peking government.

39.   FO 371/5619/A7066/18/45, 29 29, 1921, contains a discussion about who should lead the British delegation. Also discussed in a letter from Curzon to Churchill, Sep. 29, 1921, Churchill Companion vol. 4:3. As late as October the cabinet was still debating whether Lloyd George should go to Washington. Cabinet meeting of Oct. 7, 1921, CAB 23/27/V77(21), conclusion 5.

40.   Churchill to Lloyd George, Oct. 8, 1921, Churchill Companion vol. 4:3.

41.   Churchill to governor general of Canada, Borden Papers, vol. 294, reel C4448, 172672–73, Library and Archives of Canada, Ottawa.

42.   Oct. 30, 1921, Lord Riddell, *Lord Riddell's Intimate Diary of the Peace Conference and After, 1918–1923* (London: Victor Gollancz, 1933), 330.

43.   FO 371/5621/A7984/18/45, List of British Delegation.

44.   See Jason Tombs, *Balfour and Foreign Policy: The International Thought of a Conservative Statesman* (Cambridge: Cambridge University Press, 1997), especially chap. 10.

45.   The gift was made in 1917 and turned over to Lloyd George's use, as the first occupant, in January 1921.

46.   Merlo J. Pusey, *Charles Evans Hughes* (New York: Macmillan, 1951), 1:120. See also James A. Henretta, "Charles Evans Hughes and the Strange Death of Liberal America," *Law and History Review* 24, no. 1 (Spring 2006): 115–71. For an overview of the impact of Gladstone in the United States see Robert Kelly, *The Transatlantic Persuasion: The Liberal Democratic Mind in the Age of Gladstone* (New York: Alfred A. Knopf, 1969); and Stephen J. Peterson, *Gladstone's Influence in America* (New York: Palgrave Macmillan, 2018).

47.   Charles Evans Hughes, *The Autobiographical Notes of Charles Evans Hughes*, ed. David Danelski and Joseph Tulchin (Cambridge, Mass.: Harvard University Press, 1973), 210–25.

48.   Betty Glad, "Charles Evans Hughes," *American National Biography* (1999). For a comprehensive study of his statecraft see Betty Glad, *Charles Evans Hughes and*

Illusions of Innocence: A Study of American Diplomacy (Urbana: University of Illinois Press, 1966).

49. Donald S. Birn, "Open Diplomacy at the Washington Conference of 1921–2: The British and French Experience," *Comparative Studies in Society and History* 12, no. 3 (July 1970): 297–319.

50. Maurice Hankey to his wife, Nov. 13, 1921, in Michael Simpson, ed., *Anglo-American Naval Relations, 1919–1939* (Farnham: Ashgate for Naval Records Society, 2010), 41.

51. Hankey to his wife, Dec. 10, 1921, in Simpson, *Anglo-American Naval Relations*, 49.

52. An especially trenchant critique of the Washington Conference for Britain is Correlli Barnett, *The Collapse of British Power* (Gloucester: Alan Sutton, 1972), 267–73.

53. Geddes (Washington) to Irwin, Dec. 11, 1921. GEDD 5/1. Sir Auckland Geddes Papers, Churchill Archives Centre, Cambridge.

54. Beatty's immediate reaction is evident in Beatty to George V, Nov. 12, 1921, in *The Beatty Papers*, vol. II, *1916–1927*, ed. B. McL. Ranft (Aldershot: Scolar Press for the Naval Records Society, 1993), 190–91.

55. Rear Admiral Sims to Rear Admiral Andrews, Mar. 30, 1922, in Simpson, *Anglo-American Naval Relations*, 52.

56. Ian Nish, "Japan and Naval Aspects of the Washington Conference," in *Modern Japan: Aspects of History, Literature and Society*, ed. W. G. Beasley (London: Allen and Unwin, 1975), 67–80.

57. Geddes to Irwin, Feb. 17, 1922. GEDD 5/1. Sir Auckland Geddes Papers.

58. Melanie Hall and Erik Goldstein, "Writers, the Clergy, and the 'Diplomatization' of Culture: The Sub-Structures of Anglo-American Diplomacy, 1820–1914," in *On the Fringes of Diplomacy*, ed. Anthony Best and John Fisher (London: Ashgate, 2011), 127–54.

59. James Neidpath, *The Singapore Naval Base and the Defence of Britain's Eastern Empire, 1919–1941* (Oxford: Clarendon, 1981). Chapter 2 considers the period of the Washington Conference.

60. *Parliamentary Papers: House of Commons Debates*, CL, 5, 40.

61. Great Britain, *Parliamentary Debates* (Commons), CL, 5, 41.

62. Herbert A. L. Fisher, "Mr. Lloyd George's Foreign Policy," *Foreign Affairs* 1, no. 3 (Mar. 15, 1923): 69–84.

CHAPTER TWO

RETURN to GREAT POWER COMPETITION

*Imperial Japan's Rejection of
the Washington System*

Peter Mauch

Introduction

IN SEPTEMBER 1933, NAVY MINISTER ŌSUMI MINEO TOLD JOUR-nalists that success in naval arms limitation depended on the "international environment." He added that agreements on naval arms limitation were never meant to remain "in perpetuity." He noted that twelve years had passed since the original arms limitation agreements reached at the Washington Conference of 1921–22, and he insisted that the "international situation" had in the meantime "completely changed." From the viewpoint of Japanese security, he said, the existing agreements were "utterly inappropriate." Japan was "dissatisfied" with the current ratio, which limited naval shipbuilding according to a ratio of 5:5:3 for the United States, Britain, and Japan. Ōsumi concluded by asserting that Japan would demand changes to the ratio at the next conference.[1]

Japan indeed demanded changes when the second London naval conference convened in December 1935. Plenipotentiary Admiral Nagano Osami proposed equality in naval tonnage, and he suggested this ratio could best be achieved by setting a common upper limit for the navies of Britain, Japan, and the United States. Equality in tonnage was a fine-sounding term. It resonated with the Westphalian concept of sovereign equality among states. Equality would, however, have afforded Japan an unassailable operational advantage in the event of war in the western Pacific, and it was plainly unacceptable to either the United States or Britain. Nagano and his delegation withdrew, empty-handed, from the conference on January 15, 1936. In this way, Japan's Imperial Navy ended a noble, fifteen-year experiment in naval arms limitation. It sparked a new a trans-Pacific naval arms race, and rendered possible—even likely—a war that had seemed illogical throughout the era of naval arms limitation.

This chapter reexamines the public relations campaign Japan's Imperial Navy waged throughout the era of naval arms limitation. It takes the story back to the Washington Conference of 1921–22, moves through to the London Conference of 1930, and then on to the second London Conference of 1935–36. It finds that the confidential debates among uniformed naval officers about the propriety or otherwise of determining naval armaments by international agreement received remarkably accurate public airing throughout the era of naval arms limitation. It also finds that throughout the 1920s and very early 1930s, there was a proxy debate between retired officers and well-connected naval journalists who voiced the opinions of officers on active service. This essay argues that other, nonnaval voices crowded into the debate following the London Conference of 1930 and then the Manchurian Incident of 1931. It follows the Navy Ministry, as it entered the fray from 1933, and sought to reassert the service's voice in what had become a wide-ranging public debate. It argues that at this point, the Navy Ministry's focus rested with preparing public opinion for the end of international agreements on naval arms limitation.

Relatively little work has been done on the Imperial Navy and its attempts at guiding and influencing public opinion as it related to naval arms limitation. Stephen Pelz's *Race to Pearl Harbor* stands virtually alone. Pelz offered compelling insights into the public relations campaign Japan's admirals conducted in the lead-up to the second London Naval Conference of 1935–36. It was, Pelz stated, a "rousing campaign" that aimed at building public support for the repudiation of the naval arms limitation agreements that had helped regulate Anglo-American-Japanese relations since the early 1920s.[2] Pelz's work seemed so definitive that no other historian—in Japanese or English—has attempted to go over the same ground.

Other works include Sadao Asada's magisterial *From Mahan to Pearl Harbor*. It traces the Imperial Navy's enduring fascination with a trans-Pacific war and with the supposed operational imperative of a 70 percent fleet ratio vis-à-vis the U.S. Navy. It follows the navy's two factions—the so-called fleet and treaty factions—through the era of naval arms limitation. The former represented Japanese naval orthodoxy that opposed anything less than a 70 percent fleet ratio. Its members were overwhelmingly in the navy general staff, which was responsible for operational planning. The latter, generally in the Navy Ministry, were convinced that Japan could not hope to defeat the United States in war regardless of fleet ratios. They were also leery of massive naval expansion budgets and worried that a naval arms race with the United States would burden the Japanese economy.[3] These works are essential for putting the navy's public relations campaign in its correct historical context.

It seems appropriate to add a word about sources. It cannot be said that the lack of scholarly attention given to the navy's public relations campaign is attributable to a lack of materials. Booklets, pamphlets, and books penned by journalists, naval commentators, and retired officers abound. Many have been digitized as a result of the National Diet Library Digital Collections initiative.[4] Indeed, a brief glimpse at the quantity and quality of materials practically compels an effort to reconstruct the Imperial Navy's efforts at influencing public opinion throughout the era of naval arms limitation.

The Washington System

Naval arms limitation was a defining feature of the so-called Washington system, established at the Washington Conference of 1921–22 and that lasted until the second London Conference of 1935–36. The Washington system encompassed more than naval arms limitation; it was, to borrow the words of Harvard historian Akira Iriye, the "sum of all the treaties and agreements signed at the Washington Conference."[5] Besides the Five-Power Treaty on naval arms limitation, which limited capital ship building according to a ratio of 5:5:3 for the United States, Britain, and Japan (it afforded the lesser maritime powers of France and Italy a 1.75 ratio), the most important agreement at Washington was contained in the Nine-Power Treaty on policy in China. This treaty was designed to dispel mistrust arising from the decades-old practice of creating spheres of interest and exclusive opportunity in a beleaguered China. It established respect for "the sovereignty, the independence, and the territorial integrity" of China. Among other accomplishments was the Four-Power Treaty, which replaced the Anglo-Japanese alliance and provided for consultation between and among the United States, Britain, Japan, and France. Also, Japan agreed to the restoration of Chinese sovereignty in Shandong, the withdrawal of Japanese troops from that province, and the purchase by China from Japan of the province's main railroad.

The Washington system ushered in an unprecedented level of cooperation between and among the great maritime powers of the United States, Britain, and Japan. As dean of Japanese diplomatic history Hosoya Chihiro put it, it was an "international collaborative system," in which the Anglo-American-Japanese powers cooperated in pursuit of East Asian "peace and political stability." Naval arms limitation contributed to this stability, and so too did the Anglo-American-Japanese powers' disavowal of "old imperialistic diplomacy" toward China and the broadly cooperative approach they took to the issue of China's political unification.[6]

Proxy Debate over the Washington Conference

The 1920s witnessed a proxy public debate in which the Imperial Navy's treaty and fleet factions each supported and directed journalists and commentators sympathetic to their cause. The major daily newspapers were generally supportive of the 60 percent capital ship ratio agreed to at Washington; the debate played out instead in naval literature, including books, pamphlets, and booklets. The naval journalists' club known as the *kokuchōkai* (Kuroshio Current society), which the Navy Ministry had fostered and guided since the Sino-Japanese War of 1894–95, provided one source of proxies. Various clubs that brought together naval officers (both active and reservist) and others sympathetic to the Imperial Navy's cause also provided proxies. These included the *suikōsha* (sometimes referred to as the navy club or the maritime friends association), the *yūshūkai* (the perfection society), the *kaigun kyōkai* (the navy society), the *teikoku kaigunsha* (the Imperial Navy society), and the *umi to sorasha* (the sea and sky society). The Imperial Navy courted these and other clubs and societies by a program of "support" that included "proactively providing them with appropriate documents."[7] Fleet ratios, and the all-important question of the 60 or 70 percent fleet ratio, animated the public debate no less than it did the debate among uniformed naval officers.

In the immediate aftermath of the Washington Conference, naval journalist and *kokuchōkai* member Itō Masanori railed against the 60 percent ratio. Itō, whom the major daily newspaper *Jiji Shinpō* dispatched to Washington to cover the conference, argued publicly what the Imperial Navy's fleet faction was arguing behind closed doors.[8] He explained that the Imperial Navy had long since identified as necessary a fleet that was 70 percent of its U.S. counterpart, and he also explained that the difference between 70 and 60 percent was a matter of "superiority or inferiority" in the western Pacific. He was adamant that the Japanese navy could be confident of victory in a decisive naval battle if it maintained a 70 percent fleet ratio. He was equally adamant that the prospect of victory shifted to the United States if Japan's fleet strength was only 60 percent. This assessment, in Itō's analysis, explained what he regarded as the U.S. insistence at the Washington Conference on a 60 percent capital ship ratio for Japan. He seemed incredulous that Japan had (in his estimation) allowed the United States to "determine its defensive strength" at the conference. He fretted that the United States and Britain might seek to perpetuate the 60 percent ratio and extend it to other ship classes. He argued instead for an agreement that afforded each nation the "freedom" to determine the armaments it required for its own defenses.[9]

On the other side of the ledger was retired navy officer turned naval affairs commentator Ishimaru Fujita. A graduate of the Naval Academy's twenty-ninth class—his classmates included Takahashi Sankichi and Yonai Mitsumasa, both of whom rose in the 1930s to the service's highest rank— Ishimaru shot to public prominence in the mid-1920s after he published a

Japanese-language translation of Hector Bywater's *The Great Pacific War*.[10] Ishimaru was not, however, a simple war-scaremonger. Writing in 1926, he came out in unequivocal praise of the Washington system, and in particular of the naval arms limitation agreements reached at Washington. He lauded the Washington Conference for ending a trans-Pacific naval arms race. This greatly eased the Imperial Navy's budgetary demands, and the economic advantages accruing to Japan were, he insisted, enormous. Perhaps most interestingly, he insisted that the "only" nation that had lost any real "naval advantage" at the Washington Conference was the United States. He laid particular stress on the antifortification agreements reached at Washington, as a result of which the United States could not hope to defend either the Philippines or Guam in the event of war in the Pacific. He added that as a result of the agreements at Washington, the United States had had to scrap more battleships than had Britain or Japan, and it had also put an end to its ambition of overtaking the Royal Navy as the world's greatest navy.[11]

In the decade after the Washington Conference, Fukunaga Kyōsuke was another retired naval officer who publicly sang the conference's praises. A graduate of the Naval Academy's thirty-sixth class—among his classmates was Sawamoto Yorio, who later rose to the service's highest rank—Fukunaga wrote maritime tales for the highly regarded boys' magazine *Shōnen Kurabu*.[12] He also posited himself as a proxy for the Imperial Navy's treaty faction. He regarded the conference as a "great success" and regretted those voices that insisted Japan had "lost out" at the conference. He explained that such a viewpoint might perhaps hold some weight from a "specialist" or "purely naval" perspective. But he added that the United States and Britain could also argue, from just such a technical or specialist's perspective, that they too had lost out at the conference. In Fukunaga's reckoning, the Washington Conference's success was that each of the world's great navies had indeed forfeited something in the interest of establishing a more cooperative and peaceful era in the Pacific.[13]

Proxy Debate in the Lead-up to the London Conference

The public debate over naval arms limitation heated up in the lead-up to the London Conference. At issue was the question of whether the Washington

Conference's limits on battleships ought to extend to auxiliary vessels, including cruisers, destroyers, and submarines. The Imperial Navy, during the lead-up to the conference, engaged in a difficult balancing act. On the one hand, it adopted as policy the treaty faction's insistence on the strategic imperative of a 70 percent ratio in auxiliary vessels. On the other hand, it nodded to the treaty faction's insistence on the need to look beyond purely strategic imperatives in the search for national security.[14] The Imperial Navy did not publicly broadcast this position, but the treaty and fleet factions' proxies continued the public debate that had continued since the Washington Conference.

Hirata Shinsaku was a perhaps unlikely proxy. A junior high school dropout who had been imprisoned for his left-wing radicalism, he underwent an ideological conversion (*tenkō*) in the early 1920s and refashioned himself as a military and naval affairs commentator and later as an author of maritime adventure stories for boys. As was the case with many left-wing converts, he had shifted a long way to the right of the political spectrum, and according to some, he was Japan's answer to British war-scaremonger Hector Bywater.[15] On the eve of the London Conference, Hirata positioned himself as an outspoken critic of naval arms limitation, and he roundly condemned so much as the thought of extending the Washington Conference agreements beyond battleships to include auxiliary vessels. The 60 percent ratio imposed on Japan in capital ships, in Hirata's analysis, invited almost "certain defeat" in the event of war. He recounted how Japan's Supreme Military Council met in the aftermath of the Washington Conference and decided to "make up" for the deficiency in battleships by building strength instead in cruisers and submarines. A 70 percent fleet ratio was, he explained to his readers, the critical threshold for the nation's defense. Anything that threatened attainment and maintenance of a 70 percent fleet ratio, he asserted, invited "national crisis."[16]

Horinouchi Saburō also weighed in on the debate. A vice admiral who had retired from active service as recently as the mid-1920s, Horinouchi wrote for the *kaigun kyōkai*, or navy league. He explained that naval arms limitation aimed at "world peace," and he reminded his readers that arms limitation reduced what were otherwise fiscally burdensome naval budgets. He suggested that arms limitation should ideally aim at "equality" of armaments among nations, but he also allowed for disparity in nations' strengths, which bespoke a willingness to consider ratios. It was, in Horinouchi's analysis, only "natural" that the precise ratio ought to be a matter of debate among the maritime powers. On these grounds, he accepted with equanimity the 60 percent ratio agreed to at Washington, even though it was 10 percent less than the Japanese navy's long since established aim of 70 percent. He figured that the agreements at Washington had reduced the Japanese navy's offensive potential but had at the same time bolstered the Japanese navy's ability to defend in the event of war in the Pacific. The Japanese public, he wrote, ought to be thankful for the "heroic resolve" that plenipotentiary Admiral Katō Tomosaburō had displayed at Washington. He believed there were "prospects" for success at the forthcoming London Conference, and he admonished his readers to prepare for the likely possibility that Japan would have to make concessions and even scrap ships as a result of agreements reached in London. The alternative, in which the London Conference disbanded without any agreements on naval arms limitation, was in Horinouchi's analysis the "worst-case scenario."[17]

The London Conference and the Dilution of the Naval Voice

Japan received a formal invitation to the London Conference on October 7, 1929. The Imperial Navy had staked out its position several weeks before with its so-called Three Basic Principles. These included: (1) the need to secure an overall 70 percent ratio against the United States in total auxiliary tonnage; (2) the particular importance of securing a 70 percent ratio in heavy cruisers; and (3) a submarine strength of 78,000 tons.[18]

The conference opened in late January 1930. By March, Anglo-American-Japanese negotiators hammered out a compromise plan. It included a complicated formula that gave Japan an overall ratio of 69.75 percent, a cruiser ratio of at least 65 percent for several years, and an eventual cruiser ratio of 60.2 percent. It also allowed Japan to keep for several years its existing 78,500 tons in submarines, but required that Japan reduce its submarine tonnage to 52,700 tons by 1936, thereby bringing itself back to submarine parity with the Anglo-American powers. Debate over this compromise plan began from the very moment the Japanese delegation in London cabled it back to Tokyo. Even as that debate continued behind closed doors, navy

vice chief of staff (and leading fleet faction member) Vice Admiral Suetsugu
Nobumasa issued an unauthorized press release in which he stated that the
navy could "not possibly accept this kind of proposal."[19]

Despite Suetsugu's best efforts, the compromise plan formed the basis
of the London Naval Treaty, which was concluded on April 22, 1930. Even
as the Japanese government inched toward the treaty's conclusion, the main
opposition party, the Seiyūkai, publicly charged the government with having ignored the "right of supreme command." A group of 194 retired navy
officers, under the leadership of Admiral Arima Ryōkitsu (a graduate of the
Naval Academy's twelfth class), formed the *yōyōkai* (the boundless society) and publicly announced that they would "not forgive" the government
for this infraction.[20] This is not the place to consider the constitutionality
of such arguments; suffice it to quote historian Kobayashi Tatsuo on their
wider impact. "The newspapers reported these attacks in the most sensational manner and thereby sparked an explosion of discontent from the
military," he wrote. "Right wing groups immediately joined in, and among
the public there was created a mood of doubt about whether the right of
military command had not in fact been infringed."[21]

The proxy debate that the Imperial Navy had supported during the
1920s now became buried in a much larger debate. Voices included those
with connections to the Imperial Navy; also included were many commentators who had hitherto shown little interest in naval affairs. The navy effectively lost control of the public debate, as shown by two episodes. In the
first episode, Plenipotentiary Admiral Takarabe Takeshi returned to Tokyo
on June 19, only to be greeted by a placard that read, "Hang the traitorous
Plenipotentiary Takarabe!"[22] In the second, more consequential, episode, an
ultranationalistic youth who was angered by the London treaty shot Prime
Minister Hamaguchi Osachi at Tokyo Station on November 14.[23]

In this atmosphere, virulently anti-Washington system books, written
without any particular concern for debates over naval ratios, mushroomed.
To provide but one example, right-wing political scientist Satō Kiyokatsu,
in his *Teikoku kokubō no kiki* (The imperial nation's crisis) excoriated the
naval arms limitation agreements. Short on specifics, his book attributed
the Washington and London treaties to politicians who lacked any "grand
plans" and to diplomats who sought only to "flatter" foreign nations. Japan

had, in a manner akin to a nation utterly defeated in war, "surrendered" twice to the Anglo-American powers (at Washington and at London) and was on the road to "ruination." From the viewpoint of national security, Japan had now entered what Satō regarded as a "crisis." The state of Japan's armaments was such that it was now in a position of "weakness" in comparison to all its neighbors. Satō insisted that Japan's future was the "darkest of dark" unless and until the Japanese people reached the "momentous decision" to throw off the shackles imposed by their lackluster politicians and diplomats.[24]

During and immediately after the London Conference, naval writers, including the journalists, commentators, and retired officers who had joined the debate during the 1920s, sought to wrest back control of the broader narrative concerning arms limitation. Retired navy officer Mizuno Hironori was one of the first to join the fray, with a novella published even as the London Conference continued. Regarding fleet ratios, he noted that all parties at arms limitation conferences spoke of peace. He added that in reality, negotiations around issues like the 60 or 70 percent fleet ratio were conducted to ensure success in the event of war. And, although he insisted that a trans-Pacific war would come, his novella could hardly be considered war-scare literature. Mizuno was a graduate of the Naval Academy's twenty-sixth class (which included among its graduates such treaty faction luminaries as Nomura Kichisaburō and Kobayashi Seizō) and had retired from active service after rising to the rank of captain. Since the Washington Conference he had publicly supported the naval arms limitation agreements and had been outspoken in his insistence that Japan must avoid a trans-Pacific war. His 1930 novella offered a crucial explanatory insight into his concerns. Tokyo would, he asserted, become a target of U.S. air raids in the event of war. He wrote so authoritatively that fact seemed to blur with fiction. Three hundred American pilots were, he wrote, based in Hawaii and training for eventual air raids against Tokyo. Two hundred bombers were, he continued, being transferred to Hawaii. The explosives they used were so destructive, he insisted, that they had blown an unpopulated Hawaiian island out of existence. His description of the chaos that would ensue in Tokyo during air raids made for compelling reading. (Mizuno returned to the air-raid theme in a factual account published in 1932; the censors deemed large tracts of this latter book too sensitive and denied Japan's reading public the opportunity to read it and reach their own conclusions.)[25]

Other naval writers, such as Yamakawa Tadao, switched the focus more directly to the London Conference. Yamakawa's position was unique: He was a civilian advisor to the Navy Ministry who had also served as a member of the delegation to London. He acknowledged that Japan had not quite achieved its Three Basic Principles at London. This was not, in Yamakawa's estimation, cause for national despair. He reminded his readers that negotiations and concessions were the norm at international conferences and he went so far as to state that a nation should not attend an international conference if it had no intention of making any meaningful compromises. The real question, for Yamakawa, was twofold. First, did Japan's concessions at London jeopardize national security? And, second, could the conference be expected to advance or hinder Japan's overall national interest? He argued that the conference had in no way endangered Japanese security and that the arms limitation agreements were very much in Japan's national interest. He argued that arms limitation aimed at least partly at "promoting international goodwill," and he was satisfied that this goodwill was more than just a warm feeling. The alternative, he stated, was an arms race that posed even more problems for national defense than did an international agreement that limited Japanese naval armaments to a level that was a fraction beneath those deemed necessary by operational planners. Besides, national security was not, he insisted, an "issue of simply armaments." It was instead an issue of "total national strength," which included not just military and naval armaments, but also "all elements" including diplomacy, political leadership, commerce, the economy, public opinion, and scientific and technological competence. In Yamakawa's analysis, the London Conference served Japan's highest national interests insofar as it allowed some room to shift the focus away from armaments and instead toward these other critical elements of national strength.[26]

Ishimaru Fujita, the author of an appraisal of the Washington Conference, wrote in 1931 in glowing terms of the naval arms limitation agreements concluded at Washington and London. He hailed the Washington Conference for having dispelled trans-Pacific "jealousies and antipathies" as well as "fears and ideas about a coming war" between Japan and the United States. The London Conference had convened in the meantime, and Ishimaru regarded it as less successful. The Anglo-American-Japanese powers had really only agreed, as he saw it, to "maintain the status quo" in auxiliary ship strength, and this meant that an extension of the "naval holiday" to cruisers, destroyers, and submarines was unlikely, at least until the next conference, which was scheduled for 1936.[27]

Ishimaru saw good reason for Japan to desire the indefinite continuation of naval arms limitation. His stance was fundamentally similar to that of Katō Tomosaburō at the Washington Conference: it was better to work cooperatively with the United States than to invite so much as the possibility of a war from which Japan could not hope to emerge victorious. Ishimaru forecast for his readers the likely course a Pacific war might take. The U.S. Navy would, he assumed, seek to "annihilate" the Japanese fleet. That done, it would blockade Japan while at the same time launching "aerial attacks" against Japanese cities. The United States would, in other words, seek to starve and terrorize the Japanese people and thereby cause them to "lose" their "will to fight."[28]

U.S. victory in a trans-Pacific war would, Ishimaru wrote, come at considerable cost. Japan would lose its continental position, and this would afford the United States an opportunity to apply its Open Door principles throughout China. Yet Ishimaru foresaw Chinese opposition to such Open Door policies as the internationalization of the South Manchuria Railroad. The Soviet Union also stood poised to capitalize in the event Japanese power were withdrawn from the continent. In short, the removal of Japan as a perceived barrier to the Open Door would not mean the automatic enactment of U.S. policy toward China. In this way, a trans-Pacific war would yield what Ishimaru regarded as "inconclusive" results, not to mention immense "losses" for both victor and vanquished. He was convinced that a trans-Pacific war could only be "futile" for both Japan and the United States.[29]

Ishimaru also raised with his readers the most likely cause of any future breakdown in naval arms limitation, and indeed of a trans-Pacific war. It was, he wrote, the "Manchurian-Mongolian problem." He outlined two possible causes of future trouble: the United States might seek to deny Japan's "special interests" in Manchuria and Mongolia, or Japan might seek to wrest Manchurian-Mongolian sovereignty away from China. So long as these possibilities did not eventuate, Ishimaru saw every reason for the Washington system to remain intact. In this situation, he insisted, talk of a Japanese-U.S. war would remain "nothing more than a fool's dream."[30]

The Manchurian Incident and the Further Dilution of the Naval Voice

In a neat coincidence, even as Ishimaru's book hit sellers' stands, field officers attached to Japan's Kwantung Army hatched an audacious plot for the conquest of Manchuria. Lieutenant Colonels Ishiwara Kanji and Itagaki Seishirō, whom one authority has labeled the "perfect combination of brilliant planner and man of action," were the conspiratorial ringleaders.[31] In September 1931, they staged an explosion of Japanese-owned railway track just outside the Manchurian city of Mukden and blamed Chinese soldiers from a nearby military base. In so doing, Ishiwara and Itagaki created for the Kwantung Army a *casus belli*. Some officers in the War Ministry and the Army General Staff were in active connivance with this plot; the Kwantung Army otherwise left policy makers in Tokyo deliberately uninformed. This was a breathtaking act of insubordination that involved territorial conquest and, ultimately, the creation of the puppet state of Manchukuo. As if to emphasize its determination to remain on this new course, Japan responded to international criticism of its action by (among other steps) withdrawing from the League of Nations in March 1933.[32]

Sailors had not participated in either the planning or execution of the Manchurian Incident, and the navy was superfluous to the Kwantung Army's narrowly defined needs. Yet the navy could not but be concerned. The army had torn a huge territorial chunk from China and had, in the process, destroyed a defining feature of the Washington system. Japan could no longer argue that it upheld such Washington system concepts as respect for China's territorial integrity. Within Japan, the focus shifted away from naval arms limitation and instead toward the compatibility of Anglo-American-Japanese policies toward China. Jingoism and anti-Americanism were not uncommon; other voices were cautiously optimistic about the future of Japanese-U.S. relations. Either way, this shift in public debate entailed further diminution of what might be called the naval voice.[33]

Liberal journalist Kiyosawa Kiyoshi declined to see the Manchurian Incident as a stepping-stone to war in the Pacific. He acknowledged that Japan and the United States were at odds "economically," "politically," and "geographically." But he also stated outright that there should be "no war between Japan and the United States." The Manchurian Incident was, he stated, a "fait accompli." The United States would have to accept it as such, and the key question was what Japan ought to do next. Kiyosawa explained the need for Anglo-American-Japanese cooperation in southern China, and he also explained that Japan ought to invite and welcome Anglo-American (as well as German) capital and industrial expertise into Manchuria. Kiyosawa noted that Manchuria was a "splendid nation" and he argued—wishfully—that it only remained for Japan to showcase it as such to the rest of the world.[34]

Retired army officer Inoue Kazutsugu agreed that a Japanese-U.S. war was unlikely, although for different reasons. He wrote that the U.S. Navy could not "wrest control of the seas" from Japan in the western Pacific. He added that even if it were possible, the United States would then have to raise an army that could dislodge the Kwantung Army from Manchuria. This would require, at the very least, "considerable time." He also nodded to what seemed to be a growing fascination with the possibility of U.S. air raids, but he was dismissive of their actual strategic utility. For these reasons, he argued it was in the best interest of the United States to avoid war with Japan. He added that Japan could entrench such thinking in the United States by expanding its army and navy and their air arms and thereby rendering U.S. victory in a trans-Pacific war ever less likely.[35]

A sensationalist account predicting a trans-Pacific war appeared on bookstands in December 1933. Titled "Supposing Japan and the U.S. fight," the booklet opened with a discussion of Japan's role as the Asian continent's "guardian" ("*shugoshin*") against "wrongful aggressors" from across the ocean. Lest there be any confusion as to which nation might launch such transoceanic aggression, the booklet also highlighted (1) the "traditional" U.S. policy of westward expansion, which was now impelling the United States across the Pacific, and (2) that only the U.S. Navy could realistically challenge Japan's Imperial Navy in the western Pacific.[36]

The booklet offered a concise summary of the existing naval arms limitation agreements to which Japan, the United States, and Britain were parties. It opened the account with the Washington Conference of 1921–1922, which it hailed for having ended a "futile" naval arms race in the Pacific. It explained that Japan had entered the conference animated by the perceived need to attain a 70 percent fleet ratio vis-à-vis the United States and Britain but had settled for a 60 percent capital ship ratio in return for a U.S. agreement not to fortify the Philippines and Guam. (Japan, for its part, agreed not to fortify the Kurile Islands, the Bonin Islands, Amami-Oshima, the Ryuku Islands, Taiwan, and the Pescadore Islands.)[37]

The booklet next turned its attention to the London Conference of 1930. It explained that the Anglo-American-Japanese powers had, at London, sought to end an arms race in those auxiliary vessels—principally cruisers, destroyers, and submarines—not covered by the Washington agreements. It explained that Japan entered the conference seeking a 70 percent auxiliary ship ratio as well as maintenance of its actual submarine tonnage. It noted that the agreements reached afforded Japan an overall ratio of 69 percent in auxiliary vessels. This included a 60 percent ratio in cruisers, a 70 percent ratio in destroyers, and parity in submarines.[38]

The booklet next launched into a criticism of the agreements reached at London in 1930. It reported that many Japanese naval officers were "discontented" because the agreements "ignored" the needs of Japan's "national defense." It declined to explain any deficiencies—and, equally, to consider whether the agreements created similar problems for the United States—but it maintained that the assassination of Prime Minister Inukai Tsuyoshi by young naval officers on May 15, 1932, owed its origins to discontent with the naval arms limitation agreements. It also noted that the United States had begun a shipbuilding program that, although it remained within treaty limits, was of a scale that was cause for concern.[39]

The booklet concluded with a war scare. It confidently predicted a Japanese-U.S. war "in the near future." It only remained for the United States to augment its naval strength to the point it could be confident of ultimate victory over Japan. It would soon thereafter, according to this booklet, send a huge fleet to Far Eastern waters. Japan should respond, according to this booklet, by taking the Philippines. It predicted that Manila should fall within a "few days," at which point Japan's lines of communication with the resource-rich colonial regions of Southeast Asia would be opened. All the while, the U.S. fleet would sail westward from the Californian coastline toward Hawaii or perhaps Midway to engage Japan's Combined Fleet in what the booklet called the greatest naval battle "in history." The booklet recorded, in ringing tones, the likely course this battle would take. Carrier-based aircraft would locate and attack the enemy fleet. All the while, Japan's 10,000-ton cruisers would attack the enemy's advance guard. Japanese aircraft would fly from the Ogasawara Islands and would attack the enemy's aircraft carriers and destroy the enemy air forces. Japanese destroyers would wear down the enemy fleet as it sailed westward. The booklet predicted that the main fleets may be as far as 35,000 yards apart when they began engaging each other with their immense firepower. It conceded that the Japanese navy would suffer losses, but it assured its readers that Japan's Combined Fleet would emerge victorious from this engagement in the space of some twenty-four hours.[40]

Reasserting the Navy's Voice

The Imperial Navy sought, among this cacophony of perspectives, to reassert its voice. "By its 'silent existence,' the navy has until now supported both the army and foreign ministries' actions," the Navy Ministry explained after Japan's withdrawal from the League of Nations. "Henceforth, depending on how the situation develops, the navy will have to place itself in the firing line." It would be necessary, in other words, to present publicly "the navy's standpoint" as distinct from all the other viewpoints that were receiving an airing in Tokyo.[41]

The terms of the debate were now very different from what they had been during the 1920s. A proxy debate over fleet ratios now seemed quixotic, if not self-defeating. The navy determined instead to present to the public a unified stand that offered a distinctly naval perspective on such issues as the Manchurian Incident, Japanese-U.S. relations, and the future of naval arms limitation. The service continued to rely on journalists and commentators and affiliated groups such as the *suikōsha* and *yūshūkai*. Yet the proxies now presented less authoritative a voice than did the Imperial Navy itself, for the Navy Ministry's public relations office entered the public debate. Whereas it had hitherto sought to mobilize proxies, it was now determined to present the navy's voice. The language it used was by no means intemperate but neither was it conducive to international agreements on naval arms limitation.

One example of the proxies' voice was the *yūshūkai*, which in 1932 charged the American people with having failed to comprehend that Japan's military action in Manchuria was based on the "needs of [Japan's] self-defense." It maintained that Americans had exceedingly scant knowledge of the actual situation in the Far East and that they had failed to make any real effort to remedy that situation. It also viewed Americans as making common effort with the League of Nations in censuring Japan. It nonetheless argued that peace was the likely outcome, at least so long as Japan prepared for the possibility of war in the Pacific. The language used was not the language of armaments limitation. "It cannot by any means be said that a Japanese-U.S. war is impossible," it explained. "Our nation must therefore prepare incessantly for both war and peace." Preparation for war, the *yūshūkai* asserted, required nothing less than a 70 percent fleet ratio vis-à-vis the United States. It then rewrote history to delegitimize the naval arms limitation agreements reached at Washington and London. It argued that Admiral Katō had failed in his arguments for a 70 percent ratio at Washington because public opinion had not supported him ardently enough. It also insisted that the Anglo-American powers at London had imposed on Japan a ratio that left it "no prospect of victory." It reminded its readers that Japan's fleet ratio declined with each passing year, and on that basis it maintained that Japan's position was becoming increasingly "disadvantageous."[42]

The Navy Ministry's public relations office in May 1932 prepared for public consumption a booklet that considered the state of the Anglo-American navies. The focus was very much on the United States, which was building the "world's number one navy." This booklet charged the United States with having, by means of the London Naval Treaty, "restricted" other navies' construction programs while at the same time "eradicating" all "obstacles" in the way of its own construction programs.[43] In so doing, it was effectively charging the United States with chicanery: the nation spoke of peace, while preparing for war.

Some twelve months later, the public relations office followed up with a booklet that blamed the United States for the precipitous deterioration in trans-Pacific relations. It outlined the changes in U.S. policy that were necessary if Japanese-U.S. relations were to improve. These included accepting that Japan had acted in "self-defense" in Manchuria, concurring that Japan upheld "peace in the Orient," and acknowledging that Japan was neither an "aggressor" toward China nor an obstacle to China's unity. It asked searching questions of the United States. Was "unemployment relief" the sole motivating factor behind President Franklin D. Roosevelt's naval expansion program? Once the U.S. Navy possessed what it believed was the requisite strength, would it adopt a stance toward Japan that aligned with the "threats" issued by U.S. officials? It also expressed doubts about the compatibility of Japanese and U.S. policies. Even if Japanese-U.S. relations improved, it asserted that it was impossible to know whether that improvement would be "fundamental" or "superficial," or whether it would be "permanent" or "temporary." This last point was important insofar as it sought to wrest public attention away from Manchuria and the continent and instead toward the Pacific. To emphasize this last point, the booklet insisted that "threats" to Japan were both "continental" and also "maritime." The "threat which came from across the ocean," it insisted, was "particularly big."[44]

Also in 1933, the public relations office director Captain (later Rear Admiral) Sekine Gunpei wrote about the state of Japanese-U.S. relations. A graduate of the Naval Academy's thirty-seventh class, Sekine had no direct experience of the United States. He did, however, have definite views about naval arms limitation and Japanese-U.S. relations. The two nations' relations were, he stated, "exceedingly delicate." He acknowledged that the naval arms limitation agreements represented an attempt at "regulating" Japanese-U.S. relations. Yet those agreements had, in Sekine's analysis, done very little for the Japanese people's "sense of security." He added that the naval limitation agreements could only end in the "strange spectacle" of Japanese-U.S. naval arms expansion.[45]

Public Relations Offensive

The Imperial Navy in 1934 prepared the Japanese public for an end to naval arms limitation. It flooded the market with booklet after booklet providing naval perspectives. One of the earliest offerings was the innocuously titled *Kaiyō Jidai* (The age of the ocean). It argued that Japan's "fundamental" policy was "maintenance of Oriental peace." It maintained that Japan's position as an industrialized nation, as well as Japan's economic cooperation with Manchuria, ought to provide the basis for Japan's role in the "Orient's development." It insisted that threats to Japanese policy came from the continent and from across the ocean. To deal with the latter threat, the booklet insisted that Japan must expand its naval armaments. The question of naval arms limitation must, it stated, be examined first and foremost from the viewpoint of "national security." It concluded with the assertion that Japan would, at the forthcoming naval conference, face "unprecedented difficulty" but insisted there was no need for concern so long as the Japanese people remained united.[46]

The Navy Ministry followed up quickly with a booklet examining the "issue of naval arms limitation." Penned by Vice Admiral Matsushita Hajime (a member of the Naval Academy's thirty-first class), it insisted that naval arms limitation had been so harmful to Japan's national security as to leave the people feeling a sense of "great unease." The existing treaties, it stated, did "more harm than good." It was time to conclude a new treaty that "conformed" with the times. That new treaty ought to proceed from the basis of "respect for all nations' right to autonomy in national defense." The new treaty thus must enable each nation to arm itself in ways that facilitated its self-defense, and it ought to include some form of nonaggression agreement. By the terms of the new treaty, nations ought equally to commit to dispensing with "offensive power." Nations with the greatest amounts of armaments ought, it stated, agree to scrap more than nations less well-endowed. The booklet concluded by suggesting that the peace could best be assured if Japan were to lead in Asia, if the United States were to lead in the Western Hemisphere, and if Britain were to lead in Europe.[47]

Another Navy Ministry booklet published in 1934 revealed just how far the service had shifted in its perspective on naval arms limitation. It opened by denouncing the Washington Conference. Not only had the Americans imposed a 60 percent capital ship ratio, they had demanded an end to the Anglo-Japanese alliance and replaced it instead with a meaningless Four-Power alliance. The booklet likened these "disadvantageous treaties" to Tokugawa Ieyasu's actions, some three hundred years earlier, in filling the moat that surrounded Toyotomi Hideyori's castle in Osaka.

The booklet reminded its readers of Tokugawa's subsequent actions: having thus "eliminated" the very foundations of his enemy's defenses, he and his army sacked Osaka castle. It was a "clever" strategy that the Americans were now applying to Japan. The conclusion was obvious: Japan could not hope for a renewal of those agreements. One possible alternative was an end to all arms limitation agreements. Should this eventuate, the booklet conceded the possibility of a naval arms race. It also reassured its readers that such an arms race was unlikely and that the demands the Imperial Navy would make on the national budget should not be cause for "concern." Another possible alternative was a new approach to naval arms limitation. The booklet insisted that this new approach, as conceived by the Imperial Navy, should start from the premise of the "absolute equality" of each nation's "right to exist" and it must "guarantee" each nation's "sense of security." This would necessarily mean that the Anglo-American powers, as the nations possessed of the most powerful navies, would have to "reduce" their naval armaments to reassure others of their defensive (as opposed to offensive) designs. The booklet made clear the navy's insistence that political questions, such as recognition of Manchuria, be excluded from the coming conference, and it also clarified the navy's desire for an end to the nonfortification agreements reached at the Washington Conference.[48]

Another Navy Ministry booklet, published in November 1934, sought to focus the reading public's attention on the forthcoming naval conference. It warned that a "Japanese-U.S. clash" at the conference was a distinct "possibility." In this instance, the conference would end in rupture and Japanese-U.S. relations "may grow tenser." Such a possibility, while not necessarily desirable, was necessary from the twin viewpoints of Japan's national security and Japan's self-appointed role of the Far East's sole stabilizing power. It allowed for the possibility of a Japanese-U.S. arms race in the event that the conference ended in rupture, but it insisted that no nation had ever gone bankrupt as a result of "excessive expenditure" on naval armaments.[49]

The International Campaign

English-language audiences were of considerably less concern to the Imperial Navy than the Japanese reading public. The service nonetheless remained mindful of the perceived need to put Japan's case to the Anglo-American publics. An English-language translation of one of the Navy Ministry's previously mentioned booklets was published in December 1934 in the quasi-official quarterly *Contemporary Japan*.[50]

In June 1934, Admiral Nomura Kichisaburō was approached by Hamilton Fish Armstrong. Armstrong, who edited the prestigious Council on Foreign Relations quarterly *Foreign Affairs*, sought from Nomura a "frank and authoritative" essay that set forth the "Japanese point of view in the forthcoming naval discussion." Penning the essay was a distasteful task for Nomura, who identified firmly with the navy's treaty faction. But the *Foreign Affairs* audience was enormous, and the Imperial Navy wanted to reach that audience.[51]

Published in early 1935, Nomura's essay outlined his nation's position on the naval arms limitation. The message was a simple one: Japan rejected the existing agreements. Admiral Nomura acknowledged that the ratios had initially served Japan's interests no less than they had served Anglo-American interests. He argued, however, that the ratios had in the meantime become a "stigma" and a "national humiliation" that "must be abolished."[52]

Nomura offered four principal reasons for this change in Japanese naval policy. He insisted, for one thing, that although the original agreements reached at the Washington Conference of 1921–22 had taken "existing strengths" in capital ships as the "basis of calculation," the negotiations at the London Conference of 1930 had "proceeded under the apparent assumption that . . . the 5:5:3 ratio was . . . fixed and unchangeable," even though the ratio did not reflect actual strengths in auxiliary vessels. Japan had found itself, after London, having to allow the U.S. Navy to catch up. The ratio had become, in this way, an Anglo-American shackle imposed on Japan. This fed into Nomura's second point. He argued that "nationalistic sentiment" in Japan, which was "asserting itself most vigorously," stood adamantly opposed to the 5:5:3 ratio. In his reckoning, no cabinet would be "able to continue in power" unless it took "cognizance" of this. His third point centered on the twin issues of naval strategy and technology. Naval strategy, he explained, was characterized by the need to concentrate forces in the "decisive theater" of war. Advances in technology, and in particular in "mobility," meant that navies were increasingly able to concentrate their forces. A navy with a greater number of ships, no matter how widely dispersed they were, necessarily had the operational advantage. This again raised the proposition of the existing ratio as an Anglo-American restraint imposed on Japan. Nomura's fourth point centered on the notion that the "inferior ratio" imperiled Japan's "mission" of "preserving order and peace in the Far East." He suggested that "naval equality" between and among the Anglo-American-Japanese powers would better enable a world in which the United States, Britain, and Japan functioned as "stabilizing factors on the American continent, in Europe, and in the Far East, respectively."[53]

Conclusion

This chapter has traced the public relations campaign Japan's Imperial Navy waged throughout the era of naval arms limitation. It has found that the public relations campaign began, following the Washington Conference of 1921–22, as a proxy debate in which well-connected journalists and commentators voiced the views of the Imperial Navy's treaty and fleet factions. The Imperial Navy lost control of the public debate in the aftermath of the London Conference of 1930 and then the Manchurian Incident of 1931. It sought to regain control from mid-1933 by injecting its own voice into the public debate, and the Navy Ministry's public relations office became a prolific publisher of booklets and pamphlets. Throughout, the information was remarkably complete, and it accurately captured the thinking of uniformed navy officers. In this way, naval publications provide a vehicle for studying the Imperial Navy's rejection of the Washington system.

Notes

1. Kokusei Kenkyūkai, *Kaigun gunshuku kaigi sankō shiryō* [Naval arms limitation conference reference materials] (Tokyo: Kokusei Kenkyūkai, 1934), 43–44.
2. Stephen E. Pelz, *Race to Pearl Harbor: The Failure of the Second London Naval Conference and the Onset of World War II* (Cambridge, Mass.: Harvard University Press, 1974).
3. Sadao Asada, *From Mahan to Pearl Harbor: The Imperial Japanese Navy and the United States* (Annapolis, Md.: Naval Institute Press, 2005). See also David C. Evans and Mark R. Peattie, *Kaigun: Strategy, Tactics, and Technology in the Imperial Japanese Navy, 1887–1941* (Annapolis, Md.: Naval Institute Press, 1997);

Ikeda Kiyoshi, *Kaigun to Nihon* [The navy and Japan] (Tokyo: Chūkō Shinsho, 1981), esp. 67–87.

4. National Diet Library Digital Collections, https://dl.ndl.go.jp/.
5. Akira Iriye, *Japan and the Wider World: From the Mid-Nineteenth Century to the Present* (London: Longman, 1997), 51.
6. Hosoya Chihiro, "Washinton taisei no tokushitsu to hen'yō" [The Washington system's characteristics and modifications], in *Washinton taisei to nichibei kankei* [The Washington system and Japanese-U.S. relations], ed. Hosoya Chihiro and Saito Makoto (Tokyo: Tokyo Daigaku Shuppankai, 1978), 3.
7. "Shōwa 10-nendo hōji zasshi shidō tōsei keikaku (dainian)" [Plans for leadership and control of Japanese-language magazines in 1935 (second draft)], undated, in Kōbun Bikō Shōwa 10-nen E Kyōiku, Enshū, Ken'etsu, Boeishō Bōei Kenkyūjo, JACAR reference number: C05034195700.
8. Regarding Itō's dispatch to Washington, see "Kaigi ni saru beki shimbun kisha sonota (kenpei hōkoku)" [Newspaper reporters and others who will be dispatched especially for the conference (military constabulary report)], Rikugunshō dain-ikki, JACAR reference no.: C08051819500. Regarding the "revolt" against the Washington conference, see Asada, *From Mahan to Pearl Harbor*, 99–125.
9. Itō Masanori, *Kafu kaigi to sono ato* [The Washington Conference and thereafter] (Tokyo: Tōhō Jironsha, 1922), 187–88, 429–34.
10. Hector C. Bywater, *Taiheiyō sensō to sono hihan* [The Pacific war and criticisms], trans. Ishimaru Fujita (Tokyo: Bunmei Kyōkai Jimusho, 1926).
11. Ishimaru Fujita, *Beikoku yori mitaru nichibei sōhasen* [The U.S. views the Japanese-U.S. struggle for supremacy] (Tokyo: Hakubunkan, 1926), 290–98.
12. See, for example, Fukunaga Kyōsuke, "Kaima no otori" [The ocean demon's lure], in *Shōnen kurabu meisakusen: nekketsu tsūkai shōsetsushū* [A selection of masterpieces from 'shōnen kurabu': short stories to heat up your blood], ed. Katō Ken'ichi (Tokyo: Kodansha, 1969).
13. Fukunaga Kyōsuke, *Kaigun monogatari* [The tale of the navy] (Tokyo: Ichigensha, 1930), 33–34.
14. See, for example, Peter Mauch, *Sailor Diplomat: Nomura Kichisaburō and the Japanese-American War* (Cambridge, Mass.: Harvard University Asia Center, 2011), 70–74.
15. For his most famous adventure story, which was originally published in *Shōnen Kurabu*, see Hirata Shinsaku, *Shinsenkan takachiho* [New battleship Takachiho] (Tokyo: Kodansha, 1970).
16. Hirata Shinsaku, *Kokubō no kiki: nichibei kaigun no taiheiyō sakusen* [National defense crisis: The Japanese-U.S. navies' Pacific strategies] (Tokyo: Seikyōsha, 1930), 5.
17. Horinouchi Saburō, *Gunshuku mondai no shinsō* [The truth of the arms limitation issue] (Tokyo: Kaigun Kyōkai, 1929).
18. Asada, *From Mahan to Pearl Harbor*, 126.

19. Sugimoto Ken, *Kaigun no shōwashi: teitoku to shimbun kisha* [History of the navy's shōwa period: The admirals and the newspaper reporters] (Tokyo: Bungei Shunjū, 1982), 50.

20. "Tōsuiken ni kansuru iken" [Opinion concerning the emperor's right of supreme command], undated, Rondon kaigun kaigi ikken, B.12.0.0, Foreign Ministry Diplomatic Archives, JACAR reference number: B04122576100.

21. Kobayashi Tatsuo, "The London Naval Treaty, 1930," in *Japan Erupts: The London Naval Conference and the Manchurian Incident, 1928–1932, selected translations from taiheiyō sensō e no michi,* ed. James W. Morley (New York: Columbia University Press, 1984), 63.

22. Sugimoto, *Kaigun no shōwashi,* 53.

23. Hamaguchi died from the wound the following year. See Ben-Ami Shillony, *Revolt in Japan: The Young Officers and the February 26, 1936 Incident* (Princeton, N.J.: Princeton University Press, 1973), 7–8.

24. Satō Kiyokatsu, *Teikoku kokubō no kiki* [The imperial nation's crisis] (Tokyo: Hōseisha, 1931), 125–26, 214–15.

25. Mizuno Hironori, *Umi to sora: sensō shōsetsu* [The sea and the sky: A war novel] (Tokyo: Kaiyōsha, 1930), 1–2, 127–28. See also Mizuno Hironori, *Dakaika hamestuka kōbō no kono issen* [Breakthrough? Or catastrophe? This battle which will decide our rise or fall] (Tokyo: Tōkai Shoin, 1932).

26. Yamakawa Tadao, *Rondon kaigun gunshuku kaigi no seika* [The outcome of the London naval arms limitation conference] (Tokyo: Kokusai Renmei Kyōkai, 1930), 117–24.

27. Ishimaru Fujita, *Nichibei hatashite tatakauka* [Will Japan and the United States fight?] (Tokyo: Shunjūsha, 1931), 88, 139.

28. Ishimaru, *Nichibei hatashite tatakauka* [Will Japan and the United States fight?], 182.

29. Ishimaru, *Nichibei hatashite tatakauka* [Will Japan and the United States fight?], 412–13.

30. Ishimaru, *Nichibei hatashite tatakauka* [Will Japan and the United States fight?], 161–77.

31. Edward J. Drea, *Japan's Imperial Army: Its Rise and Fall, 1853–1945* (Lawrence: University Press of Kansas, 2000), 166.

32. Regarding the Manchurian Incident, see Sadako N. Ogata, *Defiance in Manchuria: The Making of Japanese Foreign Policy, 1931–1932* (Berkeley: University of California Press, 1964).

33. Historian Sandra Wilson has offered a powerful corrective to the notion of the Manchurian Incident as a stepping-stone to war in the Pacific. See Sandra Wilson, *The Manchurian Crisis and Japanese Society, 1931–1933* (London: Routledge, 2002).

34. Kiyosawa Kiyoshi, *Amerika wa nihon to tatakawazu* [America will not fight Japan] (Tokyo: Chikura Shobō, 1932), 331, 333, 362–63.

35. Inoue Kazutsugu, *Nichibei sensō no shōhai* [Victory and defeat in a Japanese-U.S. war] (Tokyo: Ichigensha, 1932), 63–65.

36. Satō Tetsujō, *Kiki 1936-nen to nichi-bei no kaigun: nichi-bei moshi tatakahaba* [The critical 1936 and the Japanese and U.S. navies: What if Japan and the U.S. fight?] (Tokyo: Chishiki to Shūyōkai, 1933), 1, 3, 42.

37. Satō Tetsujō, *Kiki 1936-nen to nichi-bei no kaigun* [The critical 1936 and the Japanese and U.S. navies], 4–6.

38. Satō Tetsujō, *Kiki 1936-nen to nichi-bei no kaigun* [The critical 1936 and the Japanese and U.S. navies], 6–8.

39. Satō Tetsujō, *Kiki 1936-nen to nichi-bei no kaigun* [The critical 1936 and the Japanese and U.S. navies], 8–17.

40. Satō Tetsujō, *Kiki 1936-nen to nichi-bei no kaigun* [The critical 1936 and the Japanese and U.S. navies], 42–52.

41. Kaigunshō Gunji Fukyūbu, eds., *Kokusai renmei dattai to teikoku kaigun* [Withdrawal from the League of Nations and the Imperial Navy] (Tokyo: Kaigunshō, 1933), 2.

42. Yūshūkai, eds., *Beikoku kaigun no shinsō* [The truth of the U.S. Navy] (Tokyo: Yūshūkai, 1932), 35–40, 380–84.

43. Kaigunshō Gunji Fukyūbu, eds., *Saikin rekkoku kaigun gunbi jōkyō* [The state of the great powers' naval armaments] (Tokyo: Kaigunshō, 1932), 1–3.

44. Kaigunshō Gunji Fukyūbu, eds., *Shōsei ni anzuru nakare* [Don't worry about me] (Tokyo: Kaigunshō, 1933), 10–13, 17–19.

45. Sekine Gunpei, *Beikoku kaigun seisaku no kaitei to sono eikyō* [Revisions to U.S. naval policy and its effects] (Tokyo: Kaigunshō Gunji Fukyūbu, 1933), 19–20.

46. Kaigunshō Gunji Fukyūbu, eds., *Kaiyō Jidai* [The age of the ocean] (Tokyo: Kaigunshō Gunji Fukyūbu, 1934).

47. Kaigunshō Gunji Fukyūbu, eds., *Gunshuku mondai ni tsuite* [About the issue of naval arms limitation] (Tokyo: Kaigunshō Gunji Fukyūbu, 1934).

48. Kaigunshō Gunji Fukyūbu, eds., *Gunshuku kaigi o chūshin to shite* [Centering on the armaments limitation conference] (Tokyo: Kaigunshō Gunji Fukyūbu, 1934).

49. Kaigunshō Gunji Fukyūbu, eds., *Kokusai jōsei to kaigun gunshuku kaigi* [The international situation and the naval arms limitation conference] (Tokyo: Kaigunshō Gunji Fukyūbu, 1934).

50. Matsushima Hajime, "The Logic of Our Naval Claims," *Contemporary Japan*, vol. 3 (Dec. 1934). This was a translation of Kaigunshō Gunji Fukyūbu, *Gunshuku mondai ni tsuite*.

51. Mauch, *Sailor Diplomat*, 90–91.

52. Kichisaburo Nomura, "Japan's Demand for Naval Equality," *Foreign Affairs*, vol. 13 (Jan. 1935). See also Mauch, *Sailor Diplomat*, 91.

53. Kichisaburo Nomura, "Japan's Demand for Naval Equality," *Foreign Affairs*, vol. 13 (Jan. 1935). See also Mauch, *Sailor Diplomat*, 91.

CHAPTER THREE

TASTING GALL

Chiang Kai-shek and
China's War with Japan

Grant F. Rhode

Introduction

THE UNITED STATES AND THE UNITED KINGDOM DECLARED WAR
on Japan on the day after the Japanese attack on Pearl Harbor on December
7, 1941. President Franklin Roosevelt and Prime Minister Winston Churchill embraced China's Nationalist Generalissimo Chiang Kai-shek as an
ally, a nominal equal in the struggle against Japan. During the previous
decade, Chiang had fought bitterly with Japan, first through resistance
following the Japanese takeover of Manchuria in 1931, and then through
full-scale war with Japan beginning in 1937. For Chiang, Pearl Harbor represented a turning point in his conflict with Japan, as it expanded from
being solely China's confrontation to a war with powerful allies against
Japan. Roosevelt and Churchill needed Chiang to preoccupy major Japanese military forces on the Chinese mainland, while they concentrated
on the naval war in the Pacific and the land war in Southeast Asia. The
three-way alliance partnership had many problems, but it ultimately

proved successful for each of the three allies, culminating in Japan's defeat in 1945.

Originally perceived as the junior partner in the alliance, Chiang's stature culminated as one of the three great power leaders at the Cairo Conference of November 1943. Together the allies laid out postwar settlement terms to be forced on Japan. Thus Chiang Kai-shek participated substantially in planning the postwar shape of the Asia-Pacific world. During the conference, Chiang gained the international face he had long desired. Evidence of Chiang's enhanced stature is demonstrated by photographs and paintings of Chiang, Roosevelt, and Churchill sitting together at the Cairo Conference that are proudly on display in both Nanjing and Taipei, the capitals from which Chiang ruled. In Nanjing, Cairo Conference photographs are placed prominently at the China Modern History Museum, formerly the Presidential Palace used by Chiang Kai-shek from 1927 to 1949; and in Taipei, they are on view at the Presidential Office Building used by Chiang from 1950 to 1975. Beyond this Cairo highpoint for Chiang Kai-shek in China's war with Japan, the story of his wartime involvement is long and complex, and it harks back to his earliest years during which his views on China's role in the world were formed.

Chiang Kai-shek's primary vision and lifetime commitment lay in restoring China to the position of wealth and power that it occupied before its "century of humiliation" during the nineteenth century. This dark, humiliating period began with the signing of the Treaty of Nanjing in 1842 at the end of the First Opium War, granting treaty port rights, extraterritoriality, and Hong Kong to the British. Chiang's vision of a restored and powerful China was shared by many of his generation, including Mao Zedong. Mao would become Chiang's archrival, leading to civil war between the founding of the Chinese Communist Party in 1921 and the establishment of People's Republic of China in 1949. Chiang commanded the Chinese Nationalist Party forces during the civil war period, ending with his forced evacuation to Taiwan in 1949.[1] China's civil war was one of Chiang's two great struggles, and in it he was unsuccessful. Chiang's other great conflict was opposing Japan's increasing domination of China between 1895 and 1945. In this struggle, he was ultimately successful. Chiang's legacy of both great failure and great success is controversial. Yet his success in the war against Japan is recognized and appreciated today even by the communists who would defeat him in the civil war.

Chiang had fought Japan for more than a decade before Pearl Harbor, and his preparation for this iteration of the Sino-Japanese War began decades earlier. Chiang was born in 1887 into a merchant family with enough means for him to study Confucian classics in the eastern coastal province of Zhejiang. Chiang was a child when China suffered a devastating loss to Japan in the First Sino-Japanese War in 1895. In the resulting Treaty of Shimonoseki, Taiwan and the Pescadores were ceded to Japan, along with rights in the Liaodong Peninsula of Manchuria. Conceptually, Chiang's war with Japan originated with his growing awareness at the age of eight of China's humiliation by Japan. Immediately following this war, Russia, Germany, and France forced Japan to vacate the Liaodong Peninsula in Manchuria. Shamed by this Triple Intervention action by the Western powers, Japan struck back and astonishingly defeated Russia in the Russo-Japanese War (1904–5). The Treaty of Portsmouth that ended the war granted Japan spheres of influence in Manchuria and Korea, as well as control of the southern half of Russia's Sakhalin Island. Observing the defeat of a major European power by an Asian power for the first time, Chiang and many other Chinese were motivated to study in Japan to discover the reforms that allowed Japan to free itself from Western domination. Chiang studied first at the Baoding Military Academy in China, and then from 1907 to 1909 attended the Tokyo Shinbu Gakko, a Japanese military academy set up for Chinese students. Returning to China, Chiang was influenced by Chinese revolutionary Dr. Sun Yat-sen. Chiang participated in the 1911 revolution that overthrew the decaying Qing dynasty by leading a "dare to die" potential suicide contingent. Chiang helped to establish the Republican government and demonstrated military courage and leadership in the service of a new China that was to emerge from the ashes of the Qing dynasty.

The new Republican government initially was unstable. Within months, warlord Yuan Shi-kai replaced Sun Yat-sen as the first president of the Republic. Divisive internal turmoil plagued China while the Western world was embroiled in World War I. In its search for regional hegemony, Japan assisted the Allies by driving Germany from the port of Qingdao in north China in 1914, and it subsequently presented its infamous Twenty-One Demands to China in 1915, which resulted in Japan taking control of Shandong Province. Much to China's chagrin, because Japan had sent many laborers to assist Europe during the war, the 1919 Treaty of Versailles awarded Shandong to the Japanese, not to the Chinese. The resulting crisis led to mass demonstrations, known as the May Fourth Movement in China, in opposition to the Treaty of Versailles. China refused to sign the treaty in protest over the Shandong decision. In attempts to unify China, Chiang spent much of World War I fighting the warlords on behalf of Sun Yat-sen's Nationalist Party. Following the war, China was split further by the Japanese occupation of Shandong, as well as by warlord fiefdoms.

By the time he was thirty-two, Chiang had prepared for and taken part in China's most important national events, and he stood poised for an even more significant future. He had fifteen years of progressive military training and experience, which included a Japanese military education, participation in the overthrow of the Qing dynasty, establishment of the Republic of China while pursuing Nationalist Party politics, and command of units competing against warlord armies within China. Steeped in Chinese history and having political, military, and international experiences as a young man living through the early twentieth century, Chiang Kai-shek stood poised to contribute substantially to China's future following World War I. Two early influences were especially formative on Chiang's life: the humiliation of China through chaotic loss of sovereignty and self-respect, and neo-Confucian thought and practice, especially that of Ming scholar-general Wang Yangming. When he was eighteen, Chiang was introduced to Wang's thought, which taught that ethics had meaning when converted to action and that stressed the Confucian values of rectitude, integrity, honesty, and loyalty. Every morning from that point on until he could no longer rise from his bed, Chiang would stand erect and concentrate every morning for fifteen minutes on his goals for the day and for his life.[2] Heading into the 1920s, Chiang was a man of discipline with military training and political aspirations, motivated by an unquenchable desire for a strong and independent China. Both China's civil war and China's second war with Japan lay before him, a lifetime of harsh experience. Later in life, Chiang was often compared to the fifth-century BCE

Chinese king Goujian of Yue, who, like Chiang, spent decades in bitter struggle "tasting gall."[3]

From Versailles to Manchukuo, 1919–31

Japan's economic and military strength expanded during the immediate post–World War I period. China remained mired in leadership chaos, most notably between northern warlord Yuan Shi-kai and Republican revolutionary Sun Yat-sen, but also with numerous other turf wars by warlords, especially in northern China. These warlord disputes were observed firsthand by Joseph Stilwell, an American Army officer who had served in France during World War I. Stilwell spent the early 1920s on U.S. Army assignment in China, immersing himself in China's language, culture, and politics. Subsequently he became recognized as a top Army China hand by both his colleagues and his mentor George Marshall.[4] Stilwell joined other observers in considering the chaos in China to be a serious problem in Asia. For instance, the British Foreign Office noted, "It is the weakness of China as much as the aggressive policy of Japan which is the constant source of danger in the Far East. The jealousies and rivalries to which it gives rise constitute the really disturbing element in the situation, for they make China a cockpit of international strife."[5]

The Treaty of Versailles failed to address many of the signatories' concerns following the First World War. Negotiations on other agreements continued until the Locarno Pact in 1925.[6] The most significant postwar Asia-related pacts were concluded at the Washington Naval Conference, which convened in November 1921 and resulted in the Five-Power, Four-Power, and Nine-Power Treaties.[7] The Five-Power and Four-Power Treaties dealt with concerns about Japan by establishing an arms control naval ship ratio among the major naval powers and by terminating the 1902 Anglo-Japanese alliance, while the Nine-Power Treaty returned the Shandong Peninsula to China from Japan.[8]

While Washington was preparing for its Naval Conference in 1921, momentous events were happening in China. In a *shikumen* building in Shanghai's Xintiandi French Concession district, the First Party Congress of the Chinese Communist Party (CCP) was held in July. CCP founding members Chen Duxiu and Li Dazhao were unable to attend, but Mao

Zedong left his work establishing communist cells in Hunan to attend the congress in Shanghai. His presence subsequently gave him higher prestige in the party, still evident on display today in the original meeting room at the *shikumen* hall building where the First Party Congress took place.[9]

Four years earlier in 1917, Sun Yat-sen had praised the Bolshevik Revolution, earning him Soviet support for the Nationalists in Guangdong in the south of China. The Comintern supported a United Front policy, namely a CCP collaboration with the KMT, to bring about a unified Chinese state.[10] Sun Yat-sen relied on assistance from Chiang Kai-shek to relocate from Guangdong to Shanghai, firmly allying Chiang to Sun until Sun's death.

Moscow financed and staffed the new Whampoa Military Academy near Guangdong with one thousand advisors when it was established in May 1924 to prepare the next generation of China's military leaders. Chiang was appointed as the academy's first superintendent. Under his leadership, it became China's premier military academy during the 1920s. Following the Confucian educational model, Superintendent Chiang personally instructed the first two thousand Whampoa students, developing bonds of loyalty, *guanxi*, with those who became known as the Whampoa Clique.[11] The early Nationalist graduates had quick success against larger, less-disciplined warlord forces,[12] first in Guangdong, and later during the Northern Expedition. By the mid-1920s, Chiang had consolidated his position as the primary Nationalist military leader, and while many Whampoa personnel were loyal to Chiang, important Communist Party leaders such as Zhou Enlai and Lin Biao were also trained at Whampoa. Despite increasing responsibilities elsewhere and the relocation of the training facilities themselves, Chiang remained superintendent of the Whampoa Military Academy until 1947. This position allowed him to oversee and track the development of military talent in China for more than two decades, although not always to the benefit of the Nationalists, as demonstrated by the examples of Zhou and Lin. The Whampoa Academy buildings were destroyed by Japanese bombing in 1938 but have since been rebuilt, including a restored entry with characters above meaning "to sleep on brushwood and taste gall,"[13] as King Goujian of Yue had been forced to do twenty-five hundred years ago.[14]

Russian aid to the Nationalists and the Communists was both military and political. Sun accepted the support of Soviet advisors, who established national and local administrative institutions, advisors who assisted in running the First Congress of the Nationalist Party in early 1924. At that event, Communist pressure modified Sun's Three People's Principles from nationalism, democracy, and people's livelihood toward national liberation, party control, and socialism. Sun continued to argue for his Three Principles even as he became ill with cancer in 1924 and would pass away in March 1925. Chiang Kai-shek mourned Sun's death, viewing himself as his protege.[15]

For Chiang Kai-shek, the second half of the 1920s was replete with important events that have become legend as well as history, including most notably the start of open civil war with the Communists, his Northern Expedition against the warlords to unite south and north China, the beginning of the Nanjing Decade of Nationalist administration of the country, and Chiang's marriage to Soong Mei-ling, instrumental in expanding the Nationalist role in economic and international affairs. Chiang's leadership of the Nationalists and China's historical fate were woven together inextricably during this period, leading up to the open confrontation with Japan.

Following Sun's death, competition for leadership of the Nationalist Party arose between Chiang Kai-shek and Wang Jingwei. Chiang represented the right wing of the Nationalist Party, and Wang, supporting the Comintern line, represented the left wing of the party. Wang had convinced Sun on his deathbed to sign a will admonishing the Nationalists to cooperate with the Soviets. In March 1926, from a position of military strength, Chiang accused the Communists of trying to kidnap him, and he declared martial law and forced Wang Jingwei into exile. Chiang also purged many Communists from the military, leaving him in charge of the government in the south.

In July 1926, Chiang launched the Northern Expedition, initially aiming to gain control of central China. Militarily successful, Chiang took his target prizes of Shanghai and Nanjing in March 1927. In Shanghai, a showdown between the Communists and Chiang's Nationalist wing occurred in April. Shanghai's underworld Green Gang joined forces with Chiang and massacred thousands of CCP members in a campaign known as the Shanghai Massacre, igniting the Chinese Civil War and prompting the Communists to flee from Shanghai.

Chiang stepped down temporarily as army commander in August 1927, nominally to allow a reunification process in the contested Nationalist Party and government, but also to give him time to take care of personal matters, in this case improving his marital status. In 1901, at age fourteen, Chiang had entered into an arranged marriage with Mao Fumei, a Zhejiang woman five years his senior. Their son Chiang Ching-kuo was born in 1910. In 1913, Chiang took a concubine, Yao Yecheng, known also as Jennie, who became the adoptive mother of Chiang Kai-shek's adopted son Chiang Wei-guo, who was born in 1916. In 1918, Chiang took another concubine, Chen Jieru, whom he married in 1921 after he divorced his first wife, Mao Fumei. By the mid-1920s, Chiang Kai-shek decided that he needed an important marriage. Over time, he wooed Soong Mei-ling, one of three daughters of the wealthy, well-connected Soong family. Mei-ling's mother opposed Mei-ling's marriage to Chiang unless he showed proof of divorce and conversion to Christianity. Chiang severed himself from his former wives and concubines to clear the way to marry Soong Mei-ling in Shanghai in December 1927. Chiang also gradually absorbed Christianity into his views as a complement to his Confucian philosophy. Mei-ling, astute, polished, and supportive in politics, became a long-term asset for Chiang.[16] Mei-ling's older sister, Ching-ling, had married Sun Yat-sen. By marrying Mei-ling, Chiang became a brother-in-law to the deceased Sun Yat-sen.

Following the 1927 wedding, Chiang quickly resumed his military career at the request of the Nationalist leadership to renew his Northern Expedition in January 1928. By February, Chiang had arranged power sharing with three warlords, consolidating his control and proclaiming the Nationalist capital in Nanjing. The Nationalists began a spring offensive against Manchurian warlord Zhang Zuolin, but the Japanese feared a Nationalist occupation of Shandong, where they had substantial economic interests despite the formal reversion of Shandong to China in the Nine-Power Treaty of 1922. Japanese and Nationalist forces clashed in the Jinan Incident of May 1928, and the Japanese were brutal in this incident, cutting out the tongue and gouging out the eyes of the Nanjing representative, Cai Gongshi, and killing his staff.

The Kwantung Army was established in 1906 after the Russo-Japanese War to secure Japanese interests in Manchuria. In a predecessor action to

Japan's occupation of Manchuria in 1931, Japanese Kwantung Army officials fatally blew up Zhang Zuolin's rail car. Now fearing the Japanese, Zhang's son, Zhang Xueliang, allied with the Nationalists, who recognized his rights in Manchuria. Chiang took control of Beijing in June and proclaimed the success of the Northern Expedition. For the first time since the 1911 fall of the Qing dynasty, China was united. Chiang turned his focus to ruling China from Nanjing in what has been called the Nanjing Decade of 1928–1937, representing the high point of Nationalist rule in China. Chiang Kai-shek consolidated his power during this period before resuming civil war campaigns against the Communists. Many Western governments recognized Chiang's Nanjing government in 1928 and 1929 and abrogated some of their former rights, including extraterritoriality, the right of Westerners to use Western rather than Chinese law to settle legal disputes in treaty port areas. By the late 1920s, Chiang's unification of major parts of China was successful in increasing order from chaos throughout the country. Yet the Japanese seizure of Manchuria was just around the corner.

From Manchukuo to Pearl Harbor, 1931–41

The historical narrative surrounding the Second Sino-Japanese War has been in flux in recent years, as the interpretations surrounding Chiang Kai-shek's contributions to the conflict with Japan have been given more credence by Beijing. Traditionally, accounts of the war's start began with the Marco Polo Bridge Incident in June 1937 and ended with the surrender of Japan in August 1945.[17] Some accounts, however, attribute the start of hostilities to 1931, when Japan invaded Manchuria, and continue with the outbreak of hostilities in central China in 1937, to the moment when the war changed from a Sino-Japanese to an Allied-Japanese war following the Pearl Harbor attack in 1941.[18]

On September 18, 1931, the Japanese military manufactured an excuse for its Kwantung Army to seize control in Manchuria by setting off a bomb on the railway line near Mukden (Shenyang). Called the "Manchurian Incident," the Japanese blamed the bombing on Chinese subversives, although the attack actually was orchestrated by Kwantung Army officers Ishiwara Kanji and Itagaki Seishiro. Kanji justified the behavior of the Japanese army by pointing to American actions during the previous century.[19]

The Kwantung Army followed up by seizing resource-rich Manchuria, an area more than twice the size of Japan and containing thirty million people. In 1932, Japan established in the region a separate puppet state of Japan called Manchukuo and installed the last Qing emperor Puyi as regent. When condemned by the League of Nations the following year for its actions, Japan withdrew from the league, foreshadowing Japan's future military intentions. Rather than fighting the Japanese during the early 1930s, Chiang Kai-shek focused on consolidating his preeminent position in Chinese politics, building his government in Nanjing, and fighting the Communists, his most serious Chinese rivals. Between 1930 and 1934, Chiang orchestrated five "encirclement campaigns" of Communist strongholds in south China,[20] which drove the Communists west, then north to Shaanxi province on the Long March.[21] During this period, Mao Zedong solidified his authority as the Communist leader. In approximate numbers, the Communists began the Long March with 100,000 troops, but suffered extreme losses due to the march's hardship, reaching the caves of Yan'an north of Xi'an with only 10,000 remaining.

In 1936, Chiang Kai-shek flew to Xi'an to execute a final blow against his exhausted Communist enemy. In the "Xi'an Incident," Chiang was captured through the treachery of General Zhang Xueliang, forcing the creation of a United Front of the Nationalists and Communists against the Japanese and giving new life to the Communist forces.[22] The capture of Chiang in the Xi'an Incident precluded what likely could have been a final successful blow against the Communists. The drama of the incident is apparent through a visit to the cottage at the Huaqing Hot Spring east of Xi'an, where Chiang leaped out a rear window to attempt escape, but, having wrenched his back, was captured.

The KMT suspended its anti-Communist operations through 1945, although fighting between Communist and Nationalist troops occurred occasionally. This incident was instrumental in transforming Chiang's primary focus and energy from anti-Communist to anti-Japanese campaigns. Chiang would be the principal Chinese military leader to oppose the Japanese through the end of World War II in 1945, bearing the brunt of casualties while the Communists increased their strength. Ultimately, the strength of the Communists became insurmountable for the Nationalists.

Six months after the Xi'an Incident, Chinese Nationalist troops pushed back against Japanese Imperial troops in a skirmish at the Marco Polo Bridge at the southwest corner of Beijing. This event, ostensibly over a missing Japanese soldier who later reappeared, traditionally has been regarded as the spark that ignited the Second Sino-Japanese War. Notably, some analysts consider this event to be the true start of World War II.

Full-scale Sino-Japanese war broke out a few weeks later on August 9, 1937,[23] after two Japanese servicemen were killed in Shanghai. The three-month Battle of Shanghai between August and November 1937 signaled Japan's intention to dominate all of China. Despite fierce Nationalist resistance, not only did Japan take the city, but the battle also displaced a tremendous wave of approximately thirty million Chinese refugees throughout the countryside in a "sea of bitterness."[24] After preserving his troops by avoiding confrontations with the Japanese in northern China, Chiang Kai-shek engaged in a fierce defense of Shanghai, attempting to bar the Japanese from the area south of the Yangzi River. A measure of recent appreciation for the Nationalist resistance against the Japanese in 1937 is visible at the entry to a building on the north side of Suzhou Creek in central Shanghai that was the last holdout of the Nationalists before they were driven south of the creek. The Nationalists held the Sihang Warehouse in the face of intense Japanese attacks for a week at the end of October 1937, an action that resonates in Chinese collective memory just as the legendary Texan defense of the Alamo resonates in American collective memory. The Nationalist commander at the warehouse was Lieutenant Colonel Xie Jinyuan. Those entering the Sihang Warehouse, still in use today as a commercial building, will find commander Xie's bronze statue at the entry, decorated with plaques and flowers.

Ultimately, a Japanese landing at Hangzhou swept from the south and drove the Nationalist troops out of Shanghai. From Shanghai, the Japanese moved up the Yangzi River to capture the Chinese capital at Nanjing. The history of the Nanjing battle remains contentious today. Present-day "history wars" between China and Japan often focus on the events at Nanjing in 1937. The number of Chinese casualties is a source of disagreement in the abundant literature containing both Chinese and Japanese narratives.[25] Nanjing's Memorial Hall of the Victims in Nanjing Massacre by Japanese

Invaders museum displays 300,000 deaths on the face of the building, representing China's accounting of Chinese casualties from Japanese aggression in Nanjing. Against a wall in the museum complex are three huge stone relief carvings called Catastrophe, Slaughter, and Mourning, which portray "scenes of horrifying crimes committed by the Japanese Imperial Army in China."

Japanese accounts of Chinese casualties at Nanjing are as low as 10 percent of the 300,000 number given by the Chinese, although there is a range in the Japanese literature. The divergent narratives of the Nanjing atrocities are evident in the catalogs of the Nanjing Museum and the Yasukuni Jinju Museum on the grounds of the Yasukuni Shrine in Tokyo. Although China considers the Shanghai and Nanjing battles to be full-fledged war with Japan and refers to the Nanjing battle as the "Nanjing Massacre" or "Rape of Nanjing," some Japanese versions only refer to it as the "Nanking Campaign." A Japanese account at the Yasukuni Shrine museum in Tokyo ends with "Nanking fell on December 13," representing what the Chinese consider to be a whitewashed version of the "Nanjing Massacre." An example of a description sympathetic to the Japanese version is "After the Japanese surrounded Nanking in December 1937, Gen. Matsui Iwane distributed maps to his men with foreign settlements and the Safety Zone marked in red ink. Matsui told them that they were to maintain strict military discipline and that anyone committing unlawful acts would be severely punished. The defeated Chinese rushed to Xiaguan, [sic] and they were completely destroyed. Chinese soldiers in civilian clothes were severely prosecuted."[26]

Following the Japanese victories in Shanghai and Nanjing, Chinese soldiers retreated into the interior, with the Japanese in pursuit. But in early April 1938, the Chinese Nationalist armies defeated the Japanese in house-to-house fighting at the Battle of Taierzhuang near Xuzhou north of the Yangzi River on the east bank of the Grand Canal. Chinese forces captured more than seven hundred Japanese soldiers and many military supplies, giving hope to both the Nationalists and to the international community that supported China. The victory was significant for shattering the myth of Japanese military invincibility,[27] but it was followed by one of the greatest tragedies of the war. To block the Japanese advance toward the Nationalist military headquarters, which had moved up the Yangzi from Nanjing to Wuhan, the Nationalists broke the dikes on the Yellow River, causing massive flooding throughout central China. The flood succeeded in slowing down the Japanese advance to Wuhan by many months, but at a tremendous human cost. More than 800,000 Chinese lost their lives in the floods, and the resulting agricultural devastation led to disease and famine in the countryside, displacing close to five million refugees.[28] The flood damage held up the Japanese advance to Zhengzhou until 1944. Chiang approved the Nationalist army's destruction of the dikes, but until the end of the war the Nationalists blamed the dikes' failing on Japanese aerial bombing. Destroying the dikes gave the Chinese forces "breathing space" so they could retreat to Chongqing, their final war capital. Still, the justification for this action does not make up for the self-inflicted casualties that caused more Chinese deaths and destruction than any other single event during the war.

The Japanese succeeded in capturing Wuhan and bombed Chongqing heavily, but the Chinese held that city even though more than 10,000 Chinese died in the Chongqing bombings and more than 17,000 buildings were destroyed. By spring 1939, the tide was turning against the Japanese both in the war with China and in its relations with the United States and other Western countries, creating the conditions that ultimately drew allies into the war for China. American public opinion, horrified by the images of Japanese bombing in China, became hostile toward Tokyo. U.S. opinion polls indicated increasing support for an embargo against Japan as the Japanese became entangled in the Chinese interior. The Japanese were outraged when the United States gave a $25 million credit to the Nationalists to purchase U.S. manufactured trucks for the war effort. In the summer of 1939, the Japanese were surprised by the Soviet Red Army defeat of Japanese troops at Nomonhon on the Mongolia-Manchukuo border. The signing of the Soviet-German nonaggression pact by Vyacheslav Molotov and Joachim von Ribbentrop in August 1939 also shocked the Japanese. A week after this pact was concluded, World War II in Europe began with Germany's invasion of Poland. Later in September, the United States placed an embargo on the sale of iron and steel scrap outside of the Western Hemisphere. Japan, under pressure from the cumulative impact of these events, concluded the Tripartite Pact with Germany and Italy. One of the pact's goals was to intimidate the United States with the possibility of a two-ocean war, but the

pact drove the United States closer to China, resulting in an increased supply of U.S. funds and arms to China, notably Claire Chennault's mercenary
Flying Tigers.

In 1940, Wang Jingwei established a Chinese collaborationist government with the Japanese in Nanjing. While the German blitzkrieg rolled
through Europe, Japan increased its pressure on Indochina and Indonesia, implementing its concept of the Greater East Asian Co-Prosperity
Sphere. The Japan-Soviet Non-Aggression Pact of April 1941 followed,
which allowed Japan to strike south without having to worry about fighting the Soviets in the north at the same time. These events prompted the
United States to take further action that Japan perceived as hostile toward
its interests. With tensions rising in the summer of 1941, the United States
froze Japanese assets in the United States and implemented an oil embargo
against Japan. Diplomatic efforts to reduce tensions with Japan by Secretary of State Cordell Hull and others failed. The Hull Note of November 26
demanded that Japanese troops withdraw from both China and Indochina,
an unacceptable ultimatum from Japan's perspective. Japan's surprise attack
on Pearl Harbor on December 7 brought the United States into the war in
the Pacific. When Germany declared war on the United States on December 11, the United States also became firmly embroiled in the Atlantic
and European war. China now had a committed American ally for its war
against Japan, even though that American obligation was tempered by an
emerging "Germany first" strategy. Britain, having lost ships and colonies
in Southeast Asia to the Japanese, was caught up in the war against Japan.
This alliance initiated a new phase in the Second Sino-Japanese War, as
China now had allies to assist them against the Japanese for the first time.

From Pearl Harbor to Japanese Surrender, 1941–45

The Japanese attack on Pearl Harbor presented an unparalleled opportunity for Chiang Kai-shek. China would no longer be on its own in the fight
against Japan, as both the United States and the United Kingdom entered
the war in Asia. The record of China's alliance with the Western powers,
however, was mixed due to the allies' competing objectives. Chiang's aim
was to expel Japan from Chinese soil, FDR's aim was to seek Japan's total
surrender, and Churchill's aim was to protect and maintain British colonies

in both Southeast and South Asia. These differing objectives led to dramatic schisms in the alliance over the next four years.

In February, two months after the Pearl Harbor attack, Chiang Kai-shek arrived in India to help plan resistance to the Japanese in South and Southeast Asia. Chiang met with Gandhi and they established anti-imperialist goals, much to Churchill's chagrin, but they failed to agree on methods. Gandhi believed in nonviolent practice, whereas Chiang understood that divesting China of the Japanese required military resistance involving violence.[29] For the remainder of the war, Chiang resented British and American pressure for Nationalist troops to fight in the British colonies in India and Burma, preferring to maintain his focus on pushing the Japanese out of China.

By the time of America's Doolittle Raid on Tokyo in April 1942, cracks in the alliance had emerged. The Doolittle Raid was a success for American self-esteem, demonstrating that American airplanes could reach Tokyo from aircraft carriers and intimidate the Japanese main islands. But because the airplanes went on to land in China after having done little actual damage in Japan, the Japanese retaliated massively against the Chinese.[30] Chiang's forces were unable to protect the airfields despite his opposition to the raid because he had succumbed to American and British pressure to reinforce their troops in Burma. Chiang lamented, "Now I know the alliance is just empty words and I don't exclude America from this." Thus differences among the Chinese, British, and Americans over how to conduct the war revealed an alliance structure in which China paid a severe price. In addition to suffering heavy Chinese losses in both Burma and eastern China, Chiang endured constant criticism from his American chief of staff, Gen. Joseph Stilwell, who mocked Chiang by referring to him as the Peanut and who asserted publicly that Chiang did little to oppose the Japanese militarily, even though the Chinese Nationalists had lost many more troops than the Americans. About four million Chinese soldiers and sixteen million Chinese civilians died in World War II; approximately 4 percent of the soldiers' deaths, about 160,000 military dead, were Communist. About 400,000 Americans lost their lives in all theaters of World War II, with very few civilian casualties. Reflecting on these statistics, it is difficult to support Stilwell's claim that Chiang did not fight.

American public opinion was divided over how much to support the Nationalist effort. Stilwell had many supporters in the United States who were skeptical about the resolve and capability of the Nationalists under Chiang's command, including his superior, Gen. George Marshall, and John Paton Davies, a U.S. diplomat who served on Stilwell's staff. Davies was more sympathetic to Mao than to Chiang, especially when Mao told him that the Communist troops would be proud to serve under Stilwell's command. On the other side of the public relations struggle in the United States, Chinese anthropologist Fei Xiaotong shifted from criticizing Chiang to criticizing Mao when he obtained information about Mao's purges in Yan'an. Fei became an advocate for the American open democratic model for China and was attacked by both the right and left in China for glorifying America.[31] Pearl Buck's *The Good Earth* (1931) also created sympathy for China, but the most effective advocate for the Nationalists was Chiang Kai-shek's wife Soong Mei-ling.[32] Madame Chiang was both the first private citizen and the first woman to address the U.S. Congress, and she was highly effective in winning friends and obtaining promises of aid for the Nationalist cause.

In China, Stilwell's vision of a land war using Chinese troops came into conflict with Claire Chennault's view of air power dominating the action, which resulted in muddled American leadership and allocation of aid and materiel. Although the United States sent a relatively small number of troops to fight alongside the Chinese in China, intelligence operations were established through the Office of Strategic Services (OSS) and the Sino-American Cooperative Organization (SACO). While OSS director William "Wild Bill" Donovan reported to President Roosevelt that SACO did not run intelligence or operations of consequence, SACO's "rice paddy navy" sank Japanese ships and blew up bridges, coordinating with KMT security chief Dai Li and establishing a model for collaboration between U.S. and local security forces in the postwar period.[33]

Chiang Kai-shek was invited to join Roosevelt and Churchill for the Cairo Conference in November 1943 even though the Western powers had committed to a "Germany first" strategy. At the conference, Chiang perceived that Churchill had a colonial mindset but was pleased that Roosevelt treated him like an "old friend," particularly with the stated commitment to return Manchuria and Taiwan to China and grant independence for Korea, a reversal of the outcomes of the First Sino-Japanese War in 1895. In return, Chiang promised to fight again in Burma, with the stipulation that the United States and United Kingdom would provide an amphibious assault in southern Burma to support Chiang's land forces. Chiang was exultant over his diplomatic success in Cairo, the greatest of his career. But it did not take long for Chiang's achievements and hopes at Cairo to be dashed. Roosevelt and Churchill met with Stalin in Tehran in December. Stalin demanded that the United States and United Kingdom focus all amphibious energy on Normandy, not on Burma. In exchange, Stalin promised to enter the war against Japan within ninety days of Germany's defeat, and he supported Roosevelt's idea of a United Nations organization. With the Soviet Union promising to assist against Japan, China's role was diminished substantially.

In December 1943, Stilwell began building a supply road from Ledo in northwest India, with the intention to cross Burma into southwest China and supply B-29 bombers flying from Chengdu to Japan. This "Road to Tokio" through Burmese leech bogs was based on faulty intelligence that Japanese forces in the area were insignificant. Stilwell's troops were unprepared for the onslaught that they faced when attacked by the seasoned Japanese forces that also had taken Singapore. Lord Louis Mountbatten, commander of the South East Asia Command (SEAC),[34] proposed delaying the Burmese operations until after the Normandy invasion. This would push back the completion of the Burma Road until 1946, too late to have an impact on the outcome of the war. Stilwell continued to conceal his plans from both of his allies, Chiang and Mountbatten, and continued to push his men relentlessly, including the unit known as Merrill's Marauders, resulting in their heavy casualties on the road-building project.

While American resources and energy remained focused on road building through Burma that would ultimately achieve little, Japan launched its largest offensive of the war in eastern China. The objective of this operation, called Ichigo[35] (Operation Number One), was to connect Manchuria with Indochina by land, resulting in Japanese control of all of eastern China. Allied ships had devastated the Japanese merchant fleet, and Japan needed a land corridor for oil and food to flow northward from Southeast Asia before crossing the Korea Strait to Japan. A secondary Japanese goal was to destroy the air bases in eastern China that Chennault had been using successfully to conduct air raids on shipping and on Taiwan. When 500,000 Japanese troops poured south across the Yellow River to begin the Ichigo offensive in April 1944, Stilwell refused to allow the use of B-29s in Chengdu against these Japanese forces. Although Chiang and Chennault pleaded for supplies for China's defense, U.S. Army Air Force chief General "Hap" Arnold denied the request, in sympathy with Stilwell, giving priority to preparing China as a springboard to attack Japan, not to assisting the Nationalist armies. That plan, called Matterhorn, was to bomb Japan from Chengdu. The distances, however, were too great for the plan to succeed and resulted in only ten attacks from Chengdu on Japan.

The Ichigo strike moved south steadily from Henan through Hubei toward Changsha in Hunan, then into Guangdong to connect with Hanoi in Vietnam. Meanwhile, Stilwell railed against Chiang for allocating Nationalist forces to fight the Japanese in China instead of sending his forces to fight in Burma. General Marshall, with Roosevelt's blessing, promoted Stilwell to full general, placing him in charge of all the Chinese armies. This was a direct insult to Chiang, and Stilwell himself delivered the note of his appointment directly to him, resulting in what Chiang considered to be the most severe humiliation of his life. Stilwell laughed and wrote in his diary: "I have waited long for vengeance, at last I've had my chance; I've looked the Peanut in the eye and kicked him in his pants." Chiang refused to accept Stilwell, and eventually he was recalled to Washington. Gen. Albert Wedemeyer, one of the Army's top planners, was appointed in Stilwell's place to serve as chief of staff to Chiang. In the end, the Ichigo offensive failed to achieve Japan's objectives. The land corridor intended by Ichigo brought only a few trainloads of supplies from Vietnam to Manchuria, but it damaged Chiang's Nationalist armies significantly. Mao's Communist armies, having been tucked away in China's northwest region, were the biggest winners in the Ichigo campaign, growing stronger as their foes, the Japanese and the Nationalists, grew weaker. The Communists were pleased to watch from a distance as battles between the Chinese Nationalists and Japanese reduced their strength and resources to the benefit of the Communists.

Although the Nationalist cause was buoyed in the United States by positive portrayals in the press and by Soong Mei-ling's persuasive messaging, by 1943 the American public began to have misgivings about reports of Nationalist incompetence and corruption, especially in relation to more positive information regarding Chinese Communist contenders for support. Stilwell, regarded as a hero in America though thoroughly reviled by Chiang Kai-shek, was impressed by Mao's band in Yan'an. The 1943 release of Chiang's book, *China's Destiny*,[36] appeared to many Americans to contain unattractive totalitarian content, such that Harvard scholar and OSS analyst John Fairbank thought it was perilous for the United States to support Chiang. Others referred to the book as the Chinese version of *Mein Kampf*. Meanwhile, the Chinese Communists were viewed increasingly as "radishes," red on the outside and pure white on the inside. Many Americans read the sympathetic accounts by Edgar Snow and Agnes Smedley about Mao's Yan'an utopia,[37] brimming with energy, goodwill, lack of corruption, and positive results, but without noting the purges of dissenting opinion that were taking place at the same time. Based on the recommendation of Stilwell and American diplomats serving in Chongqing, the Dixie Mission, led by Col. David Barrett, was sent to Yan'an to observe and establish communications with the Communists in Shaanxi Province. Barrett conducted military analysis, while Foreign Service officer John Service directed political analysis. Their reports were sympathetic to cooperation with the Communists, as were those of the OSS agents accompanying the mission, who recommended and delivered on promises to provide the Communists with radio communications equipment. In later years, both Barrett and Service recognized that they had been "unduly impressed by the Communists." Lin Yutang, one of China's major liberal intellectuals of the period, found himself forgiving Chiang Kai-shek as a farsighted humanist, and he called the Yan'an Red Zone a totalitarian dictatorship. He critiqued the Dixie Mission for not reading Chinese source documents and relying on observations during tours conducted by Communist hosts.[38]

General Wedemeyer was more sympathetic to Chiang and the Nationalists than Stilwell had been, and he provided his opinions to Chiang in private so that issues of face were not involved. Wedemeyer subsequently described his approach as using honey rather than vinegar. Burma's Ledo

Road opened under Wedemeyer's watch, but he considered it a waste of time and resources since by the time it was put into use in 1945, ten times the amount of supplies were being flown over the Hump, the eastern end of the Himalayas, than were transported on the road. Roosevelt appointed Patrick Hurley as American ambassador to China in November 1944.[39] Like Wedemeyer, he was an advocate for Chiang Kai-shek, and he eventually forced the reassignments of State Department officers John Davies, John Vincent, and John Service, the China hands who "lost China" in his opinion. Acting in tandem, Wedemeyer and Hurley managed to thwart a secretly negotiated visit by Mao Zedong and Zhou Enlai to Washington, which might have altered postwar developments had it occurred.[40]

At the Yalta Conference in February 1945, Stalin agreed to send his armies to fight the Japanese within sixty to ninety days of Germany's defeat. He notified Mao of impending Red Army support even before he shook hands with Roosevelt and Churchill to conclude the deal at Yalta. In exchange for sending his armies east, Stalin gained acceptance of his objective for Japan to return what Russia had lost in the Russo-Japanese War in 1905: a lease on the Port Arthur naval base, Manchurian railway rights, and the occupation of half of Korea. This deal was made without any input from Chiang Kai-shek, ostensibly a key ally who had a profound interest in these matters. Roosevelt kept his deal secret from Chiang. Ambassador Hurley was shocked when he finally pried out details of the deal. There had been no adherence to the principle stating that affected populations should have a say in territorial discussions. From Chiang's perspective, Roosevelt had betrayed him, though at that point FDR may have been too tired or ill to negotiate the best deal at Yalta. Two months after the Yalta Conference, Roosevelt died of a cerebral hemorrhage. Harry Truman took the presidential oath of office later that day.

In June 1945, John Service and five others in the State Department were arrested as spies, and although a grand jury cleared Service, he became a symbol of the type of person Sen. Joseph McCarthy targeted to eliminate from government service. Wedemeyer, still supporting Chiang, worried that the Nationalists, weakened by the destruction wrought upon them by the Japanese, were unprepared to fight the Communists. Indeed, the Nationalists were unable to force Japan's surrender. Japan succumbed to a combination of the atomic bombs dropped on Hiroshima on August 6 and on Nagasaki on August 9, and the Soviet Red Army invasion of Manchuria on August 8.

The story of Chiang Kai-shek's war against Japan stops here. Like King Goujian, Chiang had "slept on brushwood and tasted bile," the Whampoa Military Academy slogan over its doorway. Chiang achieved his objective, the liberation of China from Japanese domination, though with enormous suffering and bitterness on the part of the Chinese people as well as for him personally. Thus, in the end, the parallel with King Goujian held true as far as Chiang's war with Japan was concerned.

From Japanese Surrender to the Death of Chiang, 1945–75

The day before Japan formally surrendered on August 15, 1945, Chiang Kai-shek's son Chiang Ching-kuo was in Moscow to sign a treaty between China and the Soviet Union based on the Yalta terms. Stalin put pressure on Mao to fly to Chongqing for talks with Chiang in late August, a delaying tactic to give the Communists time to mobilize their troops. In China, the number of Communist forces had grown from about 40,000 in 1937 to more than a million in 1945. Compared to the Nationalists, devastated by their fight with Japan, the Communists were ready and able-bodied, and Stalin provided access to Japanese arms and munitions industries in Manchuria. With no further need for a United Front against Japan, the Communists were in an advantageous position for their ultimately successful civil war against the Nationalists that ensued over the next four years. In October 1949, the Communist People's Republic of China was founded, and Chiang and his Nationalist Republic of China were driven from the Chinese mainland to Taiwan. Chiang's flight to Taiwan was reminiscent of another figure from Chinese history, the late-Ming loyalist Zheng Chenggong, who was driven to Taiwan during the mid-seventeenth century by the Manchu in a civil war that overthrew the Ming dynasty and replaced it with the Qing dynasty.

The narrative of Zheng Chenggong, more widely known as Koxinga, is resonant because it includes a component of war against a foreign power (Koxinga against the Dutch compared with Chiang against Japan) and a component of Chinese internal war (Ming Koxinga against the Qing compared with Nationalist Chiang against the Communists). Both Koxinga and Chiang were successful against foreign powers, Koxinga against the Dutch in 1662 and Chiang against the Japanese in 1945. On the Chinese civil war front, both Koxinga and Chiang were partially successful. Koxinga established a Ming dynasty government in exile on Taiwan while the Qing dynasty controlled the mainland. Chiang established a Republic of China in exile on Taiwan while the People's Republic of China controlled the mainland. Koxinga, his son, and grandson ruled Taiwan as the last Ming remnants from 1662 until 1683, when the Qing regime took control of Taiwan through naval conquest by Shi Lang, an admiral who had defected from Koxinga's navy to the Qing. Chiang and his son ruled Taiwan from 1949 to 1988, followed by an ongoing democratic government in Taipei, opposed by Beijing's authoritarian regime.

Chiang maintained martial law in Taiwan until his death in 1975 and had a reputation for being a harsh taskmaster, as had King Goujian, who ordered some of his men, possibly captives, to cut their own throats to frighten the enemy. Chiang's public image in Taiwan, however, became softer over time, especially as he grew an avuncular mustache. He gradually transferred power to his son, Ching-kuo, who had demonstrated capable powers of administration as well as an ability to relate to the people by taking part in many public works projects. Ching-kuo is considered by some Taiwanese as Chiang Kai-shek's greatest legacy. Surprisingly, the same avuncular public image of Chiang appears in Nanjing, as his wax effigy sits on a couch in his former Presidential Palace together with effigies of his wife and other Soong sisters. This flattering depiction seems like an unusual non sequitur, considering that Chiang was the archenemy of Mao during the Chinese civil war between 1921 and 1949 and that the Taiwan question is yet to be resolved seventy years after the founding of the People's Republic of China.

The apparent non sequitur, however, fits other patterns in Chinese history. The Chinese use history to interpret the present. Returning to the Koxinga parable to think about the possibilities for historical interpretation, he served as a Ming model of Taiwanese resistance to the Qing on the mainland, with parallels to Nationalist Chiang Kai-shek's Taiwanese resistance to the ruling government of Communists on the mainland. The Nationalists therefore identify with the historic parallel between Chiang and Koxinga, while mainland Communists also consider Koxinga to be an admirable Chinese hero because he expelled foreign influence in China by driving the Dutch from Taiwan. As Chinese relations with Japan have become increasingly strained over the past two decades, the role of Chiang in the 1930s and 1940s war against Japan has been increasingly appreciated on the mainland, such that his image has been rehabilitated for driving Japan from China, even as Koxinga drove the Dutch from Taiwan. Mao died in 1976, about a year after Chiang. In the great competition between these two leaders, the China of today looks more like Chiang's vision than like Mao's vision. As with earlier great figures in Chinese history, they will each be treated with varying degrees of affection depending on the lessons the current generation wants to extract from the past.

Assessing Chiang Kai-shek

Following World War II and his defeat in the civil war in 1949, Chiang Kai-shek's contributions to the struggle against Japan were buried by Chinese scholars on the mainland and given too little attention by Western scholars. Recent reassessments have occurred in both China and in the West, and Chiang's contributions to the war against Japan are becoming more widely recognized and appreciated. This revisionism follows trends in the development of Asian great power politics since World War II and the evolution of the complex relationship between China and Japan.

In evaluating Chiang Kai-shek's contributions, biographer Jay Taylor gives Chiang the premier role in creating China's national path forward: "Truly, the vision that drives modern China in the twenty-first century is that of Chiang Kai-shek, not Mao Zedong."[41] Not all historians are as certain of Chiang's statesmanlike contributions, which is a subject of continued debate. For instance, China historian Jonathan Spence comments, "The attempt to portray Chiang as a major statesman seems to me to be flawed."[42] But Spence gives credit to many of Chiang's personal characteristics, including his toughness and concentration as recalled by Japanese officers, and his self-discipline, duty, courage, honor, and activism, as neo-Confucianist values that Chiang cultivated on the model of Wang Yangming.[43] Such positive revisionist characterizations of Chiang argue convincingly against earlier negative portrayals, such as those by Gen. Joseph Stilwell and U.S. Foreign Service officer John Service.

Scholarly analyses of the Republican period, nominally 1912–49 but now expanded to include Republican predecessors during the late nineteenth century through twenty-first century developments, and encompassing Chiang's role in this complex history, have evolved substantially over the past forty years. The partial and peripatetic opening of archives on the mainland, on Taiwan, and in the United States and Europe, has spurred this research. The new studies "marked a sea of change from the conventional wisdom about the myriad ways in which the regime's corrosive features had destroyed its chances for winning the military and political battle against the Chinese Communist Party."[44] The key role of China's war with Japan on Republican/Nationalist rule under Chiang is summarized by Mitter and Moore as part of the recent reassessment: "[T]he weight of research within the last few years has moved from an overall negative assessment to a cautiously positive analysis of many aspects of its developmental state. The outbreak of total war in 1937 becomes the key turning point, the moment at which the Guomindang's experiment in government was (ultimately fatally) blown off course by an external shock."[45] This perspective would not have been possible forty years ago, because the early war analysts uniformly assigned a much more negative view to Chiang Kai-shek, and, more recently, the economic and social changes in China now justify reconsideration of this hypothesis.

So far, Taiwan has maintained its autonomy from the mainland for seventy-one years, a better record than Koxinga's against the Qing. But the future of Taiwan is still an open question. In an unexpected parallel, the Qing built shrines on Taiwan to Koxinga, even as Communist mainlanders now visit with respect Chiang's family home in Zhejiang Province, his Presidential Palace in Nanjing, and his military headquarters in Chongqing. Over time, the meaning of Koxinga in Chinese history has changed in response to contemporary political currents. Koxinga now is highly regarded on the mainland as a successful Chinese anti-imperialist, and Chiang Kai-shek is now highly regarded on Taiwan as a successful protector of its residents against the mainland Communists, rather than as a protector against the mainland Qing, as Koxinga had been. The importance of Chiang Kai-shek's life and the interpretation of his legacy within the arc of Chinese history will vary in the future according to changing political circumstances. Subsequent historical narratives will take what they want from the parable of Chiang Kai-shek. The path of China-Taiwan relations in the future undoubtedly will affect the nature of the narrative about Chiang.

Leaning Forward

China's current narratives about its twentieth-century war with Japan and its role in World War II play a key part in China's nationalistic interpretation of its place in the world today. Increasingly, China emphasizes the importance of how its long war of attrition with Japan during the 1930s through 1945 helped set the stage for crushing Japan's ambitions on both the Asian and world stages. Surprisingly, given the bitter civil war between the Nationalists and Communists that overlapped with China's war with Japan, Nationalist historic sites and figures have become venerated on the Chinese mainland. Nationalist sites in Shanghai, Nanjing, and Chongqing now are well-kept shrines to commemorate China's resistance to Japan. China's narrative about its war against Japan has become an inclusive discourse that includes both Nationalist and Communist historical contributions.

Chiang Kai-shek's legacy in today's China is tarnished by his role as the archenemy of Chinese Communists during the civil war, but his legacy on the mainland has been enhanced increasingly through appreciation of his anti-imperialist stance, whether with regard to the Japanese or to the British. Chiang's fundamental Chinese nationalism gives core support to nationalist policies on the mainland today, such as Chinese accounts that are moving the date backward for the beginning of China's war with Japan from the 1937 Marco Polo Bridge Incident to Japan's 1931 occupation of Manchuria.[46] Thus, China's war with Japan in Chinese historical analysis has become six years longer, supporting China's narrative regarding its larger share of the burdens in fighting Japan on the world stage.

For China, "World War II is not history, it is current affairs."[47] The message of China's war with Japan and its role in World War II is twofold and clear. First, China must definitively surpass Japan's leadership role in the Asian region and never allow a repeat of its twentieth-century war with

Japan. Second, China must become and remain a global power and eschew the second-tier position it took during World War II, when it subsumed its own interests to those of its allies, the United States and the United Kingdom. Chiang Kai-shek considered this subordination of China as an unequal ally to be a personal humiliation, echoed by the current narrative of China's "century of humiliation."[48] These lessons drawn from the history of China's war with Japan and China's role in World War II are being advanced in China today, and Western strategists must recognize and understand them.

Notes

1. The Nationalist Party is known as Kuomintang or KMT in Wade-Giles romanization, or alternately as Guomindang or GMD in Pinyin romanization. The text here includes names generally in use at the time and that remain in common use. Some names will therefore be rendered in Wade-Giles romanization, while others will be Pinyin. Hence, Chiang Kai-shek, in Wade-Giles, is used rather than Jiang Jieshi, in Pinyin.

2. Jay Taylor, *The Generalissimo: Chiang Kai-Shek and the Struggle for Modern China* (Cambridge, Mass.: Belknap Press of Harvard University Press, 2011), 16–17. Chiang's relationship with his mother after his father died was close, though he referred to himself later in life as an orphan. His mother was ambitious for him. Much more detail than can be included in this chapter appears in Jay Taylor, *The Generalissimo* and in *The Generalissimo's Son: Chiang Ching-Kuo and the Revolutions in China and Taiwan* (Cambridge, Mass.: Harvard University Press, 2000). Another work of engaging and detailed scholarship on the period is Rana Mitter, *Forgotten Ally: China's World War II, 1937–1945* (Boston: Houghton Mifflin, 2013).

3. Paul Cohen, *History and Popular Memory: The Power of Story in Moments of Crisis* (New York: Columbia University Press, 2017). For a clear overview of many dimensions of the Goujian story, see chapter 3, "Chiang Kai-shek, Nationalist Policy, and the Story of King Goujian," 67–108. For a more complete history of King Goujian, see Cohen's *Speaking to History: The Story of King Goujian in Twentieth Century China* (Berkeley: University of California Press, 2009).

4. Barbara W. Tuchman, *Stilwell and the American Experience in China 1911–45* (New York: Macmillan Company, 1971).

5. David Armstrong, "China's Place in the New Pacific Order," in *The Washington Conference, 1921–22: Naval Rivalry, East Asian Stability and the Road to Pearl Harbor*, ed. Erik Goldstein and John Maurer (New York: Routledge, 1994), 251.

6. Erik Goldstein, *The First World War Peace Settlements, 1919–1925* (London: Longman, 2002), 80–90.

7. "The Washington Naval Conference, 1921–1922" (Washington, D.C.: U.S. State Department, Office of the Historian, n.d.), https://history.state.gov/milestones /1921–1936/naval-conference.

8. On the Washington Conference and the resulting treaties, see Erik Goldstein and John Maurer, eds., *The Washington Conference, 1921–22: Naval Rivalry, East Asian Stability and the Road to Pearl Harbor* (New York: Routledge, 1994).

9. *Shikumen* is a Shanghainese architectural "stone warehouse gate" style common in Shanghai from the 1860s that combines Chinese and Western elements. The wax effigy of Mao is the only standing figure in the tableau around a table of thirteen other wax effigies representing those who attended the congress, out of the fifty-seven original founding members of the CCP. The wax effigy approach to convey Chinese history at historic sites is used effectively at other sites in China as well.

10. Bruce Elleman and S. C. M. Paine, *Modern China: Continuity and Change 1644 to the Present* (Upper Saddle River, N.J.: Prentice Hall, 2010), 275–86.

11. An example of one of Chiang's Whampoa students who later became an important general for him is Hu Zongnan, whose life is recorded in a memoir being translated by Esther Hu.

12. The period of Nationalist conflict with warlords is portrayed dramatically in Richard McKenna's novel (first serialized in the *Saturday Evening Post* in 1962 and then published by Harper and Row, 1963) and the subsequent 1966 film *The Sand Pebbles*.

13. 卧薪尝胆 *woxin changdan*: "to sleep on brushwood and taste gall." See Cohen, *Speaking to History*.

14. King Goujian had been humiliated in battle and forced into servitude by King Fuchai of Wu. Goujian lived an austere life for many years, but watched for an opportunity for revenge, which he eventually achieved by defeating Fuchai in 473 BCE. The story of Yue's humiliation and subsequent recovery over a long period resonated in the proverb over the door of the Whampoa Academy. Through discipline and hard work, Whampoa students hoped to make China whole again, with enough wealth and power to repulse any adversary. In the mid-twentieth century, this moral tale of perseverance in the face of great odds galvanized China in its war against Japan.

15. Between 1926 and 1929, Chiang built a large mausoleum on Purple Mountain in Nanjing to commemorate Sun Yat-sen. The mausoleum is grand and tranquil. The architectural concept is part Chinese imperial tomb, part modern design. Innovation in layout includes the idea of the mausoleum representing an alarm bell, waking up China, lying on a green blanket when seen from the air. Some say the architect who designed the complex was inspired by the Liberty Bell in Philadelphia. An impressive construction, its cost ran about ten times over budget.

16. Two of many biographies of Soong Mei-ling include Laura Tyson Li, *Madame Chiang Kai-shek: China's Eternal First Lady* (New York: Grove Press, 2006), and

Hannah Pakula, *The Last Empress: Madame Chiang Kai-shek and the Birth of Modern China* (New York: Simon & Schuster, 2009).

17. Rana Mitter adopts this time frame in *Forgotten Ally*.

18. S. C. M. Paine adopts the 1931–1941 time frame in *The Wars for Asia, 1911–1949* (New York: Cambridge University Press, 2012). She notes on page 124, "Using 1937 as a starting date sanitizes Japanese activities." She thus regards 1937 as an escalation, rather than as a beginning. She argues that the Second Sino-Japanese War (1931–1941) was a regional war, nested between the Chinese civil war and the World War II global war.

19. Mitter, *Forgotten Ally*, 58. When being tried for war crimes in 1946, Kanji asked the American prosecutor, "Haven't you ever heard of Perry? Japan took your country as its teacher and set about learning to be aggressive. You might say we became your disciples."

20. Elleman and Paine, *Modern China*. For Encirclement Campaign locations and the Long March route, see map 19.2, 308.

21. Dick Wilson, *The Long March 1935: The Epic of Chinese Communism's Survival* (New York: Penguin Books, 1971); Harrison Salisbury, *The Long March: The Untold Story* (New York: Harper and Row, 1985).

22. For details of the Xi'an Incident, see Mitter, *Forgotten Ally*, 71–74, and Taylor, *The Generalissimo*, 123–37.

23. Peter Harmsen, *Shanghai 1937: Stalingrad on the Yangtze* (Havertown, Pa.: Casemate, 2013), 37–38. In scope, scale, and effects, Harmsen likens the battle of Shanghai to a "Stalingrad on the Yangtze, with intense battles taking place in many Shanghai neighborhoods."

24. R. Keith Schoppa, *In a Sea of Bitterness: Refugees during the Sino-Japanese War* (Cambridge, Mass.: Harvard University Press, 2011).

25. See for instance Joshua A. Fogel, ed., *The Nanjing Massacre in History and Historiography* (Berkeley: University of California Press, 2000); Katsuichi Honda and Frank Gibney, *The Nanjing Massacre: A Japanese Journalist Confronts Japan's National Shame* (Armonk, N.Y.: M. E. Sharpe, 1999); Iris Chang, *The Rape of Nanking: The Forgotten Holocaust of World War II* (1st ed.) (New York: Basic Books, 1997); Fran Stirling, *The Nanjing Atrocities: Crimes of War* (Brookline, MA: Facing History and Ourselves National Foundation, 2014). For a sensitive, historically accurate novel about American missionary Minnie Vautrin and the four thousand Chinese sheltered at Ginling College during the Nanjing battle, see Ha Jin, *Nanjing Requiem* (New York: Pantheon Books, 2011).

26. John Breen, *Record in Pictures of Yasukuni Jinja Yushukan* (Tokyo: Yasukuni Shrine, 2009), 40.

27. General Stilwell felt that the Chinese under Chiang's leadership lost their advantage by failing to pursue the Japanese after their victory at Taierzhuang, giving time for the Japanese to regroup and continue their offensive. He had no patience for the Chinese theory of winning by outlasting the Japanese. Tuchman, *Stilwell*, 244–45.

28. Mitter, *Forgotten Ally*, 162–65; Taylor, *The Generalissimo*, 154–55.

29. Mitter, *Forgotten Ally*, 246–48.

30. Japanese retaliation following the Doolittle Raid killed 30,000 Chinese troops and 250,000 civilians. John Pomfret, *The Beautiful Country and the Middle Kingdom: America, China, 1776 to the Present* (New York: Picador Henry Holt and Company, 2016), 290–91.

31. Fei Xiaotong, *Peasant Life in China: A Field Study of Country Life in the Yangtze Valley* (New York: Dutton, 1939). The book was highly regarded when published. Once China became communist in 1949, the book was dismissed as bourgeois social science. Both Fei and the book's reputation, however, were rehabilitated during the post–Cultural Revolution period. Fei helped lead a resurgence in the study of sociology in China before he passed away at age ninety-four in 2005, while he was still professor of sociology at Beijing University. As Prof. Maurice Freedman of Oxford once observed in class during the Cultural Revolution period when Fei's intellectual sun was in eclipse, "And who is Fei Hsiaotong really, other than a piece of furniture in the minds of Anglo-American liberals?" Fei's past, however, was not dead during the 1970s. It was not even past. His light shone once again during the subsequent university reforms under Deng Xiaoping's rule.

32. The couple was occasionally referred to at the time as Gissimo and Missimo.

33. Milton Miles, *A Different Kind of War* (Garden City, N.J.: Doubleday and Company, 1967); Linda Kush, *The Rice Paddy Navy: U.S. Sailors Undercover in China* (Oxford: Osprey Publishing, 2012). SACO tended to be pronounced with verve, Socko!

34. SEAC was sometimes said to stand for "Save England's Asian Colonies," a thought likely running through Chiang Kai-shek's mind.

35. Mitter, *Forgotten Ally*, 318–26.

36. Chiang Kai-shek, *China's Destiny and China's Economic Theory* (New York: Roy Publishers, 1947).

37. See Edgar Snow, *Red Star Over China* (New York: Random House, 1938); Agnes Smedley, *Daughter of Earth* (New York: G. P. Putnam's Sons, 1929); and Agnes Smedley, *The Great Road, the Life and Times of Chu Teh* (Zhu De) (New York: Monthly Review Press, 1956).

38. John Pomfret summarizes the results of the Dixie Mission succinctly: "The Chinese Communist Party's success in convincing most of the State Department diplomatic corps that it was patriotic, moderate, and willing to fight Japan had a significant outcome on China's civil war." Pomfret, *The Beautiful Country*, 328–31.

39. U.S. diplomats considered Hurley to be incompetent when he referred to Chiang and Mao as Mr. Shek and Moose Dung, respectively.

40. Pomfret, *The Beautiful Country*, 336–37.

41. Taylor, *The Generalissimo*, 595.

42. Jonathan Spence, review of Jay Taylor, "The Enigma of Chiang Kai-shek," *The New York Review of Books*, October 22, 2009.

43. Chiang named the hill north of Taipei where he located his retreat "Yangming Mountain."

44. Janet Chen summarizes the shifting conclusions of research on this period in "Republican History," in *A Companion to Chinese History*, ed. Michael Szonyi (Hoboken, N.J.: Wiley Blackwell, 2017), 171–72.

45. Rana Mitter and A. W. Moore, "China in World War II, 1937–1945: Experience, Memory, Legacy," *Modern Asian Studies* (March 2011): 229. In spite of Mitter's harsh criticism of Chiang for the flooding, he reinterprets the overall data about Chiang Kai-shek and is more sympathetic to his efforts to fight the Japanese than earlier Western histories of the period have been.

46. Rana Mitter sees part of this Chinese narrative of moving the date backward from 1937 to 1931 as a form of "affirmative action" that legitimized grievances of the three northeastern provinces against Japan. See "Memory Wars," CSIS webinar event, August 12, 2020, https://www.csis.org/events/online-event-memory-wars.

47. Mitter, "Memory Wars." Also see Rana Mitter, *China's Good War: How World War II Is Shaping a New Nationalism* (Cambridge, Mass.: Harvard University Press, 2020).

48. Zheng Wang, *Never Forget National Humiliation: Historical Memory in Chinese Politics and Foreign Relations* (New York: Columbia University Press, 2014).

CHAPTER FOUR

WINSTON CHURCHILL and the GATHERING STORM in ASIA

John H. Maurer

Introduction

ON THE EVE OF THE SECOND WORLD WAR, THE CELEBRITY GLOBE trotting American journalist John Gunther could write, "Great Britain, as everyone knows, is the greatest Asiatic power."[1] Confirmation of Gunther's claim about Britain's position in Asia could readily be grasped just by looking at a map of the world, showing British imperial possessions colored in red. The British Empire controlled a vast expanse of territory in Asia, sweeping in a great arc from New Zealand and Australia in the South Pacific to Southeast Asia and South China, and on to India and the Middle East. A quarter of the world's population, with much of it concentrated in South Asia, lived within Britain's empire. The empire, too, was rich in the resources that it possessed. Britain stood as a superpower, the leading state of the international system, with economic interests and security commitments stretching around the globe.

Despite the British Empire's strength, Britain's global leadership was already in grave danger, threatened from several quarters, by the beginning of the twentieth century. In 1874, the year of Winston's Churchill's birth, Britain was the workshop of the world, the pioneer of the Industrial Revolution, the leading financial, commercial, and manufacturing great power. This leadership was not destined to last; the spread of the Industrial Revolution to other countries was transforming the international strategic landscape. Already by 1893, the United States was surpassing Britain as an industrial power. In that year, the World's Columbian Exposition, held in Chicago, showcased American agriculture, industry, and technology. Other countries also made gains in economic development and in technological innovation. As these rising great powers converted their economic strength into armed might, they confronted Britain's leaders with difficult strategic choices about how to defend their global empire. The twentieth century's "rise of the rest" and a "return to great power competition" pointed toward a post–British international order in which Britain would no longer remain the leading actor on the world stage.[2]

In Europe, close to home, Germany emerged to menace Britain's security. German industry and technology provided the sinews that made Germany a dangerous challenger. First imperial Germany's rulers and later the Nazi regime consciously aimed to make their country into a superpower that would rival or supplant Britain in world politics. Germany's leaders threatened Britain by building up and unleashing their armed forces in desperate bids to overturn the European balance of power. While the German drive for European hegemony and world power failed in the first war, the conquest of western Europe by Hitler's Germany in 1940 put Britain's homeland in the gravest of danger. In both world wars, too, the German navy's force of submarines inflicted immense damage, sinking millions of tons of shipping, in the battle to control Atlantic sea lanes linking Britain to the rest of the world. The strategic necessity of defeating the German menace required the concentration of British armed strength in Europe and the Atlantic, which called into question Britain's ability to defend its empire on the other side of the globe in Asia.

Meanwhile, in Asia, another powerful rising great power in imperial Japan threatened the British Empire. Britain's leaders recognized the serious danger posed by Japan. Between the world wars, Japan emerged as a stiff industrial competitor to Britain and India in Asian markets. The interwar period also saw Japan make major increases in naval strength. The Imperial Japanese Navy stood second to none in the innovation and development of naval aviation. Japan's growing naval power endangered the security of Britain's empire, the defense of which required the British navy to command the Indian Ocean and the South Pacific. Not only was Japan increasing in economic and naval power, but the international ambitions of its leaders were growing as well. The increasingly belligerent behavior of Japan during the 1930s confronted Britain with the nightmare strategic problem of having to confront two powerful adversaries, bent on expansion, at opposite ends of the globe.

Of course, we know the outcome of the struggle for mastery in Asia: the destruction of two empires, that of Britain and of Japan. The outbreak of war between Britain and Japan at the end of 1941 brutally exposed British weakness in Asia. Britain's prize territories in Asia—Hong Kong, Malaya, Singapore, India, and Australia—were either seized or threatened with invasion by Japan. The Japanese seizure of Singapore, the strategic pivot of Britain's defenses in Asia, struck a staggering blow to the prestige of British arms. More than 80,000 soldiers recruited from throughout the British Empire surrendered to an invading Japanese force half their strength. Not since Yorktown had Britain's standing as an imperial power suffered such a crushing setback. Britain's humiliation might have been worse. The Japanese opening offensive drives came perilously close to pushing Britain out of India, and Australia faced imminent invasion. What saved Britain from an even greater defeat was that the overextended Japanese armed forces lacked the strength to go further in exploiting their incredible opening wartime victories.

This strategic disaster in Asia took place during the watch of Winston Churchill, Britain's prime minister and war leader. Churchill's life story coincided with the horrific, costly great power struggles that broke Britain's empire and leadership of the international system. Over his lifetime, he served in some of the most important high offices of state and at the center of British strategic decision making during both world wars. As first lord of the admiralty, minister of munitions, and secretary of state for war and air,

he confronted head-on the strategic challenges facing Britain in the struggle for world power during the era of the First World War. Throughout
the interwar period, he remained active in shaping British grand strategy.
During the late 1920s, Churchill served as Britain's chancellor of the exchequer, overseeing government expenditure and helping to set British strategic priorities. As chancellor, he downplayed the threat from Japan. In an
oft-quoted letter to Prime Minister Stanley Baldwin, the head of the Conservative government then holding office, Churchill wrote, "why should
there be a war with Japan? I do not believe there is the slightest chance of it
in our lifetime."[3] Instead of an impending clash between Britain and Japan,
Churchill foresaw a "long peace, such as follows in the wake of great wars."[4]
Of course, in one of history's cruel ironies, Churchill was fated to serve as
Britain's prime minister when Japan assaulted the British Empire less than
twenty years later.

In my chapter, I look back over the period between the two world
wars to trace Churchill's evolving views of the overall international strategic environment and the danger posed by Japan to Britain's empire in
Asia. I also explore the political and strategic options open to Churchill
as Britain's wartime leader. What foreign policy and strategy options did
Churchill have in the face of Japan's increasingly dangerous international
behavior? Did viable alternative courses of action exist that, if acted upon
by Churchill and Britain's leaders, might have averted the disasters that
befell the British Empire when Japan struck in 1941? An examination of
these questions offers an opportunity to evaluate Churchill's responsibility
for Britain's initial defeats in Asia and his reputation as a statesman and
strategist.

Britain and the Emerging Threat from Japan

Though Britain and Japan would fight a hideous war against each other in
the 1940s, the two countries had been allies at the beginning of the twentieth century. In 1902, Britain and Japan formed an alliance that served
the strategic interests of both countries for the next twenty years. Britain's
leaders cultivated a strategic partnership with Japan to manage shifts in the
global balance of power. Meanwhile, Japan sought an alliance with Britain
to gain strategic advantage over its own imperial rivals in northeast Asia.[5]

An important element of this partnership was a massive transfer of naval weaponry, technology, and know-how from Britain to Japan. British shipyards built almost all the major Japanese warships that enabled Japan to defeat China in the First Sino-Japanese War of 1894–95. A decade later, in the Russo-Japanese War of 1904–5, Japan could not have stood up to and defeated Russia without Britain's backing. Battleships built in Britain formed the backbone of Admiral Tōgō Heihachirō's fleet that won the famous victory at the Battle of Tsushima. Admiral Tōgō's flagship, the battleship *Mikasa*, was built in Britain. On the eve of the First World War, British naval architects designed and built for Japan the most powerful battle cruiser in the world, the *Kongō*. Constructed at the Vickers shipbuilding yard in Barrow-in-Furness, *Kongō* would serve in the Japanese navy for more than thirty years and take an active role in the fighting against Britain during the Second World War. In a mocking and cruel twist of fate, British workers built a ship that would go on to guard the troop transports carrying the Japanese army invading Malaya that stormed Singapore and killed and brutally imprisoned tens of thousands of Australian, British, and Indian soldiers. Japan's rapid rise as a naval power could not have occurred without the assistance received from Britain.

After the First World War, British officers and armaments firms, eager to secure lucrative contracts, continued to assist Japan's armed forces, including in the development of the Japanese naval air arm. A British pilot made the first takeoff and landing of an aircraft on the *Hōshō*, Japan's first purpose-built carrier.[6] British enterprise helped lay the foundation for the successes later achieved by Japanese naval aviation over Britain in the opening campaigns of the Pacific War. By accelerating Japan's rise as a naval and air power, Britain contributed to the decline of its own strategic position in Asia. Although Japan remained a relatively poor country when the Second World War began, with a gross domestic product per capita amounting to only a third of Britain's, its navy could nonetheless defeat the world's best in battle. In less than a generation, Japan went from an ally—a strategic understudy of Britain, heavily dependent on its ally for technology, weaponry, and expertise—to a formidable adversary, capable of inflicting crushing blows on the British armed forces at the outbreak of war in 1941. In naval aviation, the student surpassed the teacher.[7]

While Japan enjoyed immense benefits from the alliance, so too did
Britain. With Japan as an ally, Britain could concentrate its military effort
against Germany in western Europe and the Ottoman Empire in the Middle East during the First World War. As first lord of the admiralty at the
war's outbreak, Churchill was grateful for Japan's contribution in providing for the security of the British Empire in Asia. Japan seized the fortified German base at Tsingtao on the Shandong Peninsula soon after the
beginning of fighting in 1914. The Japanese navy helped to drive German
warships out of the Pacific and to police the sea lanes throughout Asia. A
Japanese warship, for example, provided escort protection for the convoy
carrying the initial deployment of Australian and New Zealand soldiers
to the Middle East. Later in the war, Japanese warships even operated far
from home waters in the Mediterranean to support Allied naval operations
against the Central Powers.

Despite the strategic value Britain derived from the alliance, British leaders grew increasingly uneasy with Japan's international behavior
during the First World War. The war raging in Europe gave Japan's leaders an opportunity to assert more control over China and enhance their
security in the Pacific. The war increased Japan's power by stimulating a
Japanese economic boom. Added wealth enabled increased armaments.
Japan began a naval buildup during the war that gave it the dominant
navy in the western Pacific, which greatly enhanced Japanese security and
standing. Japan's growing economy, foreign policy ambitions, and military
actions threatened to overturn the balance of power in Asia. Within the
British Empire, the self-governing dominions also expressed growing fears
of Japan's international ambitions and questioned the continued value of
the alliance. Whereas British leaders originally saw the alliance as a way
to contain Russia in Asia and later to concentrate on Germany's challenge
in Europe, they came to view its main purpose as being to check Japanese
expansion. In questioning the value of the alliance, Britain's leaders did
not want to risk alienating the Japanese government. They feared that an
abrupt termination of the alliance would turn Japan overnight from a strategic partner into a dangerous foe. Britain's leaders thus faced a difficult
choice of whether to continue the alliance with Japan when it came up for
renewal after the war's end.[8]

Adding to the difficulties confronting British leaders was a growing antagonism between Japan and the United States. American leaders pressured Britain to choose sides between Japan and the United States. Charles Evans Hughes, secretary of state in the Harding administration, was outspoken in demanding that Britain abrogate the alliance. In one meeting, a not-so-diplomatic Hughes shouted at the British ambassador, lecturing him that the American intervention in the war had played the decisive role in stopping Germany from winning. The British ambassador recorded Hughes as saying that Britain would have suffered defeat at the hands of the kaiser "if America seeking nothing for herself, but to save England, had not plunged into the war and (screamed) won it!"[9] Hughes' blunt message, akin to an ultimatum, underscored the dilemma confronting British leaders: renew the treaty with Japan and damage Britain's relationship with the United States, or drop the alliance and antagonize the Japanese.

Britain's leaders eventually found a way out of their awkward strategic predicament at the Washington Conference during the winter of 1921–22. In place of the alliance, Britain reached agreements with Japan and the United States to establish a multilateral diplomatic framework for cooperation to promote international stability in Asia and to achieve a reduction in naval armaments. These agreements were widely lauded at the time as a major step toward constructing an international architecture for peace, using arms control to reduce spending on naval weaponry, increasing international transparency, and thereby building confidence among world leaders. Hammered out in the aftermath of the hideous experience of the Great War, the Washington Treaty system fit the temper of the times. The statesmen at Washington believed they could avoid the mistakes of the recent past: entangling alliances and arms races, the combination of which they thought had made war between the great powers inevitable.[10]

Churchill played an active role in the British government's preparations for the Washington Conference. He insisted that Britain must work closely with the United States in shaping the postwar international system. In an article giving his views on British foreign policy, he asserted that Britain must "First: To keep firm friends with our kinsmen in the United States, and on no account lose the comradeship and sense of reunion which have sprung up during the war. This is not only first but paramount."[11] This foreign policy and strategic axiom would guide Churchill's actions for the rest of his political life.

Since the Anglo-Japanese alliance appeared to be a barrier to improved relations with the United States, Churchill wanted to remove or modify it. He contended that maintaining the alliance with Japan might even have the ill effect of driving Britain into a naval competition with the United States. He feared "A sense of antagonism, confined no doubt in the first instance to naval and military circles but gradually spreading over much wider circles, is inevitably developed by such competitions." This competition, if not checked, would produce "a ghastly disaster" like the horror of the First World War.[12] In discussions within the British government, Prime Minister Lloyd George raised the possibility that if Britain faced an American naval challenge, "the bellicose attitude of the United States might conceivably drive us into a defensive alliance with Japan." Field Marshal Sir Henry Wilson, the chief of the imperial general staff, agreed with the prime minister in seeing Japan as a counterweight to the United States in the global balance of power. Churchill strongly objected: "[N]o more fatal policy could be contemplated than that of basing our naval policy on a possible combination with Japan against the United States."[13] He also "felt uneasy" about British assistance in "training the Japanese to fly" because "it may be made a cause of misunderstanding between us and the United States."[14] Churchill was adamant that Britain must give priority to building a close relationship with the United States.

Churchill's interest in improving relations with the United States led to the rumor that he would lead the British negotiating team going to Washington. A cartoon in *Punch* magazine, titled "Disarmament and the Man," portrayed Churchill in an admiral's uniform, looking like Britain's naval hero Lord Nelson. The caption below the cartoon had Churchill "(late Minister of War by Land and Sea)" saying, "Of course my true genius is bellicose; but if they INSIST on my representing my country at the Washington Conference I must make the sacrifice."[15] But Churchill did not go to Washington. Instead, the elder British statesman and former prime minister Arthur Balfour led Britain's delegation to Washington.

Churchill applauded and supported the results of the Washington Conference. "The Pacific Agreement removes the great obstacles of the

Anglo-Japanese Alliance from the path of American friendship, without subjecting Japan to anything like the desertion or ill-usage at our hands." The arms control agreement also curbed the naval rivalry in the construction of the latest generation of large surface ships. Churchill considered the agreement curtailing the naval competition an important step in averting conflict between Britain and the United States.[16]

Within a few years, however, Churchill would change his mind about Washington's results. Instead of improving Britain's strategic position, he viewed the Washington agreements as making the British Empire less secure. Churchill contended, "That the severing of the ties between Great Britain and Japan was a misfortune to the world cannot be doubted."[17] Ending the Anglo-Japanese alliance, he maintained, "caused a profound impression in Japan, and was viewed as the spurning of an Asiatic Power by the Western world. Many links were sundered which afterwards have proved of decisive value to peace."[18]

It is not clear, however, how maintaining the alliance would have moderated Japan's international behavior. Would the alliance have stopped the assassination of Japanese political leaders who favored accommodation with Britain and the United States? Would the alliance have restrained rogue military and naval officers, intent upon an expansionist foreign policy? Would the continuation of the alliance have prevented Japanese army officers from seizing Manchuria in 1931? Puzzling over these questions indicates that the alliance would not have survived and was unlikely to have turned Japan away from wars of conquest. Japan's belligerent international behavior during the 1930s reflected the growing power of military leaders and nationalist opinion within the country's domestic politics. This shift within Japan would eventually have broken asunder any bonds of alliance with Britain. The Japanese drive for mastery in Asia would eventually have forced Britain's leaders to make a choice: either appease Japan and yield to Tokyo's foreign policy designs, or work with the United States to oppose Japanese aggression. If forced to choose, for Churchill the choice was clear: side with the United States. Thus the radicalization of Japanese politics would have doomed the alliance.

Churchill wanted to avoid a clash of arms with Japan because he apprehended the immense difficulties and costs for Britain of waging a great power war in Asia. During the 1920s, when Japanese governments showed a willingness to cooperate with Britain, Churchill downplayed the danger posed by Japan to the British Empire. This stance put him at odds in budgetary battles with the civilian and uniformed leaders of the British navy. British naval leaders believed that the restrictions imposed on the navy by the Washington Conference hurt their ability to defend the empire in Asia against Japan. They maintained that the dangers of great power naval competition and war in the Pacific had not gone away, despite good relations with Japan. British naval planners foresaw the rise of Japanese militarism and nationalism as a threat to the peace. They warned that an expansionist Japan would pose an immense danger to Britain's strategic position in Asia. Japan's industrial development, with exports employing a growing number of Japanese workers, concerned British policy makers and public commentators. Since the Japanese home islands were so poor in natural resources, Japan's industrial growth generated an increased demand for imports of raw materials. British naval leaders argued that this increased demand would lead Japan to seize direct control over sources of supply in Asia.[19] The Admiralty maintained that "the need of outlets for the population and for increased commerce and markets, especially new sources of self-supply, will probably be among the most compelling reasons for Japan to push a policy of penetration, expansion and aggression."[20]

In addition to economic motivations for conflict, the Admiralty argued that Japanese militarists, intent upon whipping up and exploiting nationalist sentiments to gain domestic political advantage, might emerge the winners in Japan's internal power struggle. In one astute appraisal, a British naval officer with considerable service in Asia maintained that "the Japanese Government and their people are entering a very critical period." He held that a struggle was "in full swing" between a "section of the ruling classes" who favor cooperation with Britain and the United States and the "military party, who have hitherto dominated Japan's policy, [and] do not take kindly to these new ideas which, as a very minimum, presuppose the subordination of armies and navies to civilian direction." The outcome of this struggle within Japan was in doubt because "the majority of the Japanese nation have been brought up very stiffly upon extreme nationalist lines."[21] If the militarists seized control, then the likelihood of conflict would increase. British weakness, the navy's leadership believed, might further encourage Japanese recklessness, leading to a breakdown of deterrence. The Japanese decision for war in 1941 followed in important respects the script written by the British Admiralty for how Japan, playing the role of an expansionist power led by aggressive military and naval leaders, might attack Britain's empire.[22] The Admiralty wanted to prepare for a showdown with Japan by recapitalizing Britain's naval forces, along with developing bases and the logistical infrastructure to pivot and forward deploy a powerful fleet to the Pacific.

This pivot to Asia, however, ran up against economic hard times in Britain. As chancellor of the exchequer during the late 1920s, Churchill wanted to curtail defense spending, not increase it. Britain suffered from sluggish economic performance throughout the interwar period: unemployment remained stubbornly high, typically hovering around 10 percent of the workforce, with older, staple industries no longer as competitive as they once were on world markets, in decline. In Asian markets, Japan presented a formidable trading competitor to Britain. Britain's overvalued currency, heavy debt burden, and growing entitlement costs weakened its competitiveness in the international economy. Meanwhile, economic policy nostrums peddled by governments of both the left and right failed to restore health to the economy. The press baron Lord Rothermere complained to Churchill: "It really looks like every economic thing in England is going wrong. We are . . . quite unsuited to the era of intensive competition which is now setting in."[23]

Confronted by straitened economic circumstances, Britain's political leaders determined that they would rather run risks in the strategic arena than jeopardize the economy's growth prospects. Spurring economic recovery as a way of preventing political and social unrest was the overriding goal of British governments during this era. Britain's economic problems thus acted as a brake on trying to defend British interests in Asia. Successive British governments during the 1920s and early 1930s curtailed the spending requests advocated by the Royal Navy for warship construction, operational readiness, and base development required to strengthen Britain's defenses in Asia. In naval aviation, an increasingly important element in determining command at sea, Britain fell behind its rivals, Japan and the

United States. By the 1920s, Britain had become a "frugal superpower" that could ill-afford an arms race against a rising great power competitor intent on gaining mastery on land and at sea in Asia.[24]

Japan's aggression against China during the 1930s gave added impetus to diplomatic efforts to avoid a return to great power competition in the Pacific. To avoid confrontation with Japan, some British leaders saw an urgent need to negotiate an accommodation with Tokyo. Neville Chamberlain, Britain's chancellor of the exchequer during the early 1930s, pressed for a diplomatic solution to protect British interests in Asia. He also mourned the loss of the alliance with Japan. He wanted diplomacy to substitute for rearmament. Chamberlain maintained that Britain could not afford "to rebuild our battle fleet. Therefore we ought to be making eyes at Japan." He ridiculed the alternative strategic course of working with the United States to contain Japan. "We ought to know by this time that U.S.A. will give us no undertaking to resist by force any action by Japan short of an attack on Hawaii or Honolulu."[25] Quite a prophetic forecast! In Chamberlain, Tokyo had a willing negotiating partner. Much to Chamberlain's chagrin, however, Japan's rulers possessed foreign policy ambitions that were incompatible with British interests and security. By refusing to cooperate in any meaningful way, Japan undercut Chamberlain, who failed to convince his colleagues within the British government that appeasing Japan would protect Britain. As Churchill would later maintain, appeasement from weakness was folly.[26]

Although Churchill had downplayed the danger posed by Japan during the 1920s, he took a much different stance during the 1930s. After Japan seized control of Manchuria, Churchill began to highlight in his newspaper and magazine articles: "The Japanese army leaders now dominate the civil government."[27] What he saw coming to pass was what the Harvard scholar Samuel Huntington would later call a clash of civilizations.[28] In one article warning of the threat from Japan, Churchill argued that Britain was "confronted with the spectacle of a great nation, equipped with all the apparatus of modern industrialism and the complete armoury of mechanized war, which is in spirit as far removed from the West, whose technical achievements it has copied, as are the Middle Ages from our own." He declared that in Japan "We have to deal with a people whose values are in many respects altogether different from our own. We have to deal with a nation in which the Army is the State and the Emperor is God."[29]

In confronting the danger from aggressor states, Churchill differed markedly from Chamberlain. Whereas Chamberlain was looking for a way to prevent an arms race, Churchill called for immediate and dramatic increases in defense spending. He held no illusions that Japan would seek an accommodation with Britain and the United States if they appeared militarily weak. Britain and the United States would need to arm if they intended to negotiate from a position of strength to preserve the peace. He believed that Japan could not win a naval competition if Britain and the United States took timely steps to rearm. "The steel-consuming power of Great Britain is in the neighbourhood of 16 million tons per annum, that of Japan is between 3 and 4 millions and the steel-consuming power of the United States is 54 millions!" Churchill believed that "these figures tend to show the scale of the various 'resources,' also how very absurd it is to talk of a naval race between the United States and Japan."[30] To protect Australia and New Zealand, he urged the completion of the base at Singapore, which he called the "key to the Pacific." On account of the sacrifices made by Australia and New Zealand on the battlefields in Europe and the Middle East during the First World War, Britain was honor-bound to defend "their own flesh and blood at the Antipodes." Nothing less than "the unity of the British Empire is directly involved," he maintained. If the base at Singapore remained unfinished, then Britain "would be taking a long step downwards upon the path of Imperial disintegration."[31] What troubled Churchill was that Britain and the United States "are sure to arm too little and too late."[32] His fears were justified: spending on the Japanese army and navy more than doubled between 1931 and 1935; meanwhile, the British defense budget showed no increase.[33] By lagging behind in the arms competition, Britain and the United States opened a window of opportunity for Japan to gain naval superiority and to strike at the end of 1941.[34]

Meanwhile, in Europe, the revival of German military power and aggressiveness under Hitler put Britain in extreme danger. By the end of the 1930s, Britain was confronted by a coalition of aggressor great powers. The prospect of having to fight both Germany in Europe and Japan in Asia was all too real. Churchill predicted that "should Germany at any time make war in Europe, we may be sure that Japan will immediately light a second conflagration in the Far East."[35] The leaders of Germany and Japan saw that their collaboration gave them added strength to advance their international ambitions. Germany and Japan negotiated first the Anti-Comintern Pact and, after the outbreak of war, the Tripartite Pact. The leaders of Germany and Japan agreed to support each other in "the establishment of a new order" in Europe and Asia.[36] A worst-case scenario was unfolding from which Britain could not hope to beat back German and Japanese aggression without the assistance of powerful allies.

Britain at War

The outbreak of war in Europe embroiled Britain in a desperate struggle for survival against Nazi Germany. The Nazi war machine appeared unstoppable as it scored one stunning victory after another and brought about the German conquest of central and western Europe. Most shocking of all was the crushing defeat German arms inflicted on France during the spring of 1940. Britain's most important ally, which had withstood repeated German offensives in the first war, had been knocked out in but a short campaign. This strategic catastrophe might also have spelled Britain's rapid defeat had it not been for the leadership of Churchill. The British people rallied around Churchill and made a heroic stand against Nazi aggression to turn back the German air assault on their homeland. This victory in the Battle of Britain was the first major reverse inflicted on Hitler and thwarted his drive to make Germany into a world power.

Heroism, however, carried a heavy price in lives lost and suffering. In 1940 almost 25,000 British civilians—people from all walks of life—were killed by German bombing of cities. To put this suffering into perspective, the civilian loss of life during 1940 amounted to the rough equivalent of seven September 11 attacks! The urban damage was immense. Still, the British people did not break under this weight of the German air assault. Churchill called this heroic stand Britain's finest hour. Indeed, the British people refused to give up and fought back even in the face of terror attacks on their homeland.

While this time of testing raised deep emotions among the British people and their leaders, sober strategic calculation also lay behind the decision by Churchill's government to fight on in 1940. Churchill, his colleagues in government, and the British military chiefs knew that Britain and its empire could not bring about the complete defeat of Nazi Germany without powerful allies. The military leadership warned Churchill that Britain's power to resist depended on whether the "United States of America is willing to give us full economic and financial support, *without which we do not think we could continue the war with any chance of success* [emphasis in original]."[37] In calculating the strategic odds, Churchill took a risk in counting on the willingness of the United States to assist Britain in the struggle against Hitler's Germany. There was nothing inevitable about the United States offering this assistance. An isolationist America, committed to a strategy of defending the Western Hemisphere, might have turned its back on Britain, opening the way to the geopolitical catastrophe of a Nazi-dominated Europe.

American domestic politics thus loomed in determining the war's course and outcome. One of the most important "known unknowns" in American politics was whether Franklin D. Roosevelt would run and be elected to an unprecedented third term as president in 1940. Would Roosevelt run again for the White House and, if he did, would he be reelected? The president added to the uncertainty by concealing his plans, telling some of those around him that he did not intend to run. He told Joseph P. Kennedy, the American ambassador to Britain, "I can't. I'm tired. I can't take it." While playing down the prospect of running again, Roosevelt also believed that he was the best man to lead the country if the United States became involved in the war.[38]

Churchill needed to understand American domestic politics because Britain's ability to wage war depended on who led the country. He asked Kennedy for the ambassador's assessment of American domestic politics. Kennedy told Churchill that he thought Roosevelt would run for a third term if the fighting escalated and the danger grew. Behind the scenes, Churchill and Britain's leaders confided their preference that Roosevelt remain as president. Churchill "said of course we want him." Churchill's political rival Lord Halifax, too, was anxious about whether Roosevelt would run for a third term and his prospects for electoral success.[39]

Churchill was fortunate that his strategic bet on America panned out: Roosevelt did run and win reelection as president. As Churchill understood,

Roosevelt was a hawk who wanted to defeat Nazi Germany. Roosevelt sought to extend the maximum assistance to Britain within the constraints imposed by the pace of American rearmament and by a deeply troubled, divided public opinion. The American president agreed with Churchill that an enduring and secure peace required the destruction of Nazi Germany. Roosevelt rejected the foreign policy and strategic advice proffered by advisors who advocated a defensive strategy of hemispheric defense. Kennedy, for example, wrote to the president at the outbreak of the war in Europe that "it is going to be a hard, difficult and dangerous world in which to live, and the United States will only be able to thrive in it by pulling itself together as a nation and being ready and prepared to protect its own vital interests. These, to my mind, lie in the Western Hemisphere."[40] Instead of adopting an isolationist, defensive crouch, Roosevelt acted to involve the United States on the side of Britain. The president rejected a foreign policy of restraint in favor of a strategy for forward engagement. He pushed to enact Lend-Lease legislation that enabled Britain to acquire American resources to wage war. Churchill called Lend-Lease the most unsordid act. In stirring rhetoric, Churchill proclaimed, "We shall not fail or falter; we shall not weaken or tire. Neither the sudden shock of battle, nor the long-drawn trials of vigilance and exertion will wear us down." He promised to "finish the job" of defeating Germany if the United States would give Britain the tools.[41] This American assistance enabled Britain to rearm and increase its military strength during 1941. To Hitler, the United States led by Roosevelt stood as a dangerous sworn enemy, frustrating his efforts to beat down British resistance. Behind the defiance of Churchill's Britain stood Roosevelt's America.[42]

Stymied by renewed British strength and resistance, Hitler looked eastward toward the Soviet Union, taking the fateful decision to attack Stalin, his erstwhile coalition partner. Churchill warned Stalin of the coming German invasion. Ivan Maisky, the Soviet ambassador in Britain, recorded that "Churchill suffers from an obsession that a war between Germany and the USSR is inevitable."[43] After Hitler's attack on the Soviet Union, Churchill did not hesitate to align Britain with the Soviet Union. In a famous speech, Churchill broadcast British resolve to help the Soviet Union. Maisky listened to "Churchill's broadcast with bated breath. A forceful speech! A fine performance! . . . Churchill's speech was bellicose and resolute: no compromises or agreements! War to the bitter end! Precisely what is most needed today."[44]

With the Soviet Union in the fight against Nazi Germany, Churchill and Roosevelt held a summit meeting off the coast of Newfoundland in August 1941 to discuss war aims and strategy, even though the United States was nominally still a neutral country. The Axis great powers held the strategic initiative and were on the offensive in the war: Britain was fighting in the Atlantic to keep the oceanic lifeline to North America open, in the air over Europe, and in the Middle East; the Soviet Union was battling for its life against the German invaders; and Nationalist China was writhing in a brutal protracted war against Japan in Asia. The desperate strategic situation of the moment did not stop Churchill and Roosevelt from looking ahead to the war's end in drafting the Atlantic Charter. This remarkable document publicly called for the rollback of Nazi Germany's conquests, the "final destruction of the Nazi tyranny," followed by the disarmament of aggressor states.[45] A later generation would call these aims regime change. Even before entering the conflict, then, the United States had made a public declaration of war aims. The Atlantic Charter provided the basis for a new international order and an enduring peace once Germany was defeated. To Churchill's dismay, however, the declaration of war aims was not followed by an immediate American declaration of war; the United States remained neutral.

While the United States held back from entering the war, a crisis emerged on the Eastern Front in the autumn of 1941. German armies surged forward and appeared on the verge of breaking Soviet armed resistance around Moscow. Stalin remained in Moscow, close to the fighting front, but the Soviet government evacuated the city to continue resistance after the capital fell into Nazi hands. As this crisis unfolded, Churchill and Roosevelt made a fateful decision: they decided there was an urgent need to develop nuclear weapons. The British had given close study to the problem of acquiring nuclear weapons. The conclusion reached by a British scientific team, contained in a famous study known as the MAUD report, was "that the scheme for a uranium bomb is practicable and likely to lead to decisive results in the war." In the view of the British scientists, the material for a nuclear weapon might be ready by the end of 1943. The British assessment was stark: "no nation would care to risk being caught without a weapon of such decisive possibilities."[46] Frederick Lindemann, Churchill's friend and scientific advisor, contended, "Whoever possesses such a [nuclear] plant should be able to dictate terms to the rest of the world." American scientific leaders agreed with the British findings. After receiving a briefing on nuclear weapons development, Roosevelt reached out to Churchill, proposing that Britain and the United States pool their resources and work together in developing these powerful new weapons. Churchill concurred: "I need not assure you of our readiness to collaborate with the United States Administration in this matter."[47] Nuclear weapons would provide an ultimate offset strategy if Soviet resistance collapsed and a Nazi superstate, stretching from the Urals to the Atlantic, emerged on the continent of Europe.

The ability of the Soviet Union to fight on also required that brakes be put on Japanese aggression in Asia. Along the border of Manchuria and the Soviet Union, the Japanese and Soviet armies fought major battles during 1938–39, and the Red Army soundly defeated the Japanese in these clashes. This fighting set the stage for negotiations between Japan and the Soviet Union. Stalin wanted to avoid the prospect of a two-front war in Europe and Asia, and he also wanted to draw the Soviet Union closer to the Axis Powers. These strategic considerations motivated Stalin to reach a nonaggression pact with Japan in April 1941. The existence of this pact, however, did not provide an ironclad guarantee that Japan would honor it if a favorable opportunity arose to strike at the Soviet Union. Japan might break the nonaggression pact and attack the Soviet Union in support of Germany, just as Hitler had broken his partnership with Stalin.

To prevent the Japanese from attacking the Soviet Union, American and British leaders deemed it essential that Japan's ambitions in Asia be contained. If Japan was not reined in, the balance of power would tilt even further in favor of Nazi Germany in Europe. In coming back to Britain after the Atlantic conference with Roosevelt, Churchill spoke publicly about British foreign policy and strategy in meeting the challenge posed by Japan. Churchill did not pull his punches. He denounced the Japanese army for the "carnage, ruin, and corruption" it was inflicting on the peoples of Asia. Japan's menacing action "has got to stop," he demanded. His hope was that Japan's leaders would accept a negotiated settlement and avoid war. "Every effort will be made to secure a peaceful settlement," Churchill stated. "The United States are labouring with infinite patience to arrive at a fair and amicable settlement which will give Japan the utmost reassurance for her legitimate interests. We earnestly hope these negotiations will succeed." In carrying out these negotiations, Churchill was a realist. He knew that the talks could break down. He warned "that if these hopes should fail we shall, of course, range ourselves unhesitatingly at the side of the United States."[48] Again, staying close to the United States remained paramount in Churchill's strategic worldview.

The aim of Churchill and Roosevelt was to deter Japan's rulers from striking against the Soviet Union in Asia, what was known as the northern advance. As the Germans began their offensive push on Moscow during the autumn of 1941, Maisky appealed for "England and the USA 'warning' Japan that any attempt to attack the USSR would mean war between Japan and the English-speaking democracies." A worried Maisky recorded in his diary, "I have no idea what the outcome will be, but I am not very optimistic."[49] Some of Japan's leaders wanted to gang up with Nazi Germany to defeat the Soviet Union. Despite signing the nonaggression pact with the Soviet Union, Japan's foreign minister Yosuke Matsuoka advocated the northern advance. Japanese army leaders were more hesitant. Japan's generals already had their forces tied down fighting Nationalist China on the Asian mainland. In addition, the alternative strategy to seize the resources of Southeast Asia, the so-called southern advance, would require the army to find the forces to attack the British Empire in Malaya and the Americans in the Philippines. Before attacking north, Japan's generals wanted first to build up their own forces and to wait until the Soviets weakened their defenses in the Far East. Stalin was fortunate that Japan's military chiefs (acting out of character) hesitated before attacking. With this respite in Asia, Stalin moved Soviet forces to Europe, where they played a decisive role in winning the Battle of Moscow, pushing back the German invaders from the outskirts of the Soviet capital.

Churchill and Roosevelt put diplomatic and economic pressure on Japan to dissuade Tokyo from embarking on further aggression. In addition, Britain and the United States strengthened their forward-deployed forces in the Pacific to build up a deterrent to give pause to Japan's leaders. Sir Robert Craigie, Britain's ambassador in Tokyo, wanted to couple the economic pressure and military buildup with a diplomatic effort to find a negotiated settlement with Japan. Craigie believed that an opportunity existed to avert war by relaxing the economic restrictions on Japan. Even if war did prove inevitable, a delay would buy time for Britain and the United States to increase their forces in the Pacific and stand better prepared to resist a Japanese attack when it did come. In Craigie's estimation, Britain had a constructive role to play by acting as a "moderating influence" in the tense negotiations between Japan and the United States. If a compromise could be reached, then "war with Japan would not have been inevitable."[50]

Churchill, however, feared that weakening the hardline stance against Japan would fail to preserve the peace and might even put Britain and the United States in a worse strategic predicament. He did not see Britain acting as a mediator between Japan and the United States. In commenting on proposals to seek a compromise with Japan, Churchill highlighted his anxiety about China: "If they collapse our joint dangers would enormously increase." While Churchill did not reject continued negotiations—indeed, he wrote Roosevelt that "we certainly do not want an additional war"—he did dampen interest among American leaders for pursuing a compromise that increased the danger of a collapse in China's resistance.[51]

Churchill was right to stress the importance of China's willingness and ability to resist in determining the balance of forces in Asia. China was tying down the bulk of the Japanese army. In 1937, Japan initiated a major regional war against Nationalist China. Chiang Kai-shek, the Nationalist leader, refused to give up against Japanese aggression despite the repeated beatings inflicted on Chinese armies. After four years of fighting, Chiang's regime and Nationalist resistance was on the verge of collapse. Japan could use a breathing space in sanctions to escalate operations against the Nationalists in an effort to force them out of the war. If Chinese resistance broke down because of a weakening of pressure by Britain and the United States, then Japan could swing additional forces against Britain in Southeast Asia. Unless the Japanese were willing to withdraw from China, the peace in Asia would remain precarious. Japan's rulers, however, refused to offer meaningful concessions to find a negotiated way out of their China nightmare. The last-minute negotiations to avoid war could not succeed because Japan's leaders showed no real willingness to admit defeat in China.[52]

As war loomed at the beginning of December 1941, the prospect that Japan might attack the British Empire in Asia but avoid fighting the United States alarmed Churchill. To deter Tokyo and reassure Washington, Churchill affirmed in public that Britain would declare war "within the hour" if Japan attacked the United States. Roosevelt, however, offered no similar public assurance if Japan attacked the British Empire. Churchill envisioned four scenarios for how the confrontation with Japan might unfold. One scenario, the outcome preferred by Churchill, was that the United States would come into the war against Germany, while negotiations with the Japanese government succeeded and Japan remained neutral. A second scenario, and the one that occurred, was that both the United States and Japan entered the war. A third scenario envisioned both the United States and Japan staying out of the war. The fourth scenario was Churchill's "worst nightmare": Japan attacking the British Empire, while the United States did not join in the fighting on the side of Britain. During the final hours before the outbreak of war, the nightmare scenario seemed to be unfolding before Churchill's eyes. Japanese forces were sighted moving to attack the British Empire in Southeast Asia, but no solid intelligence existed that Japan was about to strike American territories in the Pacific.

The Japanese attack on Pearl Harbor thus came not only as a surprise but a relief to Churchill. Japan's rulers had delivered Churchill from his "worst nightmare." As Roosevelt said to Churchill in their telephone call after hearing the news of the Japanese attack on Pearl Harbor: "We are all in the same boat now." With the United States in the war, Churchill believed that victory had been procured, even if he could not foretell when the final defeat of Germany and Japan would occur. Indeed, Churchill would later write "that to have the United States at our side was to me the greatest joy. . . . Being saturated and satiated with emotion and sensation, I went to bed and slept the sleep of the saved and thankful."[53] Japan's attack, followed soon after by Hitler's declaration of war, brought American power fully into the global struggle on Britain's side.

Disaster in Asia

Japan's victories on sea and on land at the onset of fighting in the Pacific seemed to belie Churchill's belief in the ultimate victory of the Grand

Alliance. Britain and the United States suffered one major defeat after another at the hands of Japan. The American battle line was crippled at Pearl Harbor. Just a few days later, on December 10, 1941, Japanese land-based naval aircraft, operating out of bases in French Indochina, modern-day Vietnam, struck and sank the British battleship *Prince of Wales* and battle cruiser *Repulse*—so-called Force Z—off the coast of Malaya. In sending Force Z to Singapore, Churchill had hoped to deter Japanese aggression as well as form the vanguard of a buildup of British naval power in Asia.[54] Called the "decisive deterrent" by Churchill, the forward-deployed capital ships of Force Z not only failed to achieve its strategic purpose of deterrence but instead became tempting targets to Japanese naval airmen. Churchill would later write that upon hearing the news of the destruction of Force Z: "In all the war I never received a more direct shock."[55]

More defeats at sea soon followed. Four months after the destruction of Force Z, the cruisers *Cornwall* and *Dorsetshire* quickly sank when deluged with bombs delivered by aircraft from Japanese carriers raiding into the Indian Ocean. The main fleet assembled by Britain in the Indian Ocean stood no chance in fighting the Japanese carrier force. To escape annihilation, the British fleet ran out of harm's way, retreating all the way across the Indian Ocean to the east coast of Africa to escape Japan's carrier air power.[56] By pioneering a transformation in the use of air power in naval warfare, the Japanese navy leaped ahead of rivals, gaining a first-strike strategic advantage that it used to devastating effect.

Bereft of an effective naval defense, Malaya and Singapore were open to a Japanese seaborne invasion, and their loss was inevitable. Japanese ground forces, landed on the first day of the war, quickly advanced down the Malay Peninsula. Singapore fell after a campaign of little more than two months. The rapid defeat of the British forces in Malaya and mass surrender at Singapore staggered Churchill. The British defenders on the ground outnumbered the attacking Japanese invaders, and Churchill expected and urged them to offer a determined and prolonged resistance. As the Japanese launched their final assault to seize Singapore, Churchill sent stern, fight-to-the-bitter-end orders to British commanders in Asia. "There must at this stage be no thought of saving the troops or sparing the population," Churchill ordered. "Commanders and British officers must die with their troops. The honour of the British Empire and of the British Army is at stake." Churchill exhorted his commanders to have the forces under their command fight as stubbornly as the Russian soldiers on the Eastern Front and as the Americans were doing in the Philippines.[57] But no amount of exhortation, however stirring, could change the outcome. General Arthur Percival surrendered his forces unconditionally on February 15, 1942. The British surrender did not spare Singapore's population from an orgy of violent terror unleashed by the Japanese conquerors drunk with victory, nor did it prevent the cruel treatment meted out to prisoners of war during their years of captivity.

Could these defeats have been avoided? Given Churchill's strategic priorities in the world war, Britain was practically bound to suffer opening defeats at the hands of the Japanese once Japan decided to attack. While shortchanging British defenses in Asia, his priorities nonetheless made sound strategic sense: (1) defense of the homeland from air assault and potential invasion; (2) keeping open the vital sea lanes of the North Atlantic; (3) sending whatever Britain could spare in supplies and weapons to the Soviet Union; and (4) a concentration of force to take offensive operations against the German-Italian army in North Africa and to secure the Middle East. Churchill's strategic priorities were to deploy forces and supplies to fighting fronts and not to deter Japan. He explained these strategic priorities to the House of Commons. Confident that if Japan attacked, then the United States would come into the war, Churchill wanted to use Britain's "limited resources on the actual fighting fronts." He believed that "if Japan ran amok in the Pacific, we should not fight alone."[58]

Only by changing these strategic priorities could Britain have hoped to find additional forces to mount a more effective defense against Japan. For example, Britain might have adopted a defensive stance in the Middle East and then sent more ground and air forces to Asia. Britain could also have diverted to Asia aircraft and tanks sent to the Soviet Union.[59] British weapons and supplies delivered to the Soviet Union during 1941 would have helped bolster defenses against the opening Japanese offensive drives. In particular, British Hurricane fighter aircraft, if shipped to Singapore rather than to the Soviet Union, would have helped to prevent Japan from gaining air superiority in Southeast Asia. These strategic tradeoffs, however, would have entailed running greater risk of defeat in the Middle East and on the Eastern Front. In both theaters, any weakening of the forces arrayed against the German attackers might have resulted in military disaster. The Soviet Red Army came perilously close to defeat in the Battle of Moscow and around Leningrad. Churchill and British planners feared, too, that victorious German forces in the south of Russia might break into the Middle East through the Caucasus. In North Africa, the German-Italian army inflicted major defeats on the British armed forces, which could have lost Egypt. Staving off complete defeat on the Eastern Front or in the Middle East held a higher strategic priority in the period leading up to Japan's attack.

A massive British buildup of combat forces to carry out sustained operations would have entailed a huge logistic effort over great distances. An immense commitment of shipping would have been required. Throughout the war, however, shipping was in short supply. Even after the United States ramped up merchant ship construction, a shortage of shipping would constrain Allied strategic options. A commitment to protracted fighting in Southeast Asia was perhaps beyond the available shipping resources, given the demands of other theaters of war.

A shift in strategic priorities also would have required that Britain deploy a strong air force and competitive fleet to Southeast Asia. Britain would have had to draw down its air strength in the home islands to acquire the strength needed to blunt the Japanese opening offensive. If Britain could not gain air superiority, then Japan would have the advantage in the fighting. Beating back Japan's opening offensive drive, too, would have required command of the sea. Japan's force of six large aircraft carriers, however, was markedly superior to any fleet Britain could conceivably deploy to the Pacific. If the two navies had fought a major fleet battle in the South China Sea or the Indian Ocean, the Royal Navy would have suffered a crushing defeat. Churchill was honest with the House of Commons that, with the Japanese victories at Pearl Harbor and over Force Z, "naval superiority in the Pacific and in the Malaysian Archipelago has passed from the hands of the two leading naval Powers into the hands of Japan."[60] Britain's loss of air superiority and command of the sea sealed the fate of Singapore.

An ugly strategic reality confronted Churchill in late 1941: regaining naval superiority over Japan and commanding the seas of Asia was beyond

Britain's strength while the war against Nazi Germany raged in Europe. Before the First World War, when serving as first lord of the admiralty, Churchill imagined a dreadful future scenario where the British fleet could no longer defend the empire. "If the power of Great Britain were shattered on the sea," he warned, "the only course for the five millions of white men in the Pacific would be to seek the protection of the United States."[61] Faced with the looming danger of war with Japan, Churchill reposed his confidence in the American battle fleet to deter Japanese offensive action. He believed "that over the whole of the Pacific scene brooded the great power of the United States Fleet, concentrated at Hawaii. It seemed very unlikely that Japan would attempt the distant invasion of the Malay Peninsula, the assault upon Singapore, and the Dutch East Indies, while leaving behind them in their rear this great American fleet."[62] Churchill's confidence in the striking power of the American fleet was misplaced. The American battle fleet at Pearl Harbor lacked the capability to execute war plans for an early offensive against Japan. The strike at Pearl Harbor, of course, shattered whatever deterrent effect the American battle fleet might have posed to Japanese offensive action in Southeast Asia. Allegations that Churchill had foreknowledge of the Pearl Harbor attack and withheld this information from Roosevelt, as some conspiracy theories maintain, thus make no sense, as he looked to the American battle fleet to frustrate a Japanese offensive against the British Empire. By striking at Pearl Harbor, the Japanese upset Churchill's strategic calculations and exposed Britain's weakness in Asia.

Churchill on Japan's Decision for War

The Japanese decision to attack Britain and the United States went against Churchill's conception of rational strategic assessment and decision making. Brought up to accept the optimistic tenets of classical liberalism, Churchill believed that the great powers benefited from settling their disputes without recourse to arms competitions and war. Instead of embarking on wars of conquest, Japan stood to gain in security and prosperity by joining in a partnership with Britain and the United States. The treaties achieved at the Washington Conference, twenty years before Pearl Harbor, showed the potential that existed for the great powers of the Pacific to erect an international framework to procure peace and security for themselves.

The defeat of imperial Germany in the First World War provided a recent object lesson in the folly of starting wars to overthrow the international equilibrium.[63] The kaiser's regime that initiated the great power contest did not survive at the war's end. Churchill argued that no one "outside a madhouse" would want to repeat this experience by attacking or invading another country. The risks and uncertainties of major wars were too great, while no conceivable gains could match the immense human and economic loss suffered in fighting.[64] He judged that if Japan's rulers followed imperial Germany's path of starting wars of conquest, they would suffer the same fate. Churchill asserted, "The lesson of the World War was that those who fix the moment for the beginning of wars are not those who fix the hour of their cessation."[65]

Churchill also predicted that Japanese aggression would provoke an opposing coalition of great powers to thwart Japan's domination of Asia. This prediction was rooted in Churchill's belief in the workings of the balance of power. While Churchill was brought up on the optimism of classical liberalism, he held to a realist view when it came to the workings of world politics. A coalition, to include Britain and the United States, would possess much greater potential to generate military might than Japan. Churchill sought to drive home this imbalance of forces to Japan's leaders by taking the extraordinary step of warning them to avoid "a serious catastrophe" in provoking war with Britain and the United States. The logic of Churchill's strategic assessment was clear: Japan would lose the war; hence, Tokyo should instead strive for "a marked improvement in relations between Japan and the two great sea Powers of the West."[66]

In December 1941, Japan confounded Churchill's expectations by attacking Britain and the United States. He would tell a joint session of Congress that it was "difficult to reconcile Japanese action with prudence or even sanity."[67] Churchill would later repeat this claim in his history *The Second World War*, arguing that the Japanese decision to attack "could not be reconciled with reason."[68] Although Churchill possessed a wonderful gift of imagination, he found it difficult to fathom how the leaders of a great country would run such high risks and embark upon a costly war against much stronger adversaries in which they stood little chance of winning. While Japan's initial victories did demonstrate the immense fighting power of the Japanese armed forces, they did not cause Britain, China, or the United States to drop out of the war. Japan remained mired in a costly war of attrition it was unlikely to win. In predicting that an aggressive Japanese bid for hegemony in Asia would ultimately prove self-defeating, Churchill showed that he possessed a deeper understanding of national interest and grand strategy than did imperial Japan's warlords.

While Churchill misjudged the willingness of Japan's rulers to court destruction, he fully understood that beating back German and Japanese aggression required enlisting the power of the United States. One lesson Churchill took away from the First World War was that "the Allies would have been beaten if America had not come in."[69] In these desperate contests, the British Empire could hold the line and buy time for the United States to mobilize for war. Britain, however, lacked the strength to roll back the initial victories won by Germany and Japan, let alone topple the German and Japanese regimes. Only the massive deployment of American military power overseas from the New World to the Old could accomplish that ambitious aim. This appreciation of America's importance in the global balance of power guided Churchill's strategy in both world wars. While Churchill could not prevent war in the Pacific, he did know how it would be won.

Notes

1. John Gunther, *Inside Asia* (New York: Harper, 1939), x.
2. Fareed Zakaria popularized the notion "rise of the rest" in *The Post-American World* (New York: Norton, 2008).
3. Churchill to Baldwin, December 15, 1924, in Martin Gilbert, ed., *Winston S. Churchill*, vol. 5, Companion Part 1: *The Exchequer Years, 1922–1929* (Boston: Houghton Mifflin, 1981), 307 (hereafter referred to as Gilbert, Companion).
4. Churchill memorandum, "Navy Estimates," January 29, 1925, in Gilbert, Companion, vol. 5, 366.
5. Keith Neilson, *Britain and the Last Tsar: British Policy and the Last Tsar, 1894–1917* (Oxford: Clarendon Press, 1996), 110–266; T. G. Otte, *The China Question: Great Power Rivalry and British Isolation, 1894–1905* (Oxford: Oxford University Press, 2007), 269–325.
6. David C. Evans and Mark R. Peattie, *Kaigun: Strategy, Tactics, and Technology in the Imperial Japanese Navy, 1887–1941* (Annapolis, Md.: Naval Institute Press, 1997); on British assistance in the development of the Japanese naval air arm, see

John Ferris, "A British 'Unofficial' Aviation Mission and Japanese Naval Developments, 1919–1929," *Journal of Strategic Studies* 5, no. 3 (September 1982): 416–39; and Mark R. Peattie, *Sunburst: The Rise of Japanese Naval Air Power, 1909–1941* (Annapolis, Md.: Naval Institute Press, 2001), 16–20.

7. Mark Harrison, ed., *The Economics of World War II: Six Great Powers in International Comparison* (Cambridge: Cambridge University Press, 1998), 3.

8. Ian H. Nish, *Alliance in Decline: A Study in Anglo-Japanese Relations, 1908–23* (London: Athlone Press, 1972).

9. Sir Auckland Geddes to Lord Curzon, April 15, 1921, enclosure in Curzon to Lloyd George, April 20, 1921, Lloyd George Papers, F/13/2/19, Parliamentary Archives.

10. Erik Goldstein and John Maurer, eds., *The Washington Conference, 1921–22: Naval Rivalry, East Asian Stability and the Road to Pearl Harbor* (New York: Routledge, 1994).

11. Winston Churchill, "Britain's Foreign Policy," *The Weekly Dispatch*, June 22, 1919, reprinted in Michael Wolff, ed., *The Collected Essays of Sir Winston Churchill* (London: Library of Imperial History, 1976), vol. 1, 214–17 (hereafter Wolff, *Collected Essays*).

12. Winston S. Churchill, Cabinet Memorandum, July 4, 1921, Gilbert, Companion, vol. 4, part 3, 1539–42.

13. CAB 2/3, Committee of Imperial Defence 134th Meeting, December 14, 1920, The National Archives (hereafter TNA).

14. Churchill to Lord Curzon, July 13, 1921, Gilbert, Companion, vol. 4, part 3, 1552.

15. *Punch* 161, no. 4187 (October 5, 1921): 263.

16. Churchill to the Prince of Wales, January 2, 1922, Gilbert, Companion, vol. 4, part 3, 1709–10.

17. Winston Churchill, "The Mission of Japan," *Collier's*, February 20, 1937, in Wolff, *Collected Essays*, 368.

18. Winston S. Churchill, *The Second World War*, vol. 1: *The Gathering Storm* (Boston: Houghton Mifflin, 1985 paperback edition), 13.

19. Notes by the Naval Staff, "Consequences of Suspending Work at Singapore," April 28, 1924, in B. McL. Ranft, ed., *The Beatty Papers*, vol. 2: *1916–1927* (Aldershot: Scolar Press for the Navy Records Society, 1993), 393–97.

20. Martin Gilbert, *Winston S. Churchill*, vol. 5: *Prophet of Truth, 1922–1939* (Boston: Houghton Mifflin, 1977), 103.

21. Stephen King-Hall, *Western Civilization and the Far East* (London: Methuen, 1924), 297–311.

22. John H. Maurer, "'Winston has gone mad': Churchill, the British Admiralty, and the Rise of Japanese Naval Power," *Journal of Strategic Studies* 35, no. 6 (December 2012): 775–98.

23. Lord Rothermere to Churchill, February 12, 1925, in Martin Gilbert, ed., *Winston S. Churchill*, vol. 5, Companion Part 1: *The Exchequer Years, 1922–1929* (Boston: Houghton Mifflin, 1981), 389.

24. Michael Mandelbaum, *The Frugal Superpower: America's Global Leadership in a Cash-Strapped Era* (New York: Public Affairs, 2010).

25. Neville Chamberlain to his sister Hilda, July 28, 1934, in Robert Self, ed., *The Neville Chamberlain Diary Letters*, vol. 4: *The Downing Street Years, 1934–1940* (Aldershot: Ashgate, 2005), 82–83.

26. Ann Trotter, *Britain and East Asia, 1933–1937* (Cambridge: Cambridge University Press, 1975); Peter Bell, *Chamberlain, Germany and Japan, 1933–4* (New York: St. Martin's Press, 1996); Keith Neilson, "The Defence Requirements Sub-Committee, British Strategic Foreign Policy, Neville Chamberlain and the Path to Appeasement," *English Historical Review* 118, no. 477 (June 2003): 651–84.

27. Winston Churchill, "Britain Must Hear the Truth," *The Sunday Dispatch*, November 27, 1932, in Wolff, *Collected Essays*, 308.

28. Samuel P. Huntington, *The Clash of Civilizations and the Remaking of World Order* (New York: Simon & Schuster, 1996).

29. Churchill, "Mission of Japan," in Wolff, *Collected Essays*, 365.

30. Winston Churchill, "Japan Guesses Wrong," *Collier's*, July 30, 1938, in Wolff, *Collected Essays*, 406–7.

31. Winston Churchill, "Singapore—Key to the Pacific," *Pictorial Weekly*, March 24, 1934, in Wolff, *Collected Essays*, 321.

32. Churchill, "Mission of Japan," in Wolff, *Collected Essays*, 370.

33. Richard J. Smethurst, *From Foot Soldier to Finance Minister: Takahashi Korekiyo: Japan's Keynes* (Cambridge, Mass.: Harvard University Asia Center, 2007), 265; G. C. Peden, *Arms, Economics and British Strategy* (Cambridge: Cambridge University Press, 2007), 127.

34. Stephen E. Pelz, *Race to Pearl Harbor: The Failure of the Second London Naval Conference and the Onset of World War II* (Cambridge, Mass.: Harvard University Press, 1974).

35. Winston S. Churchill, "Germany and Japan," November 27, 1936, in *Step By Step* (New York: Putnam's, 1939), 65–66.

36. Ōhata Tokushirō, "The Anti-Comintern Pact, 1935–1939," and Hosoyo Chihiro, "The Tripartite Pact, 1939–1940," in *Japan's Road to the Pacific War: Deterrent Diplomacy*, ed. James William Morley (New York: Columbia University Press, 1976), 9–111, 191–257.

37. WRP (40) 168/CoS (40) 390, "British Strategy in a Certain Eventuality," May 25, 1940, CAB 67/7/48, TNA.

38. Joseph P. Kennedy diary entry, December 10, 1939, in Amanda Smith, ed., *Hostage to Fortune: The Letters of Joseph P. Kennedy* (New York: Viking, 2001), 404–6.

39. Kennedy diary entry, March 28, 1940, in Smith, *Hostage to Fortune*, 411–12.

40. Kennedy to Roosevelt, September 30, 1939, in Smith, *Hostage to Fortune*, 385–86.

41. Winston Churchill, "Give Us the Tools," February 9, 1941, broadcast from London, https://winstonchurchill.org/resources/speeches/1941–1945-war-leader/give-us

-the-tools/#:~:text=We%20shall%20not%20fail%20or,we%20will%20finish%20
the%20job.

42. Brendan Simms, *Hitler: A Global Biography* (New York: Basic Books, 2019).

43. Ivan Maisky diary entry, May 7, 1941, in Gabriel Gorodetsky, ed., *The Maisky Diaries: Red Ambassador to the Court of St. James, 1932–1943* (New Haven, Conn.: Yale University Press, 2015), 352–54.

44. Maisky diary entry, June 22, 1941, in Gorodetsky, *Maisky Diaries*, 365–67.

45. "Atlantic Charter," August 14, 1941, https://avalon.law.yale.edu/wwii/atlantic.asp.

46. MAUD Report, 1941, https://www.atomicarchive.com/resources/documents /beginnings/maud.html.

47. Roosevelt to Churchill, October 11, 1941, National Archives, https://catalog .archives.gov/id/194884.

48. Churchill broadcast, "A Meeting with President Roosevelt," August 24, 1941, in Charles Eade, ed., *The Unrelenting Struggle: War Speeches by the Right Hon. Winston S. Churchill* (London: Cassell, 1942), 229–37.

49. Maisky diary entry, October 19, 1941, in Gorodetsky, *Maisky Diaries*, 397–98.

50. Sir Robert Craigie, Final Report, February 4, 1943, FO371/35957 F821/821/23, TNA.

51. Churchill to Roosevelt, November 26, 1941, in Warren F. Kimball, ed., *Churchill and Roosevelt: The Complete Correspondence* (Princeton, N.J.: Princeton University Press, 1984), 1:277–78.

52. Eri Hotta, *Japan 1941: Countdown to Infamy* (New York: Alfred A. Knopf, 2013), 265–68.

53. Winston S. Churchill, *The Second World War*, vol. 3: *The Grand Alliance* (Boston: Houghton Mifflin, 1950), 604–8.

54. Arthur J. Marder, *Old Friends New Enemies: The Royal Navy and the Imperial Japanese Navy* (Oxford: Clarendon Press, 1981), 1:365–506.

55. Churchill, *Grand Alliance*, 620.

56. Arthur J. Marder, Mark Jacobsen, and John Horsfield, *Old Friends New Enemies: The Royal Navy and the Imperial Japanese Navy* (Oxford: Clarendon Press, 1990), 2:81–151.

57. Winston S. Churchill, *The Second World War*, vol. 4: *The Hinge of Fate* (Boston: Houghton Mifflin, 1950), 100.

58. Churchill address, "War Situation," House of Commons, January 27, 1942, https://hansard.parliament.uk/Commons/1942-01-27/debates/d6c63f66-e4ea -4ba4-8958-3ad126eaa503/WarSituation.

59. Alexander Hill, "British Lend Lease Aid and the Soviet War Effort, June 1941– June 1942," *Journal of Military History* 71, no. 3 (July 2007): 773–808.

60. Churchill address, "War Situation."

61. Churchill speech in House of Commons, "Naval Estimates," March 17, 1914, in Robert Rhodes James, ed., *Winston S. Churchill: His Complete Speeches, 1897– 1963* (London: Chelsea House Publishers, 1974), 3:2258.

62. Churchill address, "War Situation."

63. See Winston S. Churchill, *The World Crisis, 1911–1914* (London: Thornton But-
     terworth, 1923), 9–69, 94–120, 192–213.

64. Churchill's speech, "The Causes of War," November 16, 1934, in Robert Rhodes
     James, ed., *Churchill Speaks, 1897–1963: Collected Speeches in Peace and War*
     (New York: Barnes and Noble, 1980), 586.

65. Churchill, "Mission of Japan," in Wolff, *Collected Essays*, 372.

66. Churchill to Matsuoka, April 2, 1941, in Churchill, *The Grand Alliance*, 189–90.

67. See Churchill's speech, "A Long and Hard War," December 26, 1941, in Robert
     Rhodes James, ed., *Churchill Speaks, 1897–1963: Collected Speeches in Peace and
     War* (New York: Barnes and Noble, 1980), 784–85.

68. Churchill, *The Grand Alliance*, 602–3.

69. Admiral William S. Sims recorded Churchill's comments about the war situation
     in a letter to his wife, May 10, 1917, Sims Papers, box 9, Library of Congress.

CHAPTER FIVE

FDR and AMERICA'S ROAD to WAR in the PACIFIC

Walter A. McDougall

IN 1921, THE YEAR THE WASHINGTON NAVAL CONFERENCE NEGO-
tiated a treaty limiting the fleets of the Pacific powers, the British-born strategist Hector Bywater argued that the treaty's restrictions made war *more*
likely rather than less. That was because the Japanese fleet would be concentrated in their home waters whereas the British and American fleets had
a whole world to patrol. Local hegemony, he wrote, would pose for Japan a
nearly irresistible temptation to carve out an East Asian empire.[1] Franklin D.
Roosevelt, the former Assistant Secretary of the Navy and Democratic candidate for vice president (just then convalescing from polio), did not agree.
To be sure, FDR was keenly aware of the clashes between Japan and the
United States—over commerce, immigration, and imperialism in China—
that had flared up over the previous thirty years, while his own sympathies
lay with the Chinese because his Delano forebears had made fortunes in the
China trade. But he was so enthusiastic about the Washington Conference

that he published an article in 1923 asking "Shall We Trust Japan?" and answered yes. The outstanding issues between the two countries had seemingly been resolved and in any case, he believed, advances in naval technology had rendered a Japanese attack on the U.S. fleet impossible. Hence the sort of suspicion that Bywater evinced was "exactly that outlook which I have sought to combat." FDR did not change his antagonist's mind. Instead, Bywater gathered his notes, studied his maps, and in 1925 published another blockbuster that not only foresaw a war but predicted it would begin with a sneak attack on the U.S. Navy.[2] Japanese admirals paid attention. Americans did not. Roosevelt himself wrote another essay in 1928 claiming U.S.-Japanese relations could only improve.[3]

It was the acme of irony, therefore, that FDR was fated to preside over—and to a certain extent cause—the date which would "live in infamy" thirteen years later. For as much as Japanese aggression was the obvious trigger, the fact remains it always takes two or more governments to manufacture a war. Indeed, the origins of the 1941 clash have been traced all the way back to Commo. Matthew C. Perry's voyage to open Tokugawa Japan in 1853.[4] Roosevelt himself had in his youth noticed the tensions caused by the Japanese empire's emergence as a great power in the first Sino-Japanese War of 1894–95. As a young adult FDR observed the State Department's efforts to counter European and Japanese imperialism through its anodyne Open Door Policy on trade and investment in China.[5] In 1905 his distant cousin Theodore Roosevelt brokered the treaty ending the Russo-Japanese War in hopes of restoring the Open Door and a balance of power in northeast Asia. By then Japanese immigration to Hawaii and California had become another source of tension only temporarily settled by a "Gentlemen's Agreement" in 1907. The following year, America's Great White Fleet showed the flag off of Yokohama, a not so subtle example of gunboat diplomacy that greased the skids for the diplomats. In the Root-Takahira Accord the Japanese pretended again to honor the Open Door in exchange for U.S. recognition of their domination in Korea and southern Manchuria. When the Great War erupted, Japan seized the German concession on the Shandong Peninsula and in 1915 made the notorious Twenty-One Demands on the fledgling Chinese Republic. That was the year foreign service officer Sumner Welles took up his first post in Tokyo. He quickly

concluded that only the most casual observer would fail to detect "the 'pri-
meval military instinct' behind Japan's veneer of Westernization. In every
part of Japan, the army or navy were the 'dominating' factors in daily life."[6]

By then FDR was in the Woodrow Wilson administration and applauded
the Lansing-Ishii Accord of 1917, which obliged the Japanese to walk back
their ambitions. They pledged yet again to uphold the Open Door in return
for an American pledge yet again to respect their "special interests" in China.
But at the 1919 Paris Peace Conference tensions only increased because
Wilson resisted Japan's insistence on retaining China's Shandong Province
and denied Japan's proposal for a racial equality clause in the League of
Nations covenant (lest it prohibit members from discriminating against
certain immigrants). In order to win Japan's acquiescence on the second
issue, however, Wilson caved in on the first, thereby sparking the violent
"May 4th Movement" in China.[7]

What made FDR sanguine about U.S.-Japanese relations just two years
later was the 1921–22 Washington Conference sponsored by President
Warren G. Harding's secretary of state, the former governor of New York,
chief justice, and presidential candidate Charles Evans Hughes. His deft
diplomacy leveraged Britain into terminating its twenty-year-old alliance
with Japan and substituting a system of collective security. In the resulting
Nine-Power Treaty, the powers with interests in China agreed to respect
its sovereignty and territorial integrity and to honor the Open Door. A
second Five-Power Treaty limited the capital ships in the navies of Britain,
America, Japan, France, and Italy, and fixed their respective ratios of naval
tonnage at 5 for both the American and British, 3 for the Japanese, and 1.67
for both the French and Italian. In a third Four-Power Treaty the United
States, Britain, Japan, and France agreed not to fortify any of their Pacific
islands beyond the existing bases at Pearl Harbor, Singapore, Yokohama,
and Tahiti.[8] A consortium of banks in the imperial powers, confident that
stability had been restored in East Asia, arranged for sizable loans to promote Chinese development. Moreover, the Japanese appeared to embrace
parliamentary government (Taisho Democracy) in the 1920s and to welcome Western cultural influences. Finally, Americans fostered goodwill
with the Japanese by offering them generous assistance in the wake of the
Great Kanto Earthquake of 1923. Hence, FDR wrote his sanguine article

during a brief window of sunshine in U.S.-Japanese relations, but by the time he entered the White House those hopes had been utterly dashed.

The Japanese were not primarily to blame. Throughout the rest of the 1920s they mostly practiced pro-Western "Shidehara diplomacy" led by Foreign Minister Shidehara Kijūrū, but it got them nowhere. First, the U.S. Congress passed the Japanese Exclusion Act in 1924, the "manifest object" of which, in the Japanese foreign office's official note, was "to single out Japanese as a nation, stigmatizing them as unworthy and undesirable in the eyes of the American people."[9] Second, the Nine-Power Treaty unraveled because the Chinese themselves denounced its validation of the foreign concessions and Open Door Policy which in fact violated their nation's territorial integrity and sovereignty. The result in 1928 was a Chinese boycott of foreign goods, which hit Japan hardest of all. Third, by that year the Kuomintang regime in Nanjing, led by Chiang Kai-shek, had consolidated its power in northern China as well and had begun to threaten Japanese control of southern Manchuria. John V. A. MacMurray, chief of the Far Eastern division, cabled the State Department that year: "I had hoped and expected to find even amid the known confusion definite elements of purpose and of patriotic idealism. I was disappointed to find . . . the vast complex of self-seeking jealousy and intrigue into which the movement has disintegrated. . . . [H]ere is China at its worst—its old traditions fallen into disrespect, its new sophomoric ideals curdled with cynicism—the whole thing turned into a derisive scramble for territories and taxes with no rules for the game."[10] Fourth, the Great Depression hit, world trade collapsed, and in 1930 Congress passed the protectionist Smoot-Hawley tariff. Japanese exports to the United States—nearly half of the nation's total—plummeted by 40 percent.

From the Japanese point of view, Americans' sermons on liberal internationalism had been exposed as hypocrisy. They insisted that Japan respect the Open Door on its side of the ocean but closed their own side to Japanese people and produce. To their south the Japanese faced a now unified, militant, and xenophobic China. To their north they witnessed the Soviet Union rapidly industrializing Russia, militarizing Siberia, reclaiming the tsar's sphere of influence in northern Manchuria, and turning Mongolia into a communist satellite. Japan was on the defensive, yet the civilian government in Tokyo appeared feckless. To the leadership of the army and its rural political base in Japan it seemed that decadent Western customs had corrupted the effete politicians and their allies in the zaibatsu. Only a program of "direct action" held promise. A Society for the Preservation of the National Essence (*kokutai*), especially Kita Ikki's *Outline for the Reconstruction of Japan*, gave form to such moods and married them to the Shinto cult of the emperor. A parallel intellectual movement in the military held that Japan, if it were to escape the fate of Germany in the Great War, must achieve autarky—economic self-sufficiency—and the only way to do that was through conquest. A "total war" or "control" faction coalesced around these ideas.[11]

The man who turned ideas into deeds was Lieutenant Colonel Ishiwara Kanji, a brilliant, restless young officer whose Nichiren (Sun Lotus) Buddhism prophesied a looming global conflict in which Japan must emerge victorious. In 1928 he arranged to be transferred to southern Manchuria's Kwantung Army (at the time just a military police force of about ten thousand troops) and began plotting with fellow colonels to strike a decisive blow. Their target was the provincial Chinese warlord whose father the Japanese had killed in 1928 but who had seized power in Mukden and begun a flirtation with Chiang Kai-shek. The plotters exploded a bomb on the railway in September 1931, blamed the incident on saboteurs, and hurled their soldiers in all directions in an effort to subdue the huge, mineral-rich province. The Japanese government had no choice but to throw in reinforcements and in 1932 set up a protectorate it called Manchukuo.[12] During the ensuing decade the Japanese expanded the Kwantung Army to 740,000 men and exploited Manchurian resources in the mistaken belief they could achieve autarky despite relying on American exports for 75 percent of their scrap iron, 60 percent of their machinery, and 80 percent of their oil.

The Chinese appealed to the League of Nations, which appointed a commission that scolded Japan for using "excessive force," whereupon the Japan quit the league altogether. President Herbert Hoover's secretary of state, Henry Stimson, merely issued a doctrine of nonrecognition.[13] In any case, the disarmed and depressed United States was no more able than Europeans to police northeast Asia. If anything, that was even more true under Hoover's staunchly *isolationist* successor, Franklin D. Roosevelt. Obsessed with the emergency at home, he barely mentioned foreign affairs during the 1932 campaign and only as an afterthought in his inaugural address.[14] Once in office FDR called Hoover's delegates home from the London Economic Conference, pulled the dollar off the gold standard, and left the tariff intact except for some reciprocal trade agreements with Latin American countries. Between 1935 and 1937 the overwhelmingly Democratic New Deal Congresses passed—and the president signed—Neutrality Acts that forbade Americans from selling arms, making loans, or traveling on the ships of foreign belligerents lest the United States get sucked into war as it had been in 1917.[15]

With regard to East Asia, FDR just iterated the Stimson Doctrine and reduced what American leverage remained by freezing the naval budget during years when Japan repudiated the Five-Power Treaty and launched three ambitious "Circle" plans to expand its fleet.[16] And far from assisting the Republic of China, Roosevelt inadvertently rendered that government insolvent by signing the Silver Purchase Act of 1934, logrolled through Congress by the chairman of the Senate Foreign Relations Committee, Key Pittman (D-Nev.). In what amounted to a subsidy, the act mandated U.S. government purchase of silver at inflated prices. That prompted speculators to drain China of the silver on which its currency was based, sparking severe deflation.[17] All told, one historian abruptly concluded that "the object of United States foreign policy in the Far East during 1933–1939 was to preserve traditional commercial and imperial interests, while avoiding direct conflict with Japan at virtually any cost."[18]

During his second term Roosevelt paid a good deal more attention to nefarious trends overseas, but even then his focus was almost exclusively on Europe. Adolf Hitler, who rose to power just a month before FDR's inauguration, had, in just four years, pulled Germany out of the league, launched a crash rearmament program, and reoccupied the neutralized Rhineland on the borders with France and the Low Countries. The only major democracies left in Europe—Britain and France—did nothing to hinder Nazi dynamism, or encouraged it with policies of appeasement. The only power that did resist vocally—and in the Spanish Civil War actively— was the rival totalitarianism of Joseph Stalin's Soviet Union. Many forlorn people in Depression-torn Europe began to suspect the future belonged either to fascism or communism.

Similar authoritarian spasms perturbed Japanese politics beginning in 1930, when the prime minister was shot by a nationalist. Two years later the liberal Seiyukai Party won a landslide electoral victory, only to lose its prime minister to a military assassin. Finally, in the February 26 Incident in 1936, the Kodo-ha (Imperial Way) faction in the army staged a full-blown coup d'état in which 1,500 troops seized government buildings and targeted high officials for assassination. The coup failed, but it redounded to the benefit of the Tosei-ha (Control) faction led by, among others, General Tōjō Hideki.[19]

That was the year Japan joined Nazi Germany in the Anti-Comintern Pact. Although Germany had substantial military and economic ties to China, the Japanese government was eager for insurance against another conflict with Russia. A secret military provision provided for mutual assistance in case of an unprovoked attack on either party. That pact was the first formal step toward what would become the Axis alliance, hence the initial link between the emerging theaters of conflict in Europe and Asia.

A second Sino-Japanese War was probably inevitable. For once the Kwantung Army had secured Manchuria, it faced both the need and temptation to invade the border provinces to the south in order to keep warlords, the Kuomiang, and Mao Zedong's Chinese Communists at arm's length. But each step southward was bound to inflame Chinese Nationalists, while each hostile incident was bound to inflame Kwantung officers accustomed to "direct action." They grew especially alarmed when the Communists briefly held Chiang Kai-shek captive during the sensational "Sian incident" of 1936 and pressured him into a united front aimed at the Japanese. Tōjō Hideki himself declared that "if our military power permits it, we should deliver a blow first of all upon the Nanking regime to get rid of the menace at our back." None other than Ishiwara Kanji himself now warned against an invasion of China lest Japan get dragged into "the deepest sort of bog."[20] But Tōjō got his way when skirmishes broke out around the Marco Polo Bridge near Beijing in July 1937. Both sides rushed in reinforcements and ignited an undeclared war which neither Nanjing nor Tokyo tried very hard to stop. The Japanese high command decided the way to win this war quickly was to capture the Yangtze River valley in a ruthless campaign that began with the terror bombing of Shanghai and ended with the Rape of Nanjing in which perhaps 100,000 Chinese civilians were murdered. But Chiang remained defiant, retreating first to Wuhan and in 1938 to Chongqing. The war became a protracted bloodbath.[21]

The Japanese ambassador stuck with having to explain his empire's mischief to Americans was Saitō Hirosi. Upon his arrival in December 1933, he had made an instant splash thanks to his fluent English, skill in public relations, and humor. His "chief purpose in coming here," he told reporters, "is to drink whiskey with good Americans." Over the next six years the glad-handing little man played golf, attended baseball games and night clubs, and made speaking tours reassuring audiences that the Japanese were not some band of berserks run amok. Instead, he blamed Chinese xenophobia for the occupation of Manchuria and likened the order and progress Japan brought there to the order and progress the United States brought to Latin America. He urged Americans to "turn a deaf ear when men tell you we want war."[22]

His opposite number in Tokyo, Joseph Grew, shared Saitō's sentiments. An old friend of President Roosevelt who wrote "Dear Frank" letters, he pleaded for accommodation across the Pacific. But the task of both ambassadors became far more difficult in 1937. Referring to the invasion of China, Grew reported that the "great majority of Japanese are astonishingly capable of really fooling themselves; that they really believe everything they have done is right. . . . The Westerner believes that because the Japanese has adopted Western dress, language, and customs he must think like a Westerner. No greater error can be made." Meanwhile, Saitō begged America's pardon as abjectly as he knew how; "So sorry, excuse please" was the newspapers' caricature. But the ambassador's bonhomie could not erase images and accounts of the atrocities in China. To Americans it seemed the Japanese *had* run amok, which meant Saitō was more than just a "Diplomat in the Doghouse" as *The New Yorker* wrote. He was now either a fool or a liar, a cat's paw, a con man, or (as Americans in the 1930s would have said) a Jap.[23]

Roosevelt trod carefully. He neglected to invoke the Neutrality Acts on the grounds that the Sino-Japanese War was undeclared, but the aid

Americans directed to China was paltry compared to their commerce with Japan. Secretary of State Cordell Hull, Special Advisor on Far Eastern Affairs Stanley Hornbeck, Treasury Secretary Henry Morgenthau, and Interior Secretary Harold Ickes advised FDR to impose a boycott on trade with Japan. Only Grew and MacMurray demurred, fearing the Japanese might lash out ferociously instead of stand down.[24] The president's famous Quarantine Speech of October 5, 1937, was delphic. He condemned "international lawlessness," but mentioned no names and promised Americans his intention was to "minimize our risk of involvement." Perhaps he was pondering a vague scheme for a bloc of democracies to apply moral pressure, but as yet there were "no indications that Roosevelt intended to embark on any radical program of economic sanctions, either alone or in cooperation with other nations."[25] On the contrary, when Hitler annexed Austria in 1938, then demanded the Sudetenland province from Czechoslovakia, FDR appealed to Benito Mussolini to call for a summit conference and then congratulated Prime Minister Neville Chamberlain on his policy of appeasement. Not surprisingly, he was even more passive in Asia.

During the early spring of 1939, a brief but poignant thaw in U.S.-Japanese relations occurred. Saitō, his fifty-two-year-old lungs seared by the 22,000 Lucky Strike cigarettes he smoked every year, died that February, and Roosevelt approved a State Department plan to return his ashes to Tokyo on the USS *Astoria*. Hornbeck thought the goodwill measure might have some effect inasmuch as the Japanese were "especially susceptible to and appreciative of manifestations of human kindliness and national respect." When the ship arrived on April 17, Grew reported that "a wave of friendliness for the United States swept over the country." But both men advised against elaborate ceremonies lest too much "ballyhoo" give the Japanese the wrong impression. So Saitō Hirosi—the last spirit of Japanese-American friendship—was solemnly repatriated and interred.[26]

As the Sino-Japanese War entered its third year with no sign of a truce, Roosevelt acceded to those urging him to terminate the 1911 U.S.-Japanese commercial treaty. Their ranks had swelled to include many members of Congress, led by Senator Arthur Vandenburg (R-Mich.), the influential China lobby, the American Committee for Non-Participation in Japanese Aggression, and 70 percent of citizens polled on the issue. Americans were neither willing nor able to stop aggression, but they no longer wished to abet it. In July 1939 Cordell Hull gave the Japanese government six months' notice before the United States put trade on a day-to-day basis.

In Tokyo a new cabinet featuring the pro-American admiral Nomura Kishisaburō as foreign minister hoped to repair relations with Washington before the six months ran out. But that very summer the Cabinet Planning Board adjusted to the news from America by devising a program of autarky more reckless than any before. Its studies showed that between 50 and 70 percent of the empire's needs for metals, rubber, rice, and petroleum could be recouped through the conquest of Southeast Asia. Admirals favored such a "southern strategy" because it would be largely their show, while generals refused to consider scaling back their war in China. Nomura had nothing to offer Roosevelt, who was left to hope that the progressive tightening of sanctions would dissuade the Japanese from further mischief.

On July 1, 1939, FDR appointed George C. Marshall chief of staff with these words: "There's a war coming, George. Clear out the dead wood." Historians still argue over when and why Roosevelt the isolationist turned Roosevelt the interventionist, but they all agree the cause lay in Europe. Was it the Nazi Kristallnacht pogrom in November 1938? The German invasion of Czechoslovakia in March 1939? Hitler's threat of war against Poland later that spring? What is known is that the U.S. Joint Planning Committee began work in May 1939 on the Rainbow contingency plans for possible war against multiple enemies, with a decided focus on Europe. Britain and France had just issued military guarantees in hopes of deterring a German attack on Poland, and they sought to win Stalin's support. But Nazi foreign minister Joachim von Ribbentrop outbid them in Moscow, concluding a nonaggression pact with Vyacheslav Molotov in August. The Nazi-Soviet Pact emboldened Hitler to launch an invasion of Poland on September 1, whereupon the forlorn British and French parliaments declared war on Germany. No one was more shocked than the Japanese. Their partner in the Anti-Comintern Pact had betrayed them by aligning with the USSR and had done so, in fact, just a few months after the Kwantung Army had fought (and lost) division-sized battles against the Red Army on the Manchurian-Mongolian frontier.[27] Then war broke out in Europe. The Japanese did not know how to adjust.

Roosevelt adjusted by calling on Congress to repeal its arms embargo to permit Britain and France access to the U.S. economy so long as they paid cash and carried the goods on their own ships. To mobilize public opinion, he arranged for the creation of Non-Partisan Committee for Peace through Revision of the Neutrality Act. A marathon debate ensued, but in the end comfortable majorities in both houses passed the bill, which FDR signed on November 4, 1939.

After the Nazis and Soviets partitioned Eastern Europe, a so-called Phony War set in over the winter. But in spring 1940 the German blitzkrieg quickly overran Scandinavia, the Low Countries, and France and threatened Britain with invasion. Once again shocking events on the other side of the world had profound geopolitical ramifications for Japan. Suddenly the Dutch East Indies and French Indochina were orphaned, their mother countries occupied, while the British would be sorely pressed to defend their own colonies in Southeast Asia. In other words, windows of opportunity were flung open wide for the Japanese to ameliorate their economic pinch through a strike at the European colonies. In July 1940, a month after the French surrender, the emperor asked the prestigious Prince Konoe Fumimaro to become prime minister. As a young diplomat he had attended the Paris Peace Conference and written a widely read essay, "Reject the Anglo-American-Centered Peace," which damned Wilsonian self-determination, the Open Door, and the League of Nations as hypocritical fronts for imperialism. He rose to become the leader of the House of Peers, then prime minister in 1937 just prior to the Marco Polo Bridge incident. Now he returned to power determined to impose authoritarian rule at home and win the war quickly by conquering Southeast Asia. His foreign minister, Matsuoka Yōsuke, added a third dimension: alliance with the Axis powers in Europe.

In August Matsuoka proclaimed Japan's intention to forge a Greater East Asia Co-Prosperity Sphere whose (still secret) targets included Indochina, Malaya, Thailand, Burma, the Dutch East Indies, and even India, Australia, and New Zealand. The following month he took the first step toward that goal by pressuring France's collaborationist Vichy regime to permit Japanese occupation of northern Indochina. But his boldest move followed on September 27, when his ambassador in Berlin signed a Tripartite Pact with Germany and Italy. The signatories recognized each other's plans to establish "new orders" in Europe and Asia and promised to "assist one another with all political, economic and military means if one of the Contracting Powers is attacked by a Power at present not involved in the European War or in the Japanese-Chinese conflict." That unnamed power was obviously the United States, and the purpose of the pact for the Japanese was obviously to *deter*, not provoke a Pacific War. But the Co-Prosperity Sphere and Tripartite Pact were the second and third links between the theaters of conflict in Europe and Asia.[28]

Meanwhile, U.S. rearmament, which had begun in 1938 with belated increases in naval spending, took off after the fall of France. Roosevelt replaced the secretaries of war and the Navy with the experienced Republicans Henry L. Stimson and Frank Knox, and on May 30, 1940, he summoned a committee of businessmen, led by General Motors production wizard William Knudson, to the Oval Office. He wanted to know how to convert American plant capacity to military production, preferably overnight. Knudson not only told him but gave him a slogan: arsenal of democracy. Dr. New Deal became Dr. Win the War on that day, albeit he would not reveal his new costume for another eighteen months.[29]

Roosevelt remained fixated on Europe because he believed Germany to be a much greater threat than Japan. But he also believed the United States needed to shield the British and Dutch colonies in Asia for strategic and economic reasons. Indeed, the State Department and the voice of big business, New York's Council on Foreign Relations, were warning that American prosperity could not long survive in a world of authoritarian blocs. So almost imperceptibly an American-British-Chinese-Dutch (ABCD) coalition began to gestate when FDR ordered the Pacific Fleet to permanent station at Pearl Harbor, Hawaii. Then, at a cabinet meeting on July 24, Stimson, Knox, Morgenthau, and Ickes begged the president to ban the export of metals and—most critically—oil to Japan. He almost did. But Sumner Welles argued that a total embargo might impel the "already berserk" Japanese to attack the oil-rich East Indies. Moreover, General Marshall and the chief of naval operations, Adm. Harold R. Stark, knowing the United States was not ready for war, counseled moderation. So instead, FDR signed a National Defense Action Act that empowered him to ban the export of items deemed

vital to U.S. rearmament, which did not as yet include iron and oil. His pur-
pose, too, was to *deter*, not provoke, a Pacific War. Yet in historian Robert
Divine's judgment, "The policies adopted by the United States and Japan in
September 1940 made war between the two nations nearly inevitable."[30]

During the late summer and fall the Royal Air Force won the Battle of
Britain, but the British, who now stood alone, quickly ran low on money
and ships. Following Roosevelt's reelection in November, Winston Churchill sent him a four-thousand-word letter pleading for further assistance,
and FDR pledged to "eliminate the dollar sign" through the pretense of
Lend-Lease. The public approved and so did Congress in March 1941. It
was over that winter that Marshall, Stark, and their staffs drafted Plan Dog,
which explicitly adopted a Europe-first strategy but which raised the question of what a defensive/deterrent posture in the Pacific might look like.
For instance, if the defense of Southeast Asia proved impossible, U.S. forces
might need to abandon the Philippines as well as the British and Dutch colonies and abandon support for China. The ambiguity was not resolved, but
FDR signed off on Plan Dog in January 1941, as did an Anglo-American
staff conference in March.

That was the month when Nomura, now ambassador in Washington, and
Secretary of State Hull began their sterile negotiations. In April Hull issued
his Four Points, which he considered nonnegotiable, including respect for
all nations' sovereignty and territorial integrity; noninterference in others'
internal affairs; equality of economic opportunity; and no violent distur-
bance of the status quo in the Pacific. Nomura, conscious of how those points
would be received in Tokyo, did not even forward them for a month and
then suggested they were no longer operative. Not until September did the
Japanese government realize how stubbornly Hull clung to them. In effect,
he was insisting on the restoration of the long defunct Washington Conference system, which meant that American strategy (to employ the terms of a
later era) had subtly shifted from containment to rollback. Simultaneously,
in Singapore, American, British, Dutch, and Chinese officials met to coordi-
nate operations in the first formal expression of an informal ABCD alliance.

Meanwhile, Matsuoka was busy putting the final touches on his preparations for an Axis-led new world order. After a visit to Berlin, he traveled
to Moscow where he and Molotov signed a Soviet-Japanese Neutrality Pact.

The two parties pledged neutrality in the event that either one became "the object of hostilities" with a third power. The elated Matsuoka returned to Tokyo boasting he had secured Manchuria's northern flank, forged a bloc of totalitarian states, and cleared the path for a southern advance to realize the Co-Prosperity Sphere. Just two months later on June 22, Hitler tore up his own pact with Stalin and the Wehrmacht invaded the Soviet Union. Yet again the shocked Japanese had to adjust to the inscrutable maneuvers of Europeans. Matsuoka then abruptly reversed himself, urging Konoe to attack Siberia and assist Germany in the destruction of the USSR. But the prime minister, the admirals, and a number of generals objected that a second big war on the continent would only make Japan more dependent on U.S. supplies. At length, on July 2, 1941, the Imperial Council ratified the original program to realize the Co-Prosperity Sphere even at the risk of war against Britain and the United States. Matsuoka "was discarded like a spent shot."[31]

By then top officials in the White House and the War, Navy, and State Departments were reading the Japanese embassy's mail. In September 1940 the American Signal Intelligence Service succeeded (after an eighteen-month battle) in breaking "Purple," Japan's diplomatic code. By the following year Army and Navy cryptanalysts were decoding forty to fifty messages every day, thereby giving Washington "access to Tokyo's most secret communications and thereby reopened a window on events and attitudes in various capitals, the most important being Berlin and Rome."[32]

Someone—perhaps Roosevelt himself—dubbed the process MAGIC. The decrypts were incomplete, sometimes mistranslated, and never a determining factor in foreign policy since by then the American and Japanese positions had become intractable. But MAGIC did give a small number of American leaders a good idea of the drift of opinion in Tokyo.[33] Thus, FDR told Harold Ickes in late June 1941, "The Japs are having a real drag-down . . . trying to decide which way they are going to jump. No one knows what the decision will be but, as you know, it is terribly important for the control of the Atlantic for us to help keep peace in the Pacific. . . . I simply have not got enough Navy to go around."[34]

Historian Waldo Heinrichs and others since have found circumstantial evidence to support their suspicion that the prospect Roosevelt most feared during that summer was not a Japanese strike to the south, but rather to the north, in which case the Axis might win the war before the United States could even get in. Hence he lobbied hard for Congress to extend Lend-Lease aid to Russia (which took until October 1), while denying Japan the war materials an additional Siberian campaign would require. The Japanese themselves gave him the pretext by invading the rest of French Indochina in late July. The president froze Japan's assets in the United States and embargoed refined petroleum. In Heinrichs' judgment, "Roosevelt could see the whole picture now. In July he was forceful, impatient with delay, pressing upon events, so different from the reserved, withdrawn president of the spring."[35]

Implementation of those sanctions devolved upon Assistant Secretary of State Dean Acheson, who quietly interpreted the freeze to include a full embargo on crude oil as well as refined products. In short, he closed the spigot, which meant the desperate Japanese were liable to react spasmodically. Nearly all historians have assumed that FDR did not know what Acheson had done before his departure for Newfoundland and a secret meeting with Churchill beginning on August 9. That was the conference where FDR promised to "wage war but not declare it" until such time as American clashes with U-boats forced the hand of the Congress. The leaders issued the Atlantic Charter, a Wilsonian statement of Anglo-American war aims. There, too, the military chiefs of the two powers reconfirmed their commitment to a Europe-first strategy in the event of a two-ocean war consistent with the latest U.S. contingency plan, Rainbow 5. But the leaders disagreed on policy toward Japan. Churchill, anxious to pry the United States into the war by any means possible, urged Roosevelt to deliver a clear ultimatum threatening war if the Japanese did not evacuate Southeast Asia. Roosevelt, still hoping to deter or delay a Pacific War, at least until U.S. rearmament was further along, resisted. Upon his return to Washington, he only gave Ambassador Nomura a vague warning to the effect that the United States would take "any and all steps" to uphold its interests and security in the region.[36]

Even then, most historians have thought, Roosevelt was not aware of what Acheson had done until September 1, six full weeks after the oil embargo began, at which point he must have decided he could not undo it without sending Japan the wrong signal.[37] Skeptical historian Marc Tracht-enberg has challenged that account. Is it really plausible, he asked, that Franklin Roosevelt, with the world hanging in the balance, was not even in control of the officials executing his dire instructions? Is this not more likely a case of the dog that didn't bark? After sifting through all the liter-ature and documentation, Trachtenberg concluded that if Acheson had in fact exceeded instructions "you would expect Roosevelt and Hull to have been furious when they found out what he had done." But they were not, even though they knew that the oil embargo might push the Japanese to the brink and that it lay in their power to relax the embargo at any point. Therefore, Trachtenberg reasoned that "Roosevelt had deliberately opted for a policy which he knew would in all probability lead to war with Japan."[38]

Throughout the late summer of 1941 Roosevelt had tried as hard as he could to taunt *Germany* into declaring war so that the United States could concentrate its resources on the *European* theater. He had made the destroyers-for-bases trade with the British. He had thrown the U.S. Mer-chant Marine into an undeclared Battle of the Atlantic. He had ordered destroyers to sink U-boats on sight and had established bases in Greenland and Iceland. The destroyer *Greer* was the first USN ship to shoot at a Ger-man ship on September 4. In mid-October, a U-boat torpedoed and dam-aged the destroyer *Kearny* off the coast of Iceland, killing eleven American sailors. Later in the month, the destroyer *Reuben James* was sunk in an action with a German submarine. Yet Hitler refused to be provoked, and Congress remained unmoved since a late October poll showed only 17 per-cent of Americans in favor of immediate entry into the war. So it is difficult not to conclude that for Roosevelt the outbreak of war in the Pacific had become an acceptable *pis aller*.[39]

The American embargo left the Japanese feeling "like fish in a pond from which the water was gradually being drained away."[40] The fifty million barrels of oil they had in reserve might last two years at most during which the American military buildup would become overwhelming. So their mil-itary and civilian leaders staged a series of conferences and finally decided on September 6 to give diplomacy one more chance. Indeed, Prince Konoe proposed a dramatic summit meeting in Honolulu or Juneau where he and Roosevelt might come to terms. Ambassador Grew endorsed the notion, assuring FDR that Konoe "would and could bring his country to meet whatever requirements" he laid down, whereupon he would "report immediately to the emperor and it will be the emperor who will command the army to suspend hostilities." It was "highly unlikely," wrote Grew, that "this chance will come again."[41]

The suggestion got nowhere in Washington. Hornbeck could not imagine the Japanese ever agreeing to withdraw from Indochina and China, refused to trust them if they did so agree, and in any event rejected a bilateral summit. Hull argued forcefully that a U.S.-Japanese summit was bound to do irreparable damage to the ABCD coalition. FDR deferred to his secretary of state. On October 2 Hull told Nomura in no uncertain words that the summit would not take place and that acceptance of his Four Points remained the precondition for any negotiations.[42] Konoe resigned on October 18. General Tōjō became prime minister.

Roosevelt had met with his own military and civilian leaders two days before and said candidly, "We face the delicate question of the diplomatic fencing to be done so as to be sure that Japan was put in the wrong and made the first bad move—overt move."[43] The president ordered Gen. Douglas MacArthur to take command in the Philippines and approved the Army's plan to build up a bomber force at Clark Field, well within range of Japanese cities. The ostensible purpose was deterrence but it was more likely meant as a provocation. Meanwhile, in a series of meetings on November 1–2 the Tōjō cabinet reconsidered the decision of September 6 in light of three options. The first—prolonged perseverance and patience—was unacceptable to the military because the ABCD coalition would only grow stronger over time while Japan's oil reserves would be depleted. The second—immediate initiation of hostilities—was resisted by the foreign and finance ministers. The third—one last bid to reach a modus vivendi with Washington—was adopted *faute de mieux*. But Tōjō gave the diplomats a deadline of November 30, after which war against the ABCD powers was the only alternative. On November 5 Admiral Yamamoto Isoroku received the order to assemble the combined fleet for a surprise attack on Pearl Harbor.

The eleventh-hour negotiations were a waste of time. American officials already knew through MAGIC the final terms Nomura would propose.[44] They contained five points: (1) Japan and the United States undertake not to make armed advances into any new region of Southeast Asia; (2) Japan to withdraw from its current positions there upon restoration of peace with China; (3) Japan and the United States to cooperate in securing materials they required from Dutch East Indies; (4) Japan and the United States agree to restore their commercial relations prior to the freezing of assets; and (5) the United States to refrain from acts prejudicial to restoration of general peace between Japan and China. To accept that proposal would have meant acquiescence in Japanese domination of East Asia, betrayal of the Chinese, and abandonment of the British. Hull's final proposal required the Japanese to withdraw from Indochina and *all of China*, recognize Chiang's regime, make a nonaggression pact with other Pacific powers, and repudiate the Tripartite Pact. To accept that proposal would have meant surrender of Japan's whole empire in exchange for abject dependency on the ABCD powers. Tōjō's deadline passed and—thanks to MAGIC—the War and Navy Departments knew a Japanese attack, no doubt on the Philippines, was imminent. But U.S. intelligence and surveillance lost track of Japan's aircraft carrier force after it left port on November 29. It would steal across the ocean under radio silence and a cover of fog in anticipation of the sneak attack on Hawaii scheduled for December 8 (Tokyo time).

The strongest argument against a backdoor theory has always been that Roosevelt's real aim was to get the United States into the European war and that he could not have been sure that war with Japan would do the trick. Hitler might not keep his word under the Tripartite Pact. Nor might Congress—hot for vengeance against Japan—gratuitously declare war against Germany. In fact, MAGIC decrypts had already provided circumstantial evidence that might have emboldened FDR. In August 1941 the Japanese embassy in Berlin reported that Hitler would honor his word and open hostilities with the United States "at once" in the event of a Japanese-American collision. Again on November 29, Ribbentrop assured the ambassador that "Should Japan become engaged in a war against the United States, Germany, of course, would join the war immediately. . . . The Führer is determined on that point." Finally, on December 7 itself, Hull told the British ambassador Lord Halifax that Roosevelt and his cabinet never thought of war against Japan alone because they expected a declaration from Germany.[45]

But something fishy also occurred. A top-secret copy of Rainbow 5, all 350 pages of it, fell into the hands of Cissy Patterson and her cousin Robert McCormick, the isolationist publishers of the *Washington Times-Herald* and *Chicago Tribune*. On December 4, the front pages of both newspapers screamed "F.D.R.'S WAR PLANS!" Who leaked it and why? The mystery has never been solved. But Gen. Albert Wedemeyer, an initial suspect later exonerated, confided this in 1983: "I have no hard evidence but I have always been convinced, on some sort of intuitional level, that President Roosevelt authorized it." Indeed, the day the story appeared Roosevelt had nothing to say and his press secretary merely refused to confirm or deny its accuracy: another dog that didn't bark. Did FDR leak the war plan to give Hitler added incentive to declare war on the United States? There were certainly grounds from the German perspective. Rainbow 5's Europe-first strategy would be badly hindered by war in the Pacific, while Germany would be free to wage unlimited submarine warfare in the Atlantic. Moreover, the plan conceded that American forces could not intervene decisively in Europe before July 1943, by which time Hitler expected the war to be over and won. What is known is that Hitler congratulated the Japanese on their surprise attack and instructed the Reichstag to declare war on the United States four days after Pearl Harbor. The reason he gave was that Germany had been provoked by American newspapers which revealed "a plan prepared by President Roosevelt . . . according to which his intention was to attack Germany in 1943 with all the resources of the United States. Thus our patience has come to a breaking point."[46]

In the end, the turbulent, confusing events of 1941 played out in such a way that the leader most pleased with the result was undoubtedly Joseph Stalin. He got his first choice: peace on his Far Eastern flank while the United States went to war with Germany as well as Japan. Roosevelt settled for his second choice: a two-ocean war. To be sure, he never expected his beloved battleships would be mauled from the air two-thirds of the way across the Pacific. But inasmuch as that was what happened, he was able to lead the American people into the war more united and determined than he ever dared hope. For Roosevelt, the proof that he had been wrong when he wrote those articles back in the 1920s turned out to be a blessing in disguise.[47]

Notes

1. Hector Bywater, *Sea Power in the Pacific: A Study of the American-Japanese Naval Problem* (London: Constable, 1921).
2. Hector Bywater, *The Great Pacific War* (London: Constable, 1925).
3. William L. Neumann, "Franklin D. Roosevelt and Japan, 1913–1933," *Pacific Historical Review* 22, no. 2 (1953): 143–53.
4. See Walter Lafeber, *The Clash: A History of U.S.-Japanese Relations* (New York: W. W. Norton, 1997); and Walter A. McDougall, *Let the Sea Make a Noise: A History of the North Pacific from Magellan to MacArthur* (New York: Basic Books, 1993).
5. George Kennan, "Mr. Hippisley and the Open Door," in *American Diplomacy* (Chicago: University of Chicago Press, 2012 [1951]), 23–40. The Open Door, like so many other allegedly American novelties in foreign affairs, was originally a British idea.
6. Benjamin Welles, *Sumner Welles: A Biography* (New York: St. Martin's, 1997), 42.
7. Paul Gordon Lauren, "Human Rights in History: Diplomacy and Racial Equality at the Paris Peace Conference," *Diplomatic History* 2 (1978): 257–78.
8. Erik Goldstein and John Maurer, eds., *The Washington Conference, 1921–22: Naval Rivalry, East Asian Stability and the Road to Pearl Harbor* (New York: Routledge, 1994).
9. "International Documents," in the American Peace Society, *Advocate of Peace* 86 (1924).
10. Akira Iriye, *After Imperialism: The Search for a New Order in the Far East 1921–1931* (New York: Atheneum, 1969), 216–17; Dorothy Borg, *American Policy and the Chinese Revolution, 1925–1928* (New York: Macmillan, 1947).
11. W. G. Beasley, *Japanese Imperialism 1894–1945* (Oxford: Clarendon Press, 1987); Michael Barnhart, *Japan Prepares for Total War: The Search for Economic Security, 1919–1941* (Ithaca, N.Y.: Cornell University Press, 1987); Richard J. Smethurst, *A Social Basis for Prewar Japanese Militarism: The Army and the Rural Community* (Berkeley: University of California Press, 1974).
12. Mark R. Peattie, *Ishiwara Kanji and Japan's Confrontation with the West* (Princeton, N.J.: Princeton University Press, 1975). The puppet ruler of Manchukuo was Puyi, the deposed Ch'ing (Manchu) emperor of China.
13. See Christopher Thorne, *The Limits of Foreign Policy: The West, the League, and the Far Eastern Crisis of 1931–1933* (New York: Capricorn, 1973).
14. "In the field of world policy I would dedicate this Nation to the policy of the good neighbor—the neighbor who resolutely respects himself and, because he does so, respects the rights of others." That was all FDR said or intended to say. While drafting the speech FDR asked Sumner Welles, who by then had become a Latin American specialist in the State Department, to give him no more than "two paragraphs" about foreign policy, which FDR trimmed down to one sentence. See Welles, *Sumner Welles*, 148–49.

15. Robert A. Divine, *The Illusion of Neutrality: Franklin D. Roosevelt and the Struggle over the Arms Embargo* (Chicago: University of Chicago Press, 1962).

16. Emily O. Goldman, *Sunken Treaties: Naval Arms Control between the Wars* (University Park: Pennsylvania State University Press, 1994), 189–237; Mark R. Peattie, *Kaigun: Strategy, Tactics, and Technology in the Imperial Japanese Navy, 1887–1941* (Annapolis, Md.: Naval Institute Press, 1982).

17. The act was a pork-barrel windfall for seven silver-producing western states whose fourteen senators FDR needed to pass New Deal legislation. Hence American domestic politics once again had nefarious consequences for foreign policy. See Milton Friedman, "Franklin D. Roosevelt, Silver, and China, " *Journal of Political Economy* 100, no. 1 (1992): 62–83.

18. Arnold A. Offner, *The Origins of the Second World War: American Foreign Policy and World Politics, 1917–1941* (New York: Praeger, 1975), 135.

19. Barnhart, *Japan Prepares for Total War*; James Crowley, *Japan's Quest for Autonomy: National Security and Foreign Policy, 1930–1938* (Princeton, N.J.: Princeton University, 1966).

20. Meirion and Susan Harries, *Soldiers of the Sun: The Rise and Fall of the Imperial Japanese Army* (New York: Random House, 1991), 207.

21. Iris Chang, *The Rape of Nanking: The Forgotten Holocaust of World War II* (New York: Basic Books. 1997).

22. Saitō Hirosi, *Japan's Policies and Purposes: Selections from Recent Addresses and Writings* (Boston: Marshall Jones, 1935).

23. Joseph C. Grew, *Ten Years in Japan* (New York: Simon & Schuster, 1944), 84; Jack Alexander, "Profiles: Diplomat in the Doghouse," *The New Yorker*, April 30, 1938, 22–27.

24. Waldo Heinrichs, *American Ambassador: Joseph C. Grew and the Development of the American Diplomatic Tradition* (New York: Oxford University Press, 1986); Joseph Grew, *Turbulent Era: A Diplomatic Record of Forty Years, 1904–1945*, 2 vols. (Boston: Houghton Mifflin, 1952).

25. Divine, *Illusion of Neutrality*, 210–13.

26. Roger Dingman, "Farewell to Friendship: The *U.S.S. Astoria*'s Visit to Japan, April 1939," *Diplomatic History* 10, no. 2 (1986): 121–39.

27. Stuart D. Goldman, *Nomonhan, 1939: The Red Army's Victory That Shaped World War II* (Annapolis, Md.: Naval Institute Press, 2012); Alvin D. Coox, *Nomonhan: Japan Against Russia, 1939*, 2 vols. (Stanford, Calif.: Stanford University Press, 1990).

28. David John Lu, *Agony of Choice: Matsuoka Yosuke and the Rise and Fall of the Japanese Empire* (Lanham, Md.: Lexington Books, 2002); Ken Ishida, *Japan, Italy and the Road to the Tripartite Alliance* (Cham, Switzerland: Palgrave Macmillan, 2018).

29. On rearmament see Christopher Layne, *The Peace of Illusions: American Grand Strategy from 1940 to the Present* (Ithaca, N.Y.: Cornell University Press, 2006); Warren F. Kimball, *The Juggler: Franklin Roosevelt as Wartime Statesman* (Princeton,

N.J.: Princeton University Press, 1991); Paul A. C. Koistenen, *Arsenal of World War II: The Political Economy of American Warfare, 1940–1945* (Lawrence: University Press of Kansas, 2004); Arthur Herman, *Freedom's Forge: How American Business Produced Victory in World War II* (New York: Random House, 2013).

30. Robert A. Divine, *Reluctant Belligerent: American Entry into the Second World War* (Hoboken, N.J.: Wiley, 1965), 102; on Welles' intervention see Welles, *Sumner Welles*, 265–66.

31. Ian Nish, *Japanese Foreign Policy, 1869–1942* (London: Routledge & Kegan Paul, 1977), 239–49. On the neutrality pact see George Alexander Lensen, *Strange Neutrality: Soviet-Japanese Relations during the Second World War 1941–1945* (Tallahassee, Fla.: Diplomatic Press, 1972).

32. David Alvarez, *Secret Messages: Codebreaking and American Diplomacy, 1930–1945* (Lawrence: University Press of Kansas, 2000), 80–82, 97–101.

33. Keiichiro Komatsu, *Origins of the Pacific War and the Importance of MAGIC* (New York: St. Martin's, 1999), 243, concludes with the surprising observation that "Roosevelt seemed to have only the vaguest notion of what the codebreakers were doing for him," and Komatsu, like Alvarez, downplays the influence of MAGIC decrypts over U.S. foreign policy.

34. Harold Ickes, *The Lowering Cloud: The Secret Diary of Harold L. Ickes* (New York: Simon & Schuster, 1955), 567.

35. See Waldo Heinrichs, *Threshold of War: Franklin D. Roosevelt and American Entry into World War II* (New York: Oxford University Press, 1982), 118–45, quote, 145.

36. Lafeber, *The Clash*, 188–90.

37. See, for instance, Jonathan G. Utley, *Going to War with Japan, 1937–1941* (Knoxville: University of Tennessee Press, 1985), 154–55.

38. Marc Trachtenberg, "Developing an Interpretation through Textual Analysis: The 1941 Case," in *The Craft of International History* (Princeton, N.J.: Princeton University Press, 2006), 79–139, passage on Acheson and the embargo, 94–101. David Kaiser, *No End Save Victory: How FDR Led the Nation into War* (New York: Basic Books, 2014), 254–59, reveals that on July 31 Sumner Welles presented a summary of the State Department plan to implement the asset freeze to Roosevelt, who duly initialed it. Hence, he also concluded that "there seems to be no doubt that everyone involved, including the President, knew that all petroleum exports to Japan were about to cease."

39. Walter A. McDougall, *The Tragedy of U.S. Foreign Policy: How America's Civil Religion Betrayed the National Interest* (New Haven, Conn.: Yale University Press, 2016), 208–10.

40. Robert Butow, *Tojo and the Coming of the War* (Princeton, N.J.: Princeton University Press, 1961), 245.

41. Grew, *Turbulent Era*, 2:1333–34; Trachtenberg, "The 1941 Case," 110–11. For data on Japanese oil imports, see Herbert Feis, *The Road to Pearl Harbor* (Princeton, N.J.: Princeton University Press, 1950), 268.

42. Akira Iriye, *Origins of the Second World War in Asia and the Pacific* (New York: Routledge, 2013 [1987]), 159–67.

43. Kaiser, *No End Save Victory*, 304–6.

44. As the historian of intelligence bluntly states, "Such information would have been of inestimable value to the United States if Washington and Tokyo had been engaged in real give-and-take negotiations. Unfortunately they were not." See Alvarez, *Secret Messages*, 100–101.

45. F. H. Hinsley, *British Intelligence in the Second World War: Its Influence on Strategy and Operations* (Cambridge: Cambridge University Press, 1981), 2:75; Kaiser, *No End Save Victory*, 324; Trachtenberg, "The 1941 Case," 124–29, also cites evidence to the effect that the overwhelming majority of Americans polled in late 1941 believed the Axis alliance was ironclad and the Japanese were acting as "Hitler's puppets." Hence there is reason to believe FDR might have been able to persuade Congress to declare war on Germany in the event of a Japanese attack.

46. Thomas Fleming, *The New Dealers' War: Franklin D. Roosevelt and the War Within World War II* (New York: Basic Books, 2001), 1–48. Joseph Connor, "Who Leaked FDR's War Plans?" History Net, https://www.historynet.com /who-leaked-fdrs-war-plans.htm, describes the FBI investigation in some depth. Kaiser, *No End Save Victory*, 325–26, records that in his autobiography published much later, "the isolationist Senator Burton K. Wheeler claimed to have received the Joint Board draft from an unnamed Army captain." If so, was that anonymous captain carrying out the wishes of his commander-in-chief?

47. Hector Bywater had died in 1940, but one well-placed American anticipated an air raid on Pearl Harbor. Edwin T. Layton, then a staff officer of the Commander in Chief Pacific Fleet, had served as a military attaché in Tokyo. To perfect his language skills, he had translated a book published in 1932 by Hirata Shinsaku. It was called *Not If, but When We Fight* and included a vivid description of a raid by "a fast striking force of cruisers and aircraft carriers." Layton was so impressed that he wrote an article, which he submitted to magazines under a cover letter that said, "Whether or not it is a preview of Japanese-American naval warfare is a matter for history to determine." Every editor rejected it out of hand. See Layton, *"And I Was There": Pearl Harbor and Midway—Breaking the Secrets* (New York: William Morrow, 1985), 70–71.

CHAPTER SIX

IGNITING the U.S.-JAPAN WAR, 1941

Richard B. Frank

The Asia-Pacific War and China

FEW AMERICANS OF THAT ERA BEYOND EARLY CHILDHOOD EVER forgot where they were and how they learned about the Pearl Harbor attack on December 7, 1941. It appeared to still an extremely divisive conflict over intervention or nonintervention by the United States into World War II. *Time* magazine declared, "But the war came as a great relief, like a reverse earthquake, that in one terrible jerk shook everything disjointed, distorted, askew back into place. Japanese bombs had finally brought national unity to the US."[1] But not all noninterventionists accepted that there had been no alternative to war. The same day as Roosevelt's address, former president Herbert Hoover wrote in a private letter, "You and I know this continuous putting pins in rattlesnakes finally got the country bitten. We also know that if Japan had been allowed to go without these trade restrictions and provocations, she would have collapsed from internal economic reasons alone within a couple of years."[2]

Important context framed Hoover's immediate reflection. Americans classed Pearl Harbor as a disaster, but many found it inexplicable. Further, that the United States swiftly found itself at war with Germany thanks to Hitler's decision to declare war on the United States also seemed as mysterious as consequential. Over the next seven decades, theories materialized to explain these interlocked puzzles. They go now most prominently under the short titles "The Back Door to War" and "Advanced Knowledge." The first interpretation posits that the Roosevelt administration plotted to provoke Japan's attack that they knew would automatically achieve the administration's goal: the United States at war with Germany. This theory started from the well-founded belief that President Roosevelt deemed it vital that the United States enter the war against Germany. The theory then spun out an argument that after he failed to achieve this goal via direct provocations in Europe and the Atlantic Ocean, he then devised a fiendish subterfuge to provoke Japan's attack with foreknowledge that this would get the United States into war with Germany. The "Advanced Knowledge" theory arises from the premise that Roosevelt and British prime minister Winston Churchill, or both, knew in advance of the attack by various means and did nothing to prevent or ameliorate it, again with an eye toward creating a link to war with Germany.[3]

Now let me add a personal note. Although my area has been the Asia-Pacific War for decades, I exercised great wariness about Pearl Harbor. I became convinced early that the topic lurked as a fever swamp into which many a historian, good or otherwise, has trekked, succumbed to conspiracy fevers, and never regained mental balance. When I embarked on my trilogy on the whole Asia-Pacific War, I realized it was time to take up this topic in depth and—there being no approved vaccine—risk the consequences.

Two outstanding takeaways emerged from my Pearl Harbor expedition. First came confirmation of my long-standing view that Pearl Harbor must be recognized at least at the tactical and operational level as a Japanese victory, not just an American defeat. At the strategic level it was a Japanese disaster. Further, on the U.S. side, there rises a long, melancholy litany of mistakes, misjudgments, and failed communications in both Hawaii and Washington.[4]

I had no inkling my research would reveal my second major takeaway. I reached this conclusion because certain choices of themes and research areas steered me there. One planned theme of the trilogy would be a continual examination of how the Asia-Pacific and the European phases of the war did—or did not—relate. That theme took me to a revealing quote.

Joseph C. Grew was the long-serving U.S. ambassador to Japan in 1940. He had known Franklin Roosevelt when they were boys together at the elite Groton School. Grew thus exercised the privilege of addressing letters to the president, "Dear Frank." In December 1940, Grew asked for Roosevelt's views on "Japan and all her works." Roosevelt replied, "I believe that the fundamental proposition that we must recognize is that the hostilities in Europe, in Africa, and in Asia are all parts of a single world conflict." This statement reinforced my approach to remember the war was global and it captured the essence of Roosevelt's profound insight that all the components of the war were linked. These two points proved the foundation for my account of the road to Pearl Harbor.[5]

The World in 1941

For eleven months in 1941, the overwhelming locus of the Asia-Pacific War was China. The war had touched northern French Indochina in 1940 and the rest of French Indochina from July 1941, but otherwise had not engulfed other areas. In July 1941, China passed over the four-year mark in the struggle against Japan, already longer than the United States, United Kingdom, or other allies would fight Japan. Maps showing limited Japanese occupied areas of China deceive because Japan's soldiers dominated the most densely populated and wealthy sectors of China. More than half of China's 450 million people lived under at least nominal Japanese rule. The fighting obliterated the Chinese economic growth of the previous seventy years. The conduct of Japanese soldiers—summarily executing Chinese servicemen (or just males from teenage years upward who might become soldiers) and horrifying treatment of Chinese women—sparked what one Chinese writer called "the greatest migration in human history." Estimates vary between 45 million and 80 million refugees. Among the approximately 7.5 million Chinese dead by mid-1941—some 80 percent noncombatants— hundreds of thousands had perished in this gigantic, terrorized flight. Even after Hitler invaded the Soviet Union in June and inflicted deaths measured in millions for the first time, the death toll in China was higher than that in Europe to the end of 1941.[6]

When fighting broke out in July 1937 at what was called in the West the Marco Polo Bridge Incident near Beijing, worldwide expectation projected that after a few weeks or months, Japan would crush China's armies and the Chinese government would kneel to Japanese dictates. This vision stemmed from literally almost a century of recent history, when China failed to mount sustained and effective resistance to a Westernized power. Japanese victory in the Battle of Shanghai by November 1937, followed by the fall of the Nationalist capital of Nanjing in December, appeared to erase any hope raised by the stalwart fighting for months in Shanghai that China would reverse a century of military futility. But the Chinese did not quit. In a protracted, costly struggle almost through 1938, the Japanese would strive to capture Wuhan, where Chiang Kai-shek had pitched his military headquarters. Wuhan fell in October. Not only did the Chinese resistance continue, but the secret war diary at Imperial General Headquarters admitted that Japan lacked the capability to force China to cease resistance by military means alone.[7]

This brings us to the first examples of China's contribution to the cause of what became known in 1942 as the United Nations. The most obvious is China's role in tying down massive numbers of Japanese troops that might have been deployed against the Soviet Union to the north, or the Allied nations fighting in the Pacific or in South or Southeast Asia. An example of this role is the Battle of Changsha in September and October 1941. Changsha was the nexus of the south China railway network and a vital access portal for recruits for Chinese armies and food for the nation. A Japanese offensive eventually numbering eight divisions and four brigades attempted to score a huge victory and even knock China out of the war by capturing Changsha. The Japanese got to the city, but a furious Chinese counterattack drove them back. By December 1941, as Japan embarked on a huge expansion of the war, the largest portion of the Imperial Army sat in China (twenty-two divisions) and Manchuria (thirteen, plus two in Korea as backup). Only ten divisions of fifty-one (including four in Japan) could be spared for "Southern Operations."[8]

In the political realm, China rendered an invaluable contribution. Japan claimed its noble mission was to liberate other Asians from Western colonialism. That the Chinese maintained an armed struggle against Japan was by far the most potent rebuttal to Japan's claim that the heart of the Asia-Pacific War was race.[9]

The Signal Chinese Contribution in 1941

But in 1941 China would make a combined military and political contribution central to the ultimate victory over the Axis powers. The essence of this story is that the root of the Pearl Harbor attack grew from recognition that keeping the Soviet Union in the war with Hitler required that the United States not abandon China, as Japan demanded.

When the German onslaught against the Soviet Union began on June 22, 1941, Washington and London both expected an inevitable Soviet collapse, just as all of Hitler's targets to date had fallen, save by a slender margin Great Britain in 1940. The U.S. War Department projected the Soviets would last from one to three months. By June 30, a London War Cabinet meeting termed the Soviet situation as "grave."[10]

Neither Germany nor the Soviets permitted foreign observers to conduct independent views of the colossal struggle. The dueling daily communiques from Berlin and Moscow provided the only open information on what soon was termed the Eastern Front. The *New York Times*, as it did throughout the war, printed the communiques of all the major belligerents each day on page two, often with helpful maps. There was seldom, if ever, any resemblance between the two communiques in the daily depictions of battlefield results. Over a period of days or weeks, the sole data point on which Berlin and Moscow roughly agreed was the location of the fighting. This validated German claims of deep penetrations into the Soviet Union until abruptly in the last ten days of July, the communiques confirmed the German advances had halted.[11] We know now this was due to a combination of ferocious fighting by the Red Army (although with staggering casualties) wearing down the cutting edge of the German army and massive German logistical miscalculation.[12]

Stalin swiftly grasped the relationship between Soviet survival and Chinese resistance. He ordered the Chinese communist leader Mao Zedong to provide intelligence and commence diversionary attacks. But Mao balked. Due to gross deficits in weaponry and ammunition in the Red Army (about twenty rounds per rifle, claimed Mao), Mao rejected embarking on conventional battle and instead prioritized a buildup of his forces.[13]

Roosevelt and Churchill immediately recognized the import of the halt: the Soviets might survive, a prospect of supreme strategic importance. But the British were overstretched and the United States unready to do much in the realm of material support of the Soviets in 1941. Further, huge logistical hurdles stood between the aspiration to deliver aid to the Soviets in 1941 and actual timely arrival. Washington and London identified one vital contribution they could render the Soviets: keep Imperial Japan from entering the war against the Soviet Union and potentially delivering a knockout blow. Japan was ensnarled in a quagmire in China, and this constituted the foremost impediment to a Japanese attack on the Soviets. Thus keeping China in the war was fundamental to Soviet survival.

The Japanese Advance into Southern Indochina

Coinciding with the halt of the German offensive into the Soviet Union was Japan's occupation of southern Indochina in late July 1941. Although the Japanese claimed this furthered their war in China, this transparently was not so. Unlike northern Indochina, which did provide a logistical route to support China (via the port of Haiphong and the road and rail net into southern China) until Japanese occupation in July 1940, there was no such logistical connection between southern Indochina and the Sino-Japanese War. The move was, however, obviously purposed to give Japanese forces a springboard to attack British, Dutch, and American possessions in the Far East.[14]

The Japanese advance confronted Roosevelt with a critical decision. The United States was supplying Japan about 75 to 80 percent of its petroleum.[15] Powerful currents of American public opinion calling for sanctions against Japan due to the horrific stories and images emerging from China had beset the Roosevelt administration. Roosevelt had walked a tightrope between responding to congressional pressure reflecting this public outrage by cutting off potential enhancements of Japan's war-making capabilities like aircraft and scrap iron, but he had steadfastly rejected cutting off petroleum.

He feared Japan would react to the cutoff by swooping down and seizing the abundant petroleum sources in the Dutch East Indies (now Indonesia). Roosevelt did not believe the American public would support a war to rescue a European colonial possession in the Far East. The Japanese would thus obtain an alternate source of oil, fortify their strategic position, and continue their war in China. Roosevelt did, however, now authorize what was initially intended as a flexible control system over petroleum exports to Japan in response to the direct threat to the U.S. position in the Philippines. The intent was carefully calculated pressure to get Japan out of southern Indochina without provoking an attack on the Dutch East Indies.[16]

This action coincided in turn with what became known as the Atlantic Conference between Roosevelt and Churchill August 9–12, 1941, on warships anchored in Placentia Bay, Newfoundland. Churchill brought with him Roosevelt's most trusted aide, Harry Hopkins, who was fresh from a candid interview in Moscow with Joseph Stalin. The Soviet dictator had imparted to Hopkins by far the most candid disclosures about the fighting to date, and he convinced Hopkins he intended to fight on and survive. Soviet officials also urged Hopkins to have the United States issue a public declaration that if Japan attacked the Soviet Union, the United States would enter the war against Japan. When Hopkins divulged this to Roosevelt and Churchill, it was clear that keeping China in the war to tie down the Japanese was a shared objective in Washington, London, and Moscow. Following the Atlantic Conference, Roosevelt made the embargo on oil to Japan permanent.[17]

There are two further critical aspects of the U.S. oil embargo. The first of these is moral. By mid-1941, Japan's four-year war in China had resulted in the deaths of millions of Chinese, overwhelmingly noncombatants. U.S. oil was not only fueling Japan's economy, but also Japan's war machine that was perpetrating these horrors. (Imagine what the historiography would read like if the United States had been supplying Hitler's Germany 75 to 80 percent of its oil from September 1939 to December 1941.) But Roosevelt made the agonizing decision that a U.S. cutoff of oil would only incite Japan to seize a secure supply from the Netherlands, East Indies, and continue its war in China. The other aspect is strategic. As Japanese historian Yoshitake Oka explicitly noted in his biography of Japanese prime minister

Fumimaro Konoe, the oil cutoff quashed any realistic plan to attack the Soviet Union.[18]

The View from Tokyo

From the Tokyo perspective, the supreme strategic issue was extricating Japan from the China quagmire. News of Hitler's attack on the Soviets triggered some Japanese army and navy officers to advocate that Japan join the assault. The Imperial Army commenced a huge buildup of forces in Manchuria that eventually reached 700,000 men. In Tokyo, officers in the cautious Army Ministry became alarmed that field commanders in Manchuria might unilaterally launch an attack on the Soviet Union without authorization. Given the history of the Imperial Army in the Manchurian Incident of 1931 and repeated episodes of such insubordination in China, these fears were well-grounded. Tokyo began to curtail the buildup based on those fears.[19]

Other parts of the leadership outside the Army Ministry also were wary about taking on the Soviets unless they were plainly about to collapse, and they also recognized that securing a supply of oil must take precedence over any action against the Soviets. Further, sober minds even in the Imperial Army also realized that without U.S. oil, an immediate attack on the Soviets was impossible. The manifest connection between the cutoff of U.S. petroleum and blocking a Japanese attack on the Soviets is a point much of the historical literature has ignored. The Japanese strategic debates in July accorded absolute primacy to ending the war in China. After that came "Southern Operations" aimed at securing the oil of the Dutch East Indies. "Northern Operations" to enter the war against the Soviets dangled in standby status, only to be considered if the Germans were about the crush the Soviets.[20]

Thus the diplomatic negotiations between the United States and Japan between July and December 1941 pivoted around China. The Japanese placed two alternative demands before the United States. First was that the United States cooperate with Japan to impose a peace treaty on China that would end the conflict in a clear Japanese triumph that Japan's leaders could present to their people as justifying the sacrifices made for four years, including nearly 200,000 battle deaths. The second or alternative demand was that the United States end all political, military, and economic support to China. The Japanese believed this would lead inevitably to the collapse of Chinese resistance.[21]

To understand the Japanese diplomatic objectives, it is essential not only to read the bland official language of their written proposals, but to grasp what Japan sought with this language as divulged in the statements of Japanese diplomats in Washington and Tokyo and in decryptions of secret Japanese diplomatic cables. For example, on September 6, 1941, Japanese diplomats presented the formal Japanese note requiring that the United States "refrain from any measures or actions which will be prejudicial to the endeavor by Japan concerning the settlement of the China Affair." Four days later, Japanese officials made clear to the State Department that these seemingly mild words required that the United States withdraw all support for China.[22]

Likewise, while by 1941 the American public strongly opposed Hitler and Germany, the public remained ambivalent at best about Joseph Stalin and the Soviet Union, with many seeing them as twins morally. Roosevelt thus avoided publicly making an explicit link between the oil embargo and its role in supporting the Soviets. We do have solid evidence on the true foundation of his policy. William L. MacKenzie King, the prime minister of Canada, enjoyed close relations with both Churchill and Roosevelt. Indeed, the American president confided more to the Canadian than probably any foreign leader apart from Churchill. After discussions with Roosevelt in early November, King wrote in his diary, "A break in Chinese resistance will probably mean a break in Russian resistance."[23]

And Canada contributed more than MacKenzie King's diary entry. Canada dispatched two infantry battalions to Hong Kong in late November 1941. The original official accounts presented this as triggered by the recommendation of an outgoing Hong Kong (Canadian) military commander that such a reinforcement could make Hong Kong's defenses far more imposing. But as Christopher M. Bell revealed, the real reason for this action was to support the Soviet Union by buttressing China in conjunction with American and British measures.[24]

The other key figures who recognized the true engine of U.S. policy were Japanese ambassador Kichisaburō Nomura and special envoy Saburō

Kurusu in Washington. Nomura fundamentally grasped, as he put it in one message to Tokyo, "the United States will not favor us at the sacrifice of China."[25] Nomura and Kurusu realized the complete unreality of Tokyo's pursuit of U.S. abandonment of China. They also recognized that events were careening swiftly toward war. In desperation, they extracted their own proposal from ingredients in various terms Tokyo had provided. This essentially called for restoration of the status quo ante of July: Japan would withdraw from southern Indochina and the United States would restore the oil flow. They presented this as Japan's proposal on November 18. When they reported their initiative to Tokyo, they received a harsh rebuke and preemptory orders to withdraw their proposal and substitute another variant specifically requiring the U.S. abandonment of China. When Nomura and Kurusu delivered this to Secretary of State Cordell Hull on November 20, Hull demonstrated that he grasped that the key Japanese demand was the abandonment of China. Hull asked the envoys what they thought the administration's reaction would be to a demand that the United States abandon Great Britain; in short, the United States would no more consider abandoning China than abandoning Great Britain.[26]

Hull initiated a further exploration of diplomatic measures after this meeting. Drafts were transmitted to London. After reviewing them, Churchill responded in words that made clear his understanding of the vital importance of continued Chinese resistance: "There is only one point that disquiets us. What about Chiang Kai-Shek? Is he not having a very thin diet? Our anxiety is about China. If they collapse our joint dangers would enormously increase."[27] While at first blush these comments might be taken as related only to dangers in the Asia-Pacific region, Churchill's actual frame of reference is documented in a memorandum he sent to Anthony Eden, his foreign secretary, on November 23. Replying to Eden's exploration of alternatives in negotiations with Japan, Churchill allowed that a partial relaxation of pressure on Japan might be acceptable, but only if it did not encompass the abandonment or suspension of aid to China or make it possible for Japan to attack the Soviet Union.[28]

Then Hull read decrypted Japanese cables to the Washington envoys on November 24 disclosing not only that the United States absolutely must agree to abandon China, but also that the final deadline for this was

November 28 (Tokyo time), just four days later. These cables, coupled with the withdrawal of the terms presented by Nomura and Kurusu on November 18, made the futility of further diplomacy clear to Hull.[29]

Hull then had prepared what became labeled the "Hull Note" that was delivered to Nomura and Kurusu on November 26. Some histories present this as an "ultimatum," not only breaking off what are depicted wrongly as ongoing and still hopeful negotiations, but also as forcing Japan to go to war. The "ultimatum" charge fails because it was marked "Strictly Confidential, Tentative and Without Commitment," and it lacked both a deadline for acceptance and a threat that failure to accept it would result in war. What Hull intended, with the shameful Munich capitulation firmly in mind, was to state firmly for history the principled American position on all measures required to halt Japan's aggression in Asia and sever her ties to Hitler's Germany.[30]

The "Hull Note" did cause glee among the militarists in Tokyo pressing for war with the United States. But the "Hull Note" was based on an accurate understanding that the negotiations could not possibly succeed, especially in the four days between November 24 and 28, because of the irreconcilable objectives of the United States and Japan over China's global role in the anti-Axis coalition. Actual Japanese expectations can be judged by the fact that the Pearl Harbor attack force sailed on November 25, the day before the "Hull Note."[31]

The failure in much of the historiography to acknowledge the connections between Hitler's attack on the Soviet Union and the recognition in Washington and London of the vital role of China in preventing Japan from striking what was feared to be the fatal blow to Soviet resistance ultimately links to a larger failure to acknowledge for decades the significance of China in the global conflict. The role of China was perhaps never greater in the whole war than the last months of 1941.

Notes

1. "The US at War: National Ordeal," *Time*, December 15, 1941.
2. Small collections, Elinor and James Hendrick, etc. Herbert Hoover to Morgan H. Hoyt, Folder Hoover, Herbert, Pearl Harbor Materials, Franklin D. Roosevelt Presidential Library.

3. An immense amount has been written about the "Back Door to War" and "Advanced Knowledge" theories. A representative list of the notable works on these theories includes John Thomas Flynn, *The Truth about Pearl Harbor* (Glasgow: Strickland Press, 1945); Charles A. Beard, *President Roosevelt and the Coming of the War 1941* (New Haven, Conn.: Yale University Press, 1948); Robert A. Theobald, Rear Adm. USN (Ret.), *The Final Secret of Pearl Harbor—The Washington Contribution to the Japanese Attack* (New York: Devin-Adair Company, 1954); Robert B. Stinnett, *Day of Deceit: The Truth about FDR and Pearl Harbor* (New York: Free Press, 1999).

4. Richard B. Frank, *Tower of Skulls: A History of the Asia Pacific War July 1937–May 1942* (New York: W. W. Norton & Company, 2020), chaps. 10 and 11.

5. Joseph C. Grew, *Turbulent Era: A Diplomatic Record of Forty Years 1904–1945* (Boston: Houghton Mifflin, 1952), 2:1255–61.

6. Frank, *Tower of Skulls*, 106–7, 167–68, 178.

7. Edward J. Drea, *Japan's Imperial Army: Its Rise and Fall 1853–1945* (Lawrence: University Press of Kansas, 2009), 203; Edward Drea and Hans van de Ven, "Overview of Major Military Campaigns during the Sino-Japanese War, 1937–1945," in *The Battle of China: Essays on the Military History of the Sino-Japanese War 1937–1945*, ed. Mark Peattie, Edward J. Drea, and Hans van de Ven (Stanford, Calif.: Stanford University Press, 2010), 35; Ryōichi Tobe, "The Japanese Eleventh Army in Central China, 1937 to 1941," in *The Battle of China: Essays on the Military History of the Sino-Japanese War 1937–1945*, ed. Mark Peattie, Edward J. Drea, and Hans van de Ven (Stanford, Calif.: Stanford University Press, 2010), 215; Stephen R. MacKinnon, *Wuhan, 1938: War, Refugees and the Making of Modern China* (Berkeley: University of California Press, 2008), 42–43; Hans van de Ven, *War and Nationalism in China 1925–1945* (London: RoutledgeCurzon, 2003), 227; Diana Lary, *The Chinese People at War: Human Suffering and Social Transformation, 1937–1945* (Cambridge: Cambridge University Press, 2010), 46; Kazuo Yagami, *Konoe Fumimaro and the Failure of Peace in Japan 1937–1941* (Jefferson, N.C.: McFarland Publishers, 2006), 68; Frank, *Tower of Skulls*, 84.

8. Frank, *Tower of Skulls*, 212–13; Leland Ness, *Rikugun: Guide to Japanese Ground Forces 1937–1945*, Volume 1: *Tactical Organization of the Imperial Japanese Army and Navy Ground Forces* (Solihull, U.K.: Helion & Company, Ltd, 2014), 26–32.

9. Eri Hotta, *Pan Asianism and Japan's War 1931–1945* (New York: Palgrave Macmillan, 2007), esp. chap. 5; Rana Mitter, *Forgotten Ally: China's World War II, 1937–1945* (Boston: Houghton Mifflin, 2013), 143.

10. See the Diary of Henry S. Stimson, Yale University, June 23, 1941; Martin Gilbert, *Winston S. Churchill*, vol. 6, *Their Finest Hour* (Boston: Houghton Mifflin, 1983), 1125–26, 1128.

11. *New York Times*, June 23 to July 31, 1941, 2 (the reprint of daily communiques from Berlin and Moscow). The maps with the communiques further illuminate

the movement of the battlefield. Waldo Heinrichs, *The Threshold of War: Franklin D. Roosevelt and American Entry into World War II* (New York: Oxford University Press, 1988), 137–39, makes the point that Roosevelt himself derived critical information on the Eastern Front from Berlin and Moscow communiques reprinted in the *New York Times*. These communiques also occasioned news headlines about the halt along the front. Heinrichs also itemizes other sources supporting the import of the communiques.

12. David Stahel, *Operation Barbarossa and Germany's Defeat in the East* (Cambridge: Cambridge University Press, 2009). See pages 127 to 138 on the completely deficient German logistics and the details in following chapters on the fierce fighting and high losses of German units. Much the same analysis appears in the numerous works by David Glantz that contain vast detail from Soviet archives. Of note is *Barbarossa Derailed: The Battle for Smolensk, 10 July to 10 September 1941* (Solihull, U.K.: Helion & Company Limited, 2012), 1:576–78.

13. See Kuisong Yang, "The Evolution of the Relationship between the Chinese Communist Party and the Comintern during the Sino-Japanese War," in *Negotiating China's Destiny in World War II*, ed. Hans van de Ven, Diana Lary, and Stephen R. MacKinnon (Stanford, Calif.: Stanford University Press, 2015), 85–86.

14. Eri Hotta, *Japan 1941: Countdown to Infamy* (New York: Alfred A. Knopf, 2013), 128–36, 139–40, 144–46, 151–53; James Morley, ed., *Japan's Road to the Pacific War; The Fateful Choice: Japan's Advance into Southeast Asia, 1939–1941* (New York: Columbia University Press, 1980), 209–95.

15. Edward S. Miller, *Bankrupting the Enemy: The US Financial Siege of Japan before Pearl Harbor* (Annapolis, Md.: Naval Institute Press, 2007), 162.

16. Heinrichs, *The Threshold of War*, 10–11, 75, 121, 132–33; Robert Dallek, *Franklin D. Roosevelt and American Foreign Policy, 1932–1945* (Oxford: Oxford University Press, 1981), 274–76; Gerhard Weinberg, *The World At Arms: A Global History of World War II*, 2nd ed. (Cambridge: Cambridge University Press, 2005), 84–85, 154–60, 243–45.

17. See U.S. Department of State, *Foreign Relations of the United States* (hereafter *FRUS*), *1941*, vol. I, general, Soviet Union, ed. Matilda F. Axton, N. O. Sappington, Shirley L. Phillips, Rogers P. Churchill. Irving L. Thomson (Washington, D.C.: Government Printing Office, 1958), 341–69; Heinrichs, *The Threshold of War*, 141–42; Kenneth S. Davis, *FDR: The War President 1940–1943* (New York: Random House, 2000), 235–49; Miller, *Bankrupting the Enemy*, 203–4; William L. Langer and S. Everett Gleason, *The Undeclared War* (New York: Harper, 1953), 646.

18. Yoshitake Oka, *Konoe Fumimaro: A Political Biography*, trans. Shumpei Okamoto and Patricia Murray (Tokyo: Tokyo University Press, 2015), 136.

19. Frank, *Tower of Skulls*, 179–80, 196–97.

20. Frank, *Tower of Skulls*, 196–97, 200–206; Oka, *Konoe Fumimaro*, 136. Oka is explicit that the oil cutoff quashed any realistic plan to attack the Soviet Union.

21. Jun Tsunoda, "The Decision for War," in *Japan's Road to the Pacific War; The Final Confrontation: Japan's Negotiation with the United States 1941*, ed. James Morley (New York: Columbia University Press, 1994), 261–65, app. 9; Nobutaka Ike, *Japan's Decision for War: Records of the 1941 Policy Conferences* (Stanford, Calif.: Stanford University Press, 1967), 209–11; Frank, *Tower of Skulls*, 206–9.

22. *FRUS*, Japan 1931–1941, ed. Joseph V. Fuller, vol. 2, 608–9. The same source contains a whole series of documents demonstrating how Japanese officials in Japan and in the United States explained the actual meaning of the terms Japan formally proposed; see 604–19, 623–24, 633, 637–41, 656–61, 672–87.

23. MacKenzie King Diary, November 6, 1941, 3, www.bac-lac.gc.ca/eng/discover /politics-governemtn/primeministers/william-lyon-mackenzie-king/pages. Weinberg, *A World at Arms*, 286–87, notes that the U.S. public not only was quite distressed over the lack of freedom of religion in the USSR, but also that the Soviet attack on Poland and Finland further undergirded great hostility. In this atmosphere, it is scarcely remarkable that Roosevelt avoided candid explanation of measures to help the Soviets.

24. Christopher M. Bell, "Our Most Exposed Outpost: Hong Kong and British Far Eastern Strategy, 1921–1941," *Journal of Military History* 60, no. 1 (January 1996): 61–88. Bell meticulously lays out the case that the real reason two Canadian infantry battalions were dispatched to Hong Kong in November 1941 was part of a series of coordinated actions by the United States, United Kingdom, and Canada to bolster Chinese resistance to support the Soviet Union.

25. U.S. Department of Defense, *The "Magic" Background to Pearl Harbor* (Washington, D.C.: Government Printing Office, 1977), no. 110, Washington (Nomura) to Tokyo, no. 1090, November 14, 1941, appendix IV, A-56-7.

26. Peter Mauch, *Sailor Diplomat: Nomura Kichisaburō and the Japanese American War* (Cambridge, Mass.: Harvard University Asia Center, 2011), 208–10. Mauch uses Japanese foreign minister versions of the relevant cables. *FRUS*, Japan 1931–1941, vol. 2, 744–751, 753–56.

27. *FRUS*, 1941, The Far East, vol. 4, ed. John G. Reid, Louis E. Gates, Ralph R. Goodwin, 665.

28. David Klein and Hilary Conroy, "Churchill, Roosevelt and the China Question in Pre-Pearl Harbor Diplomacy," in *Pearl Harbor Reexamined: Prologue to the Pacific War*, ed. Hilary Conroy and Harry Wray (Honolulu: University of Hawaii Press, 1990), 134.

29. Tokyo to Washington, November 22, 1941, SDRJ, 16849, 16850, 16852 (translated November 24), box 20, SDRJ Series, record group 457, National Archives and Records Administration; Tokyo to Washington, no. 823, November 24, 1941, *The "Magic" Background to Pearl Harbor*, app. 4, A89.

30. Memorandum of a Conversation, November 26, 1941, *FRUS*, Japan 1931–1941, vol. 2, 764–68; Document Handed by the Secretary of State to the Japanese Ambassador (Nomura) on November 26, 1941, *FRUS*, Japan 1931–1941, vol. 2,

768–70. The multiple reasons why the "Hull Note" was not an ultimatum is laid out in Takeo Iguchi, *Demystifying Pearl Harbor: A New Perspective from Japan* (Tokyo: International House of Japan, 2010), 137–38, 168, 265.

31.   Frank, *Tower of Skulls*, 223–27, 236.

CHAPTER SEVEN

CHINESE VIEWS of FUTURE WARFARE in the INDO-PACIFIC

*First Strike and U.S.
Forward Bases in Japan*

Toshi Yoshihara

IT HAS BECOME FASHIONABLE TO ENTERTAIN THE PROSPECTS for war between the United States and China. Over the past decade, leading scholars and practitioners have debated how the intensifying great power rivalry might lead to the use of force.[1] They point to major sources of great power competition, ranging from the rapid power transition to local disputes over territory to miscalculation to incompatible ideologies, that could unravel the long peace in Asia. Most are concerned with underlying and proximate causes of war. Yet few have paid attention to how each side might start the fighting. Fewer still have examined the possible opening military moves of a Sino-American war.

The outbreak itself is an area worthy of deep study because the first hours and days of a shooting war between Chinese and American armed forces will determine the war's scale, intensity, geographic scope, and duration. A massive conventional first strike could prove highly escalatory, whereas a limited attack involving nonkinetic means, such as cyber weapons, might give room for the great powers to find an exit from conflagration. How statesmen and commanders on both sides consider operational and tactical options at the war's outset will have a profound influence on the war's course.

This chapter assesses how Beijing thinks about its opening act in a prospective armed conflict with Washington. It argues that the People's Liberation Army (PLA) is predisposed to delivering a decisive first blow against U.S. forward-deployed forces in the western Pacific, particularly those in Japan. The evidence, drawn from Chinese-language open sources, suggests that China could reprise a Pearl Harbor–like attack in the opening phases of a Sino-American war.

To advance this argument, this chapter first examines how PLA strategists perceive the U.S. military challenge. It surveys the Chinese literature on America's military basing arrangements in Asia, its dependence on forward bases in the western Pacific, and its logistical vulnerabilities stemming from such dependence on overseas infrastructure. The chapter then explores the PLA's doctrinal writings on offensive campaigns against the adversary's logistical systems and on the importance of surprise in future operations. It concludes with a critical assessment of the PLA's thinking about its first move in a war against the United States.

The PLA's Views of the U.S. Military Challenge

The United States looms large in Chinese war planning. Beijing must always weigh the likelihood of U.S. intervention in a range of possible regional conflicts that directly involve China. The local actors against which China might use force in various contingencies, from a cross-strait war to a second Korean War to fighting over territorial disputes in the East and South China Seas, are either formal treaty allies or close partners of the United States. In a war with Beijing, Washington would mobilize those same high-quality alliances and partnerships, some of which host bases and facilities from which the U.S. military projects power. In the eyes of Chinese strategists, the American armed forces remain the most credible threat to the PLA's ability to fight and win wars along China's maritime periphery. Chinese leaders thus must account for Washington's strategic calculus and potential military and diplomatic responses across various flashpoints.

Should the United States militarily oppose Beijing's use of force, the gravest danger to China is a direct attack on the mainland. According to the authoritative *Science of Military Strategy*, "The most serious threat of war is a large-scale strategic raid initiated by a powerful enemy intended to destroy China's war potential to force us to yield."[2] The terms "powerful enemy" and "strong enemy," which appear regularly in PLA doctrinal writings, are code for the United States. Should deterrence fail, the U.S. military would be in position to unleash its forces to destroy major targets across China, imposing heavy costs on Beijing. The strategy report goes on to assert, "In particular, the strong enemy will rely on its comprehensive expeditionary superiority from the oceanic direction to threaten our homeland at greater distances, allowing it to strike us while it is out of reach and to deter us in peacetime while quickly wrecking our combat system in wartime."[3]

American naval and air forces could launch long-range strikes against the mainland from distances well beyond the reach of PLA defenders. In other words, the United States could pummel China while the Chinese military would lack the wherewithal to hit back.

Moreover, China's most important political, economic, and cultural hubs are located along its long coastline clustered around the Beijing-Tianjin, Shanghai-Nanjing, and Guangzhou-Shenzhen corridors. These three seaward-facing megalopolises are essential to powering China's ascent. Yet they are also the most exposed to the striking power of the U.S. military operating offshore. As *Science of Military Strategy* observes, "These [coastal] areas directly face the powerful enemy's superior sea, air, space, and cyber combat systems. In wartime, they very likely will become the strike areas of first choice by the powerful enemy."[4] The military asymmetry in operational reach, then, compounds China's geographic vulnerabilities.

Chinese assessments of the U.S. military challenge to Beijing's ambitions is the essential context for understanding the PLA's war plans and its opening moves. Chinese commanders must anticipate how American naval and air forces might be employed to interfere in PLA operations.

China must protect its crown jewels along its shores from the long reach of U.S. firepower. A major wartime requirement for the PLA is to hold American expeditionary forces at arm's length while balking U.S. military threats that are already within striking distance of the mainland.

Over the past two decades, the PLA invested in capabilities designed to hold at risk U.S. forces operating across the western Pacific and to interdict reinforcements arriving from other theaters. The plan is to complicate, hinder, and delay U.S. operations, affording the PLA adequate time and maneuver room to achieve its objectives before the United States can marshal enough power and rally allies to reverse China's gains on the battlefield. Frequently described as a "counterintervention" (反介入) strategy, the PLA intends to project power as far forward from the homeland as possible to meet American forces within and along an extended defensive perimeter. As *Science of Military Strategy* avers, "For some time to come, we must consider an outward extension of the strategic frontier from the coastal and borders regions of the three northeast, southeast, southwest directions to form an arc-shaped strategic zone covering the limited areas of the western Pacific and the northern Indian Ocean."[5] Notably, this arc covers and extends well beyond U.S. forward bases in Japan.

This counterintervention strategy is the basis for discerning how the PLA plans to make its first move should deterrence fail. The PLA's war plans for targeting U.S. basing infrastructure in the western Pacific are a particularly important component of the strategy. After all, the forward-deployed forces on those bases will be the first responders to any crisis or war involving China. Disrupting their ability to rapidly react would clearly be a top priority for the PLA. Indeed, given the centrality of those bases to the U.S. operational posture in the region, it is likely that the basing network would be among the top candidates on the PLA's target list. The extensive doctrinal writings surveyed next demonstrate that the PLA has fixed its sights firmly on American bases in Asia.

The PLA's Views of U.S. Forward Bases in Asia

PLA analysts have subjected U.S. forward bases, including naval bases, to close study. Chinese strategists are intimately aware that forward bases in Asia are essential to U.S. regional strategy. They understand that Washington relies on access and use of bases located across the western Pacific, without which it would be hard-pressed to fulfill its security commitments.

Senior Captain Ouyang Wei of the National Defense University describes "strategic forward deployment" as a critical element of the U.S. global military posture. Proximity to overseas threats enables the United States to engage in preventive defense, deterrence, rapid crisis response, and even first strikes. Such forward defense requires bases on foreign soil that can be reliably accessed in peace and in war, the stationing of personnel, equipment, ammunition, supplies, and other stores at those bases, and reinforcements in the strategic rear that could be rapidly deployed to the frontlines. According to Ouyang, the United States possesses some eighty overseas military bases in Asia, forming "an arc of military basing network" (弧形军事基地网) stretching south from the Japanese Islands through the Philippines to Thailand.[6]

Yang Jianhua, a senior engineer of the PLA, depicts the U.S. basing architecture in the Indo-Pacific as concentric rings of island chains. The first line of islands runs through Aleutians, the Japanese home islands, Singapore, and Diego Garcia. The second chain extends southward from Guam through the South Pacific and terminates at Australia and New Zealand. The third island chain centers on Hawaii. Yang further perceives an integrated "web of bases" (基地网) that ties together these islands chains, extending from America's west coast through the central Pacific to the littorals of the western Pacific. Beginning with San Diego serving as the hub of naval power in North America, the U.S. basing infrastructure radiates outward to a constellation of bases in Alaska, Hawaii, and Guam. The "western island chain zone" (西部岛屿锁链区)—encompassing U.S. bases and facilities in Japan, South Korea, and Singapore—marks the maximum forward extension of this basing network.[7]

PLA analysts see U.S. forward bases on the first island chain—the transnational archipelago that runs south from Japan through Taiwan to the Philippines—as essential to fulfilling America's security commitments in the western Pacific. They pay close attention to the role of naval bases on the island chain in supporting American strategy. As Senior Captain Ouyang Wei notes, "Naval power, whether in the form of surface combatants and submarines, even as they operate on or beneath the seas respectively, must still rely on shore bases and island bases. As such, the navy's various bases constitute the basic form and system of its deployment. . . . Shore bases will always be the foundation of sustaining naval power."[8]

Yokosuka naval base in Japan—the largest overseas U.S. naval installation in the world and the home to the Seventh Fleet and the only permanently forward-deployed aircraft carrier—draws perhaps the most attention from PLA analysts. Senior Captain Fan Gaoyue of the Academy of Military Science and Senior Captain Gong Xuping of the Air Force Command College describe Yokosuka as a "core base" (核心基地) and a "powerful support point" (强大支撑点) among the military bases in the western Pacific. To them, Yokosuka is the operations, command and control, and logistics center for the Seventh Fleet and is the "ideal forward base" (最佳前进基地) from which U.S. and Japanese naval forces can control passage through such key chokepoints as Tsugaru, Soya, and Tsushima Straits.[9] To the authors, the naval bases in Yokosuka, Sasebo, Pusan, and Guam constitute a mutually supporting basing network in the region.

Yang Jianhua observes that Yokosuka is the largest comprehensive base of its kind in the western Pacific, boasting six drydocks, world-class piers, the largest ship-repair facilities in the region, and the largest ammunition depot in Japan.[10] The author notes that the naval base is the only one in the western Pacific with the facilities to provide major repairs and maintenance on aircraft carriers. Lieutenant Commander Cao Xiaoguang, the author of a nearly seven-hundred-page tome on Japanese naval power, concurs that Yokosuka's strategic value is derived from its logistical infrastructure. Yokosuka is the only base west of Hawaii boasting the facilities and highly skilled shipyard workers to keep the forward-deployed forces at sea. Without it, ships would have to fall back to Hawaii or the continental United States for maintenance and repairs.[11]

Cao goes on to illustrate the logistical centrality of Yokosuka. Tellingly, he provides detailed information about the U.S. Navy's massive fuel storage facility located on Azuma Island across from Yokosuka's naval piers. Relying on open-source intelligence, primarily through Google Earth overhead satellite imagery, Cao reveals the scale of the storage area, which measures more than 800,000 square meters. The author then identifies the above-ground storage tanks, pipeline connections, pumping stations, and marine terminals on Azuma.[12] Cao reports that the Azuma storage area is only one of six major oil depots scattered across Japan that supports U.S. naval operations across the Indo-Pacific.[13] The PLA analyst also uses satellite imagery to identify Yokosuka's Urago ammunition depot, including the underground storage site spanning nearly 200,000 square meters.[14]

The impressive knowledge that Cao and others display in their writings reflect how much value the PLA attaches to understanding U.S. dependence on forward bases in Asia. This awareness has in turn helped to inform the PLA's assessment of modern logistics and its importance to American expeditionary operations.

The PLA's Views on Logistics in Modern Warfare

Chinese military analysts foresee the need to prepare for and fight "local wars under informationized conditions" (信息化条件下局部战争). They believe that the PLA must anticipate the outbreak of regional wars along China's periphery in such hot spots as the Taiwan Strait and the Korean Peninsula. They further expect high-tech, information-based weaponry to feature prominently in these local wars. Their assessments of modern warfare are based on decades of closely studying America's major wars over the past three decades. Drawing upon lessons from these conflicts, PLA strategists anticipate that future large-scale conventional wars between great powers will be short, high-tempo, and extraordinarily intense. They recognize that logistics, of which military bases are an integral part, will be crucial to success in future wars.

To PLA strategists, modern wars between advanced militaries will involve multiple combat arms and services with fighting taking place in all domains, including land, sea, air, space, cyberspace, and the electromagnetic spectrum. Combat will be continuous, conducted day and night under all weather conditions, while the lines dividing the front and the rear areas will blur as long-range strikes cover the entire battle zone.[15] Combatants will consume inordinate quantities of materiel, such as precision-guided munitions. PLA analysts foresee spasms of violence, with opponents hurling the full weight of their firepower against each other.

Local wars under informationized conditions thus place enormous burdens on the logistical system. Each side must produce prodigious amounts of expensive high-tech weaponry and munitions to feed its war machine. Each will be highly dependent on a well-functioning and efficient logistical infrastructure that can sustain the flow of materiel. Conversely, bottlenecks and disruptions to resupply could severely undermine the momentum of military operations. Logistics could be the difference between seizing and ceding the initiative on the battlefield.

PLA analysts also acknowledge that logistic systems will be highly vulnerable in future local wars under informationized conditions. Modern militaries possess "hard kill" (硬杀伤) and "soft kill" (软杀伤) weapons that could be directed at the opponent's logistical infrastructure. The former refers to precision-strike munitions that physically destroy their targets, while the latter refers to electronic and cyber warfare that disrupts or puts out of action the enemy's ability to perform key functions. As a PLA doctrinal study on joint logistics notes, "During local wars under informationized conditions, 'soft-kill' and 'hard-kill' informationized weapons are used to damage the key points of the enemy's command and control information systems, cutting off the information flow and thus cutting off the flow of materiel. At the same time, some hard-kill informationized weapons are used to destroy and wreck the enemy's transportation lines, equipment, and facilities on the ground, at sea, and in the air."[16]

PLA analysts point to additional risks to logistics. The concentration of supplies in a single location or in a few places exposes such war materiel to the danger of being wiped out in a single raid or a few attacks. Indeed, such concentrated stocks could tempt the adversary to conduct preemptive strikes to seize an early advantage in a conflict. As Yu Chuanxin of the Academy of Military Science observes, "The materiel needed for waging informationized war are frequently those with very high levels of information technology content, making them very high value. If the materiel stocks are concentrated and they suffer enemy destruction, this would not only impact the campaign, but it would also incur tremendous economic losses."[17]

Another potential risk is the lack of stockpiles to sustain a protracted war. The failure to amass adequate amounts of materiel in peacetime could prove disastrous in war when crucial resources run low or run out. Yu, for example, points to Argentina's experience during the Falklands War.[18] The Argentine military had only acquired small numbers of Exocet antiship missiles in the prewar period. When war broke out, France embargoed Argentina, preventing the latter from obtaining more missiles. Yu speculates that had Buenos Aires purchased more Exocet missiles before the war, it might have inflicted even more harm on the Royal Navy, perhaps enough to change the course of the conflict. These PLA writings show an appreciation for the importance—and the potential vulnerability—of the logistics infrastructure in a high-end conventional war.

The PLA's Views on Campaigns against Enemy Logistics

The Chinese military holds a holistic view of modern warfare. America's recent wars have had a powerful influence on the PLA's understanding of future conflicts. A key finding drawn from these U.S.-led wars is that tactical victories achieved by frontline units will no longer decide the war's outcome. Rather it is the supporting architecture, such as the command and control system and the logistical infrastructure, that will determine success. The side that possesses a superior architecture or a "system of systems" would enjoy a significant advantage. At the same time, the side that can wreck its opponent's architecture would be in a superior position to seize the high ground.

One PLA study on waging campaigns calls on the armed forces to systematically attack the enemy in areas akin to the vital organs of the human body. Invoking two sets of four-character idioms, the study states, "Attack and destroy the enemy system, strike precisely to paralyze the enemy (体系破击, 精打瘫体) refer to the comprehensive use of various means and measures to implement disruptive or destructive attacks against the enemy's operational system and the enemy's war potential that directly supports its operational system. The goal is to dismember or paralyze the entire system and to collapse the will to fight, thereby achieving campaign victory."[19]

The study specifically identifies "command hubs, *logistical support systems* [emphasis added], and informationized weapons systems" as key elements of the enemy's operational system, describing them as "key points" (要穴) and "junctions" (关节点). Key points and junctions refer to physical surface areas or joints of the human body, respectively. These anatomical metaphors convey the idea that certain vital parts of the body, when hit precisely, can do outsized harm to the body. In Chinese martial arts lore, for example, it is believed that a fighter can apply pinpoint pressure on the right acupuncture point to paralyze the opponent. Similarly, according to the PLA study, strikes on the adversary's operational system could "cause the enemy's combat system to collapse into disorder, its power to lose balance, and its overall operations to malfunction, ultimately leading to the complete paralysis of the enemy's entire combat system." Targeted attacks, then, could enable the Chinese military to "defeat the enemy in a single blow" (一招制敌).[20]

In an offensive campaign, the PLA envisions the use of "joint firepower strikes" (联合火力打击), which employ medium- to long-range precision strike weaponry, to cripple the adversary's operational system. According to one doctrinal study, such attacks are designed to "suppress, disrupt, and destroy the enemy's important military, political, and economic targets, weaken the enemy's combat power and war potential, and collapse the enemy's will to resist."[21] A joint firepower strike campaign divides its targets into the frontline warfighting platforms, such as ships and aircraft, and the support architecture located in the enemy's strategic rear areas. As the study states, "The targets of key-point strikes typically include such vital objects as the enemy's combat units and the enemy's command and control, logistics, and war potential—such as the C4ISR [command, control, communications, computers, intelligence, surveillance] systems, airports, ports, communication lines and hubs, logistical support systems, sources of energy production, and so forth—that support the combat units."[22]

The study goes on to explain the operational importance of wrecking the enemy's logistical system and industrial base. It contends, "Under informationized conditions, the enemy's logistics facilities and military industries are the fountainhead of sustaining its war potential and combat power. In the process of executing decisive operations against the enemy, campaign commanders—based on the overall operational needs of the joint offensive campaign—must select and confirm the enemy's important logistics facilities and military industries as targets and must employ air, missile, special forces, and other attacks to destroy and wreck them."[23]

In a study of precision-strike warfare, Peng Chengcang of the National Defense University identifies the system of systems as the adversary's primary weakness. Peng states, "The enemy's critical vulnerabilities (敌之要害)

typically refer to the opponent's operational command and control centers and automated command systems as well as the key nodes of the adversary's weapons systems and the key nodes of enemy's rear-area resupply systems that pose the greatest threat to our forces."[24]

The author then vividly describes the importance of the logistical system to the enemy and its corresponding value to the PLA as a target. Peng explains, "The logistical support system is the lifeblood and the lifeline of military operations. It must be considered an important target. In combat, troops rely on logistical support to obtain supplies, equipment, ammunition, medical goods while the use of precision-guided weaponry is dependent on the logistical system for technical support, maintenance, and munitions resupply. The place and function of logistics are decisive. Once the logistics supply lines are cut off or the logistics bases are destroyed, combat units lacking fuel, water, ammunition, and food would descend into disorder."[25]

Peng contends that precision strikes against the adversary's logistical system would paralyze or dismember its combat system, depicting the operational effects on the enemy in anatomical terms. As the author explains, "If effective strikes were delivered against the enemy's many supply bases and long supply lines, then the attack would disrupt, even paralyze, the enemy's logistical support system and weaken its overall combat functions. The enemy would not be able to continue and it would ultimately lose its combat power."[26] Peng's view echoes the doctrinal writings' contention that targeted attacks against the key nodes of the enemy's war-fighting architecture would bring down the entire edifice.

The PLA's Views of Surprise Attacks

The PLA has long prized surprise attacks, and it remains predisposed to view surprise attack as an efficacious way to use force. As Mao Zedong noted in 1936, "The Red Army generally operates by surprise attacks."[27] In his assessment of the struggle against Japan's invasion of China, Mao averred that "Offensives in guerrilla warfare generally take the form of surprise attacks."[28] In another less-well-known work, Mao described surprise attacks as the "basic combat form in a guerilla war."[29] He went on to explain that the specific goals of surprise attacks were to destroy the enemy's small units, harass the opponent's larger units, wreck the adversary's facilities located in the rear areas, and disrupt the foe's lines of communications.

Major actions by Mao's armies, from the Communist insurgency's earliest days to Japan's invasion of China to the Chinese civil war's endgame to the Korean War, reflected the centrality of surprise attacks. While Mao's forces did not distinguish themselves in the fighting against the Imperial Japanese Army, their engagements with the enemy frequently featured surprise. In its first victory on the battlefield against the Japanese, the Communists sprung an ambush on an enemy column that delayed Japan's advance on North China in September 1937. Two months later, Mao's Eighth Route Army ambushed another Japanese unit to delay its march toward the Central Plains. The PLA's historiography holds up both battles as classic "ambush warfare" (伏击战).

The Eighth Route Army also engaged in "sabotage warfare" (破袭战) that destroyed rail lines, train stations, and bridges through sudden attacks to disrupt Japan's movement of forces and resupply. The PLA today classifies the assaults on the Pinghan railway in the spring of 1938 and the Baijin railway in the spring of 1940 as prime examples of its traditional excellence in surprise attacks. During the Chinese civil war, the PLA launched large-scale sabotage operations from July to October of 1947. The series of surprise attacks destroyed some four hundred kilometers of rail lines, cut off two main lines of communication running through the Central Plains, and wiped out some 45,000 Nationalist troops.

During the Battle of Kumsong as the Korean War drew to its end, the Communists launched a daring special operations assault that won—and continues to win—wide acclaim in China. Members of a Chinese reconnaissance unit disguised themselves in enemy uniforms and penetrated the position of South Korea's Capital Division. The "unorthodox raid" (奇袭) was meant to sow confusion and chaos deep behind enemy lines. As the infiltrators made their way to the division's rear area, some nine kilometers from the front lines, they clashed eleven times with surprised defenders, causing considerable tactical disruptions to traffic and resupply.[30]

While these engagements were relatively minor within much larger-scale wars, the PLA nevertheless views them as exemplars of its fine tradition in surprise attacks. Indeed, these operations remain an essential part of the Chinese military's institutional memory. The PLA's recent doctrinal writings still hark back to these past events to extol its combat history of derring-do.

Chinese military doctrine still incorporates surprise attacks as a core element of combat. Tellingly, the PLA defines surprise attacks in four-character idioms, conveying their importance and familiarity to domestic audiences as collected Chinese wisdom. The PLA's official dictionary on military terms defines surprise attacks (袭击) as sudden attacks that "strike the enemy at a time or place or in a manner for which it is unprepared" (出敌不意) or that "catch the enemy off its guard" (乘其不备).[31]

According to PLA doctrine, there are at least six different types of surprise attacks. A rapid raid (急袭) involves quick strikes that deliver devastating blows against the enemy when it is unprepared. An ambush (伏击) springs an attack from hidden locations against an adversary traveling along a key line of communication. A sneak attack (偷袭) is to approach an opponent in utmost secrecy to unleash paralyzing firepower against the enemy's vital targets or core leadership. A long-range raid (奔袭) uses power projection forces to attack the foe from different directions to knock the enemy off balance. A sabotage raid (破袭) aims to limit the enemy's mobility, cut off resupply from the rear, and paralyze the command and control of forces. Finally, a harassment attack (袭扰) seeks to deplete, exhaust, tie up, or confuse the adversary.[32]

The PLA sees the continuing relevance of surprise attacks in the current era when China must prepare for and fight to win local wars under informationized conditions. To Chinese defense planners, the methods for conducting surprise attacks have multiplied while the speed of such assaults have accelerated. At the same time, the geographic space within which surprise would take place has expanded. Doctrinal writings, for example, refer to "firepower surprise attacks" (火力袭击) to bypass enemy defenses, directly destroy enemy targets, swiftly engage the opponent, and conduct deep attacks well behind enemy lines.[33]

But Chinese strategists recognize that surprise attack by itself would not be enough to achieve Beijing's war aims. Rather, PLA doctrine calls for a combination of "frontal assaults" (强攻) and surprise attacks to defeat the opponent. A frontal assault involves the concentration of superior military power to overwhelm the enemy. Such a direct attack seeks to a punch a hole through the opponent's well-prepared defenses and exploit the breakthrough with follow-on operations to encircle and annihilate the adversary's forces or to occupy key terrain.[34] Frontal assaults and surprise attacks are to complement each other. Their timing, sequencing, and locations are subject to variation depending on the operational circumstances. Surprise attacks, then, are not a panacea in the PLA's eyes. Based on the specific situation, they can either deliver a decisive blow or serve as a force multiplier to the main military effort.

The PLA's Means for an Offensive Campaign

The PLA possesses a growing arsenal of weaponry, including long-range ballistic and cruise missiles, to engage in a joint firepower strike campaign against U.S. forward bases, including those in Japan. Among various projectiles that can reach the Japanese archipelago, China's ground-launched theater-range missile forces have increased—in some cases dramatically—in number over the past decade. For illustrative purposes, the following focuses on three types of missiles that could be employed to knock out U.S. naval and air bases in Japan.

The most likely weapon of choice for the PLA's Rocket Force is the DF-21C, a conventionally armed land-attack medium-range ballistic missile (MRBM). According to the Defense Intelligence Agency's (DIA) 2019 report on Chinese military power, "The Rocket Force is fielding conventional MRBMs to increase the range at which it can conduct precision strikes against land targets and naval ships (including aircraft carriers) operating from China's shores out to the first island chain—the islands running from the Kurils, through Taiwan, to Borneo, roughly encompassing the Yellow Sea, East China Sea, and South China Sea."[35]

The agency estimated that the DF-21C has a range of at least 1,500 kilometers, putting the entire Japanese archipelago within its range.[36]

The Pentagon's 2020 annual report on Chinese military power concurred that "China also deploys the land-attack CSS-5 Mod 4 (DF-21C) and the ground-launched CH-SSC-9 (CJ-10) LACM [land-attack cruise missile], placing infrastructure on Okinawa and the main Japanese islands at risk."[37] For the DF-21C, the document estimated that the Rocket Force had fielded 150 launchers and more than 150 missiles.[38] By comparison, the 2010 edition reported that China possessed 75 to 85 launchers and 85 to 95 missiles.[39] Since the DF-21 missiles are assigned three roles—nuclear strike, land attack, and antishipping—only a portion of those are assigned to conventional land-attack missions. The two reports did not specify how many of those missiles were dedicated to land attack. Nevertheless, over a ten-year period, the number of launchers in this missile class may have doubled and the number of missiles may have increased by 76 percent.

The National Air and Space Intelligence Center (NASIC) publishes occasional reports on worldwide ballistic and cruise missile threats. The 2017 version stated that "The CSS-5 Mod 4 (DF-21C) is intended to hold at-risk or strike logistics and communication nodes, regional military bases including airfields and ports."[40] According to NASIC, there were at least 16 launchers for the conventional land-attack version of the DF-21 missile. Noting that launchers can reload and fire additional missiles, NASIC stated that the "missile inventory may be much larger than the number of launchers." The report did not, however, provide an estimate of the missile count. The 2013 edition stated that "These systems [conventional land-attack DF-21 missiles] are likely intended to hold at-risk or strike logistics nodes, regional military bases including airfields and ports, and naval assets."[41] It estimated that China possessed fewer than 30 launchers.

To complement the DF-21C, the Rocket Force has deployed the CJ-10 ground-launched cruise missile (GLCM) with a range exceeding 1,500 kilometers, putting the Japanese islands well within reach. According to the DIA, "The CJ-10 . . . offers flight profiles different from ballistic missiles, enhancing targeting options. Because of overlap in the kinds of targets China is likely to engage with either ballistic missiles or cruise missiles, GLCMs . . . provide key operational and planning flexibility. These weapons are likely to reduce the burden on ballistic missile forces. . . . This will complicate an adversary's air and missile defense problem."[42]

In 2020, the Pentagon reported that the Rocket Force had as many as 100 launchers and more than three hundred CJ-10 missiles.[43] The 2010 edition estimated that there were forty-five to fifty-five launchers and two hundred to five hundred missiles, suggesting that the number of launchers may have more than doubled in ten years.[44]

The conventional land-attack version of the DF-26 intermediate-range ballistic missile (IRBM) could potentially take part in a bombardment against U.S. bases in Japan, although its range suggests that it is destined for more distant targets such as Guam. The DIA observed that "The DF-26 is capable of conducting precision strikes against ground targets and contributes to China's counterintervention posture in the Asia-Pacific region."[45] The missile can be armed with nuclear or conventional warheads and has a range of four thousand kilometers.[46]

The Department of Defense noted that "The multi-role DF-26 is designed to rapidly swap conventional and nuclear warheads and is capable of conducting precision strikes in the Western Pacific, the Indian Ocean, and the South China Sea from mainland China."[47] It explained that "The DF-26 IRBM has a maximum range of 4,000 km and is capable of precision strikes against ground and ship targets, potentially threatening U.S. land and sea-based forces as far away as Guam."[48] The Pentagon estimated that there were two hundred launchers to fire more than two hundred DF-26 missiles.[49] By comparison, the 2018 edition, the first time the Defense Department tallied the number of DF-26 launchers and missiles, estimated that the Rocket Force fielded sixteen to thirty launchers and sixteen to thirty missiles.[50] If the reports are correct, then this class of missiles may have grown sixfold in just two years.

The 2017 NASIC report described the DF-26 as an element of China's strategy "specifically designed to prevent adversary military forces' access to regional conflicts."[51] The Intelligence Center estimated that the missile has a range of more than three thousand kilometers and that the Rocket Force had fielded more than sixteen launchers.[52]

Nongovernmental sources provide some data about China's missile force. The International Institute for Strategic Studies estimated that the Rocket Force had deployed twenty-four DF-21C ballistic missiles, fifty-four CJ-10 cruise missiles, and seventy-two DF-26 ballistic missiles.[53] Janes listed sixteen or more DF-21s but did not offer specific figures of its own about the number of CJ-10s and DF-26s.[54]

The bottom line is that the PLA's Rocket Force has clearly acquired the capabilities to hold at risk U.S. bases across the Japanese archipelago. If the other services' striking power, including air- and ship-launched platforms and prospective capabilities such as the hypersonic weapons, are included, the danger to those bases is even more severe.

Beyond the physical means to harm U.S. forward basing, the PLA has also demonstrated its ability to pull off a missile raid with precision and lethality. In their 2017 report, Thomas Shugart and Javier Gonzalez unearth evidence based on Google Earth searches that the Chinese military has conducted assaults against mock sites to simulate attacks against naval bases.[55] The authors show that the PLA has practiced strikes against port facilities and warships moored pierside, which are fixed vulnerable targets. They speculate that Beijing may be purposively permitting observation of its test sites as an element of its deterrence signaling to Washington and other Asian capitals.

Tellingly, the overhead satellite imagery reveals that the size and configuration of the mock harbors are roughly comparable to that of Yokosuka naval base and that the mock warships' length is about the same as the *Arleigh Burke*–class destroyer, the workhorse of the U.S. Navy. The report further shows that the impact craters on the mock buildings and ships indicate the use of submunitions, demonstrating the PLA's ability to hit targets with impressive precision. These photographs also demonstrate that Chinese defense planners have been rehearsing a preemptive strike, since only an enemy caught flatfooted would leave its ships tied up at pierside. An adversary with adequate early warning would sortie its fleet out to sea to escape a possible missile raid.

Critical Assessment of the PLA's Threat to U.S. Bases

Chinese strategists recognize that the U.S. military depends heavily on forward bases and their associated logistical support for peacetime and wartime operations. They assess that attacks against these large, concentrated, and vulnerable bases across the western Pacific would have an outsized impact on the U.S. armed forces' ability to carry out their missions. At the same time, PLA doctrine calls for systemic attacks against the enemy's strategic rear, including the logistical infrastructure, to cut off support to the opponent's frontline combat units. Given the PLA's judgment that the system of systems is essential to American power projection and to sustaining operations, Chinese commanders likely see U.S. command and control hubs and logistical centers as priority targets to be knocked out at the outset of a conflict. The PLA's penchant for surprise and its demonstrated capability to launch rapid long-range attacks further reinforce the imperative to deliver the first blow.

The PLA's threat to U.S naval bases in Japan would constitute only one element of a larger campaign. Indeed, a first strike would likely encompass a much wider range of targets. The PLA would likely launch a barrage of missiles against major airbases such as Kadena in Okinawa—the hub of American airpower in the region—Iwakuni, and Misawa as well as against major command elements located at Yokota and elsewhere. The Rocket Force possesses an arsenal of ship-killing DF-21 and DF-26 ballistic missiles that would be aimed at U.S. carrier strike groups and other surface combatants operating west of Guam. In the near future, a larger proportion of the missile force will be armed with hypersonic weapons. Bombers armed with air-launched cruise and ballistic missiles would join the fray. Nuclear-attack submarines equipped with land-attack cruise missiles would stealthily approach their shore targets beneath the waves. Cyber-attacks against critical nodes on the American homeland and space warfare to destroy or blind the constellations of U.S. military satellites would be an element of China's opening move.

While the doctrinal writings illustrate the operational logic of a first strike, they do not consider the strategic considerations that would preoccupy Chinese policy makers. Strikes against U.S. bases in Japan and elsewhere would almost certainly guarantee vertical and horizontal escalation. They might compel Washington to retaliate with counterstrikes against the mainland, the very outcome that PLA doctrine describes as the most serious threat. They would draw in Japan, the third largest economy in the world and possessing a first-rate military, as a combatant in the war. They could accelerate China's international isolation as U.S. allies and friends in Asia and beyond rallied around the United States. Such a blitzkrieg campaign would also take place under the shadow of nuclear weapons. In short, a surprise attack may be operationally efficacious, but it could very well prove strategically counterproductive, if not disastrous, for Beijing. It is therefore highly unlikely that Chinese leaders would take lightly any decision to launch a first strike. They would more likely decline to pull the

trigger first if it were apparent to them that such a move would significantly complicate the war effort or dim the chances of success. Whether
to strike first or not, then, is an intrinsically uncertain political question
rather than a straightforward operational or technical one. It is anyone's
guess, including possibly Chinese policy makers themselves, how Beijing
will weigh the risks and benefits of a first strike in that moment of decision.

Looking ahead, the tensions between the operational logic of first strike
and the strategic calculations of restraint will likely sharpen. The prolifer-
ation of new technologies and capabilities, including hypersonic weapons
and artificial intelligence, could substantially increase the speed and lethality of modern warfare. Indeed, the reach and velocity of precision firepower
could shrink the battlefield further still while truncating the precious time
political leaders and commanders need to deliberate critical decisions.
The temptation to hit first and hard to seize the initiative will thus grow.
The PLA's core institutional beliefs and values, as exemplified by the doctrine surveyed previously, will only incentivize calls for going first. It thus
behooves Western observers to discern the circumstances under which
Chinese leaders would yield to pressures of a first strike when they find
themselves on a collision course with the United States.

Notes

English translations of Chinese titles are used after first mention.

1. See John J. Mearsheimer, *The Tragedy of Great Power Politics*, updated edition
   (New York: Norton, 2014); Graham Allison, *Destined for War: Can America and
   China Escape Thucydides's Trap?* (Boston: Houghton Mifflin Harcourt, 2017);
   Kevin Rudd, "Beware the Guns of August—in Asia: How to Keep U.S.-Chinese
   Tensions from Sparking a War," *Foreign Affairs*, August 2, 2020; and Christopher Layne, "Coming Storms: The Return of Great-Power War," *Foreign Affairs*,
   November/December 2020.
2. 寿晓松 [Shou Xiaosong, ed.], 战略学 [Science of Military Strategy] (Beijing:
   Academy of Military Science, 2013), 100.
3. Shou Xiaosong, *Science of Military Strategy*, 106.
4. Shou Xiaosong, *Science of Military Strategy*, 209–10.
5. Shou Xiaosong, *Science of Military Strategy*, 106.
6. 欧阳维 [Ouyang Wei], 战略部署论 [On Strategic Deployment] (Beijing: Liberation Army Press, 2011), 43.

7. 扬建华 [Yang Jianhua], 世界军事地理要览 [Overview of Global Military Geography] (Beijing: Academy of Military Science, 2010), 124–25.

8. Ouyang Wei, *On Strategic Deployment*, 38.

9. 樊高月 宫旭平 [Fan Gaoyue and Gong Xuping], 美国全球军事基地览要 [Overview of U.S. Global Military Bases] (Beijing: Liberation Army Press, 2014), 80.

10. 扬建华 [Yang Jianhua], 世界战略要地概览 [Overview of Global Strategic Locations] (Beijing: Liberation Army Press, 2012), 54–55.

11. 曹晓光 [Cao Xiaoguang], 深度解密日本海军 [Decoding the Japanese Navy] (Beijing: Qinghua University Press, 2013), 211.

12. Cao Xiaoguang, *Decoding the Japanese Navy*, 242–44.

13. Cao Xiaoguang, *Decoding the Japanese Navy*, 282–83. The other five terminals are located at Tsurumi Depot in Yokohama, Hachinohe Depot in Hachinohe, Akasaki and Iroizaki Depots in Sasebo, and Yokose Depot in Saiki.

14. Cao Xiaoguang, *Decoding the Japanese Navy*, 245.

15. 于川信 [Yu Chuanxin], 联勤教程 [Course Materials on Joint Logistics] (Beijing: Academy of Military Science, 2012), 35.

16. 于川信 [Yu Chuanxin], 联勤概论 [Introduction to Joint Logistics] (Beijing: Academy of Military Science, 2011), 122.

17. Yu Chuanxin, *Introduction to Joint Logistics*, 106.

18. Yu Chuanxin, *Introduction to Joint Logistics*, 107.

19. 乔杰 [Qiao Jie], 战役学教程 [Course Materials on the Science of Campaigns] (Beijing: Academy of Military Science, 2012), 143.

20. Qiao Jie, *Course Materials on the Science of Campaigns*, 142.

21. 李有升 [Li Yousheng], 联合战役学教程 [Course Materials on the Science of Joint Campaigns] (Beijing: Academy of Military Science, 2012), 201.

22. Li Yousheng, *Course Materials on the Science of Joint Campaigns*, 203–4.

23. Li Yousheng, *Course Materials on the Science of Joint Campaigns*, 227.

24. 彭呈仓 [Peng Chengcang], 精确作战 [Precision Warfare] (Beijing: National Defense University, 2011), 46.

25. Peng Chengcang, *Precision Warfare*, 15.

26. Peng Chengcang, *Precision Warfare*, 16.

27. Mao Zedong, "Problems of Strategy in China's Revolutionary War," in *Selected Military Writings of Mao Tse-tung* (Beijing: Foreign Language Press, 1963), 135.

28. Mao Zedong, "Problems of Strategy in Guerrilla War against Japan," in *Selected Military Writings of Mao Tse-tung* (Beijing: Foreign Language Press, 1963), 155.

29. 毛泽东 [Mao Zedong], "论抗日游击战争的基本战术—袭击 [On Basic Tactics in Guerrilla War against Japan—Surprise Attack]," in 毛泽东文选 第二卷 [Collected Works of Mao Zedong, Volume II] (Beijing: People's Press, 2000), https://www.ixyread.com/read/ID1608076541p3uh/OEBPS-Text-Section0311.html.

30. For the various historical examples of surprise attacks, see 程晋明 [Cheng Jinming], 合同进攻战术教程 [Course Materials on Combined Attack Tactics] (Beijing: Academy of Military Science, 2013), 51.

31. Cheng Jinming, *Course Materials on Combined Attack Tactics*, 50.

32. Cheng Jinming, *Course Materials on Combined Attack Tactics*, 55–58.

33. Cheng Jinming, *Course Materials on Combined Attack Tactics*, 53.

34. Cheng Jinming, *Course Materials on Combined Attack Tactics*, 45.

35. Defense Intelligence Agency, *China Military Power: Modernizing a Force to Fight and Win* (Washington, D.C.: Defense Intelligence Agency, 2019), 91.

36. Defense Intelligence Agency, *China Military Power*, 94.

37. Office of the Secretary of Defense, *Military and Security Developments Involving the People's Republic of China* (Washington, D.C.: Department of Defense, 2020), 81.

38. Office of the Secretary of Defense, *Military and Security Developments*, 2020, 166.

39. Office of the Secretary of Defense, *Military and Security Developments Involving the People's Republic of China* (Washington, D.C.: Department of Defense, 2010), 66.

40. National Air and Space Intelligence Center, *Ballistic and Cruise Missile Threat* (Wright-Patterson Air Force Base, Ohio: National Air and Space Intelligence Center, 2017), 22.

41. National Air and Space Intelligence Center, *Ballistic and Cruise Missile Threat* (Wright-Patterson Air Force Base, Ohio: National Air and Space Intelligence Center, 2013), 14.

42. Defense Intelligence Agency, *China Military Power*, 92.

43. Office of the Secretary of Defense, *Military and Security Developments*, 2020, 166.

44. Office of the Secretary of Defense, *Military and Security Developments*, 2010, 66.

45. Defense Intelligence Agency, *China Military Power*, 91.

46. Defense Intelligence Agency, *China Military Power*, 93.

47. Office of the Secretary of Defense, *Military and Security Developments*, 2020, 56.

48. Office of the Secretary of Defense, *Military and Security Developments*, 2020, 81.

49. Office of the Secretary of Defense, *Military and Security Developments*, 2020, 166.

50. Office of the Secretary of Defense, *Military and Security Developments Involving the People's Republic of China* (Washington, D.C.: Department of Defense, 2018), 125.

51. National Air and Space Intelligence Center, *Ballistic and Cruise Missile Threat*, 2017, 3.

52. National Air and Space Intelligence Center, *Ballistic and Cruise Missile Threat*, 2017, 25.

53. International Institute for Strategic Studies, *Military Balance* (London: International Institute for Strategic Studies, 2020), 259.

54. See Janes online at https://www.janes.com/.

55. Thomas Shugart and Javier Gonzales, *First Strike: China's Missile Threat to U.S. Bases in Asia* (Washington, D.C.: Center for a New American Security, 2017).

BIBLIOGRAPHY

PRIMARY SOURCES: GOVERNMENT ARCHIVES
United Kingdom
The National Archives, London
CAB 2 Committee of Imperial Defence Minutes
CAB 23 Cabinet Minutes
CAB 32 Imperial Conferences
CAB 34 Committee of Imperial Defence Memoranda
CAB 67 War Cabinet Memoranda
FO 410 Foreign Office, Confidential Print Japan
FO 371 Foreign Office, General Correspondence

United States
National Archives and Records Administration
RG 457 Record of the National Security Agency/Central Security Service

PRIMARY SOURCES: PRIVATE PAPERS
Borden, Sir Robert, Library and Archives of Canada, Ottawa
Geddes, Sir Auckland, Churchill Archives Centre, Cambridge
Lloyd George, 1st Earl, Parliamentary Archives, London
Rennell of Rodd, Bodleian Library, Oxford
Roosevelt, Franklin, Franklin D. Roosevelt Presidential Library
Sims, Admiral William S., Library of Congress
Stimson, Henry S., Diary, Yale University

PUBLISHED DOCUMENTS
Eade, Charles, ed. *The Unrelenting Struggle: War Speeches by the Right Hon. Winston S. Churchill.* London: Cassell, 1942.

Gilbert, Martin, ed. *Winston S. Churchill, 1874–1965*, vol. 4, Companion Part 3. London: Heinemann, 1977.

———. *Winston S. Churchill, 1874–1965*, vol. 5, Companion Part 1: *The Exchequer Years, 1922–1929.* Boston: Houghton Mifflin, 1981.

Gorodetsky, Gabriel, ed. *The Maisky Diaries: Red Ambassador to the Court of St. James, 1932–1943.* New Haven, Conn.: Yale University Press, 2015.

James, Robert Rhodes, ed. *Winston S. Churchill: His Complete Speeches, 1897–1963.* London: Chelsea House Publishers, 1974.

Ranft, B. McL., ed. *The Beatty Papers*, vol. II, *1916–1927*. Aldershot: Scolar Press for the Navy Records Society, 1993.

Self, Robert, ed. *The Neville Chamberlain Diary Letters*, vol. 4, *The Downing Street Years, 1934–1940*. Aldershot: Ashgate, 2005.

Shugart, Thomas, and Javier Gonzales. *First Strike: China's Missile Threat to U.S. Bases in Asia*. Washington, D.C.: Center for a New American Security, 2017.

Smith, Amanda, ed. *Hostage to Fortune: The Letters of Joseph P. Kennedy*. New York: Viking, 2001.

GOVERNMENT DOCUMENTS
China
Cao Xiaoguang [曹晓光]. 深度解密日本海军 [*Decoding the Japanese Navy*]. Beijing: Qinghua University Press, 2013.

Cheng Jinming [程晋明]. 合同进攻战术教程 [*Course Materials on Combined Attack Tactics*]. Beijing: Academy of Military Science, 2013.

Fan Gaoyue and Gong Xuping [樊高月 宫旭平]. 美国全球军事基地览要 [*Overview of U.S. Global Military Bases*]. Beijing: Liberation Army Press, 2014.

Li Yousheng [李有升]. 联合战役学教程 [*Course Materials on the Science of Joint Campaigns*]. Beijing: Academy of Military Science, 2012.

Ouyang Wei [欧阳维]. 战略部署论 [*On Strategic Deployment*]. Beijing: Liberation Army Press, 2011.

Peng Chengcang [彭呈仓]. 精确作战 [*Precision Warfare*]. Beijing: National Defense University, 2011.

Qiao Jie [乔杰]. 战役学教程 [*Course Materials on the Science of Campaigns*]. Beijing: Academy of Military Science, 2012.

Shou Xiaosong, ed.[寿晓松]. 战略学 [*Science of Military Strategy*]. Beijing: Academy of Military Science, 2013.

Yang Jianhua [扬建华]. 世界军事地理要览 [*Overview of Global Military Geography*]. Beijing: Academy of Military Science, 2010.

———. 世界战略要地概览 [*Overview of Global Strategic Locations*]. Beijing: Liberation Army Press, 2012.

Yu Chuanxin [于川信]. 联勤教程 [*Course Materials on Joint Logistics*]. Beijing: Academy of Military Science, 2012.

———. 联勤概论 [*Introduction to Joint Logistics*]. Beijing: Academy of Military Science, 2011.

Great Britain
Parliamentary Papers: House of Commons Debates, 5th series. London: H.M.S.O., 1922.

Japan
Kaigunshō Gunji Fukyūbu, eds. *Gunshuku kaigi o chūshin to shite* [Centering on the armaments limitation conference]. Tokyo: Kaigunshō Gunji Fukyūbu, 1934.

———. *Gunshuku mondai ni tsuite* [About the issue of naval arms limitation]. Tokyo: Kaigunshō Gunji Fukyūbu, 1934.

———. *Kaiyō Jidai* [The age of the ocean]. Tokyo: Kaigunshō Gunji Fukyūbu, 1934.

———. *Kokusai jōsei to kaigun gunshuku kaigi* [The international situation and the naval arms limitation conference]. Tokyo: Kaigunshō Gunji Fukyūbu, 1934.

———. *Kokusai renmei dattai to teikoku kaigun* [Withdrawal from the League of Nations and the Imperial Navy]. Tokyo: Kaigunshō, 1933.

———. *Saikin rekkoku kaigun gunbi jōkyō* [The state of the great powers' naval armaments]. Tokyo: Kaigunshō, 1932.

———. *Shōsei ni anzuru nakare* [Don't worry about me]. Tokyo: Kaigunshō, 1933.

Kimball, Warren F., ed. *Churchill and Roosevelt: The Complete Correspondence.* Princeton, N.J.: Princeton University Press, 1984.

Kokusei kenkyūkai. *Kaigun gunshuku kaigi sankō shiryō* [Naval arms limitation conference reference materials]. Tokyo: Kokusei Kenkyūkai, 1934.

United States

Defense Intelligence Agency. *China Military Power: Modernizing a Force to Fight and Win.* Washington, D.C.: Defense Intelligence Agency, 2019.

Department of Defense. *The "Magic" Background to Pearl Harbor.* Washington, D.C.: Government Printing Office, 1977.

Department of State, *Foreign Relations of the United States, Japan, 1931–1941,* vol. 2. Washington, D.C.: Government Printing Office, 1943.

———. *Foreign Relations of the United States, 1941,* vol. 1. Washington, D.C.: Government Printing Office, 1958.

———. *Foreign Relations of the United States, 1941,* vol. 4, *The Far East.* Washington, D.C.: Government Printing Office, 1956.

National Air and Space Intelligence Center. *Ballistic and Cruise Missile Threat.* Wright-Patterson Air Force Base, Ohio: National Air and Space Intelligence Center, 2013.

———. *Ballistic and Cruise Missile Threat.* Wright-Patterson Air Force Base, Ohio: National Air and Space Intelligence Center, 2017.

Office of the Secretary of Defense. *Military and Security Developments Involving the People's Republic of China.* Washington, D.C.: Department of Defense, 2010.

———. *Military and Security Developments Involving the People's Republic of China.* Washington, D.C.: Department of Defense, 2018.

———. *Military and Security Developments Involving the People's Republic of China.* Washington, D.C.: Department of Defense, 2020.

NEWSPAPERS AND PERIODICALS

Advocate of Peace
Collier's
New York Times
Pictorial Weekly

Punch
Sunday Dispatch
Time
Weekly Dispatch

SECONDARY SOURCES

Adams, R. J. Q. *Arms and the Wizard: Lloyd George and the Ministry of Munitions, 1915–1916*. College Station: Texas A&M University Press, 1986.

Alexander, Jack. "Profiles: Diplomat in the Doghouse." *The New Yorker*, April 30, 1938, 22–27.

Allison, Graham. *Destined for War: Can America and China Escape Thucydides's Trap?* Boston: Houghton Mifflin Harcourt, 2017.

Alvarez, David. *Secret Messages: Codebreaking and American Diplomacy, 1930–1945*. Lawrence: University Press of Kansas, 2000.

Armstrong, David. "China's Place in the New Pacific Order." In *The Washington Conference, 1921–22: Naval Rivalry, East Asian Stability and the Road to Pearl Harbor*, edited by Erik Goldstein and John Maurer. New York: Routledge, 1994.

Asada, Sadao. *From Mahan to Pearl Harbor: The Imperial Japanese Navy and the United States*. Annapolis, Md.: Naval Institute Press, 2005.

Baker, Ray Stannard. *Woodrow Wilson: Life and Letters*. New York: Doubleday, Page & Co., 1927.

Barnett, Correlli. *The Collapse of British Power*. Gloucester: Alan Sutton, 1972.

Barnhart, Michael. *Japan Prepares for Total War: The Search for Economic Security, 1919–1941*. Ithaca, N.Y.: Cornell University Press, 1987.

Beard, Charles A. *President Roosevelt and the Coming of the War 1941*. New Haven, Conn.: Yale University Press, 1948.

Beasley, W. G. *Japanese Imperialism 1894–1945*. Oxford: Clarendon Press, 1987.

Bell, Christopher M. "Our Most Exposed Outpost: Hong Kong and British Far Eastern Strategy, 1921–1941." *Journal of Military History* 60, no. 1 (January 1996): 61–88.

Bell, Peter. *Chamberlain, Germany and Japan, 1933–4*. New York: St. Martin's Press, 1996.

Bennett, G. H. *The Royal Navy on the Age of Austerity: Naval and Foreign Policy under Lloyd George*. London: Bloomsbury Academic, 2016.

Best, Antony. "The 'Ghost' of the Anglo-Japanese Alliance: An Examination into Historical Myth-Making." *Historical Journal* 49, no. 3 (2006): 811–31.

Biagini, E. F. "Gladstone's Midlothian Campaign of 1879: The Realpolitik of Christian Humanitarianism." *Journal of Liberal History* 42 (Spring 2004): 6–12.

Birn, Donald S. "Open Diplomacy at the Washington Conference of 1921–2: The British and French Experience." *Comparative Studies in Society and History* 12, no. 3 (July 1970): 297–319.

Borg, Dorothy. *American Policy and the Chinese Revolution, 1925–1928*. New York: Macmillan, 1947.

Bowring, John, ed. *The Works of Jeremy Bentham*. New York: Russell & Russell, 1962.

Boyle, Timothy. "New Light on Lloyd George's Mansion House Speech." *Historical Journal* 23, no. 2 (June 1980): 431–33.

Breen, John. *Record in Pictures of Yasukuni Jinja Yushukan*. Tokyo: Yasukuni Shrine, 2009.

Buckley, Thomas. *The United States and the Washington Conference, 1921–1922*. Knoxville: University of Tennessee Press, 1970.

Butow, Robert. *Tojo and the Coming of the War*. Princeton, N.J.: Princeton University Press, 1961.

Bywater, Hector. *The Great Pacific War*. London: Constable, 1925.

———. *Sea Power in the Pacific: A Study of the American-Japanese Naval Problem*. London: Constable, 1921.

———. *Taiheiyō sensō to sono hihan* [The Pacific war and criticisms]. Translated by Ishimaru Fujita. Tokyo: Bunmei Kyōkai Jimusho, 1926.

Chang, Iris. *The Rape of Nanking: The Forgotten Holocaust of World War II*. New York: Basic Books, 1997.

Chen, Janet. "Republican History." In *A Companion to Chinese History*, edited by Michael Szonyi, 171–72. Hoboken, N.J.: Wiley Blackwell, 2017.

Chiang Kai-shek. *China's Destiny and China's Economic Theory*. New York: Roy Publishers, 1947.

Churchill, Winston S. "Germany and Japan." November 27, 1936, in *Step By Step*. New York: Putnam's, 1939.

———. *The Second World War*, vol. 1: *The Gathering Storm*. Boston: Houghton Mifflin, 1985 paperback edition.

———. *The Second World War*, vol. 3, *The Grand Alliance*. Boston: Houghton Mifflin, 1950.

———. *The Second World War*, vol. 4, *The Hinge of Fate*. Boston: Houghton Mifflin, 1950.

———. *The World Crisis, 1911–1914*. London: Thornton Butterworth, 1923.

Cohen, Paul. *History and Popular Memory: The Power of Story in Moments of Crisis*. New York: Columbia University Press, 2017.

———. *Speaking to History: The Story of King Goujian in Twentieth Century China*. Berkeley: University of California Press, 2009.

Conroy, Hilary, and Harry Wray, eds. *Pearl Harbor Reexamined: Prologue to the Pacific War*. Honolulu: University of Hawaii Press, 1990.

Coox, Alvin D. *Nomonhan: Japan against Russia, 1939*, 2 vols. Stanford, Calif.: Stanford University Press, 1990.

Cosgrove, Richard. "A Note on Lloyd George's Speech at the Mansion House." *Historical Journal* 12, no. 4 (Dec. 1969): 698–701.

Crowley, James. *Japan's Quest for Autonomy: National Security and Foreign Policy, 1930–1938*. Princeton, N.J.: Princeton University Press, 1966.

Dallek, Robert. *Franklin D. Roosevelt and American Foreign Policy, 1932–1945*. Oxford: Oxford University Press, 1981.

Davis, Kenneth S. *FDR: The War President 1940–1943*. New York: Random House, 2000.

Dayer, Roberta Allbert. "The British War Debts to the United States and the Anglo-Japanese Alliance, 1920–1923." *Pacific Historical Review* 45, no. 4 (Nov. 1976): 569–95.

Dingman, Roger. "Farewell to Friendship: The *U.S.S. Astoria*'s Visit to Japan, April 1939." *Diplomatic History* 10, no. 2 (1986): 121–39.

Divine, Robert A. *The Illusion of Neutrality: Franklin D. Roosevelt and the Struggle over the Arms Embargo*. Chicago: University of Chicago Press, 1962.

———. *The Reluctant Belligerent: American Entry into the Second World War*. Hoboken, N.J.: Wiley, 1965.

Drea, Edward J. *Japan's Imperial Army: Its Rise and Fall, 1853–1945*. Lawrence: University Press of Kansas, 2000.

Drea, Edward J., and Hans van de Ven. "Overview of Major Military Campaigns during the Sino-Japanese War, 1937–1945." In *The Battle of China: Essays on the Military History of the Sino-Japanese War 1937–1945*, edited by Mark Peattie, Edward J. Drea, and Hans van de Ven. Stanford, Calif.: Stanford University Press, 2010.

Elleman, Bruce, and S. C. M. Paine. *Modern China: Continuity and Change: 1644 to the Present*. Upper Saddle River, N.J.: Prentice Hall, 2010.

Evans, David C., and Mark R. Peattie. *Kaigun: Strategy, Tactics, and Technology in the Imperial Japanese Navy, 1887–1941*. Annapolis, Md.: Naval Institute Press, 1997.

Feis, Herbert. *The Road to Pearl Harbor*. Princeton, N.J.: Princeton University Press, 1950.

Ferris, John. "A British 'Unofficial' Aviation Mission and Japanese Naval Developments, 1919–1929," *Journal of Strategic Studies* 5, no. 3 (Sept. 1982): 416–39.

Fisher, Herbert A. L. "Mr. Lloyd George's Foreign Policy." *Foreign Affairs* 1, no. 3 (March 15, 1923): 69–84.

Fleming, Thomas. *The New Dealers' War: Franklin D. Roosevelt and the War within World War II*. New York: Basic Books, 2001.

Flynn, John Thomas. *The Truth about Pearl Harbor*. Glasgow: Strickland Press, 1945.

Flournoy, F. R. "British Liberal Theories of International Relations (1848–1898)." *Journal of the History of Ideas* 7, no. 2 (April 1946): 195–217.

Fogel, Joshua A., ed. *The Nanjing Massacre in History and Historiography*. Berkeley: University of California Press, 2000.

Frank, Richard B. *Tower of Skulls: A History of the Asia Pacific War July 1937–May 1942*. New York: W. W. Norton & Company, 2020.

Friedman, Milton. "Franklin D. Roosevelt, Silver, and China." *Journal of Political Economy* 100, no. 1 (1992): 62–83.

Fukunaga Kyōsuke. *Kaigun monogatari* [The tale of the navy]. Tokyo: Ichigensha, 1930.

———. "Kaima no otori" [The ocean demon's lure]. In *Shōnen kurabu meisakusen: nekketsu tsūkai shōsetsushū* [A selection of masterpieces from 'shōnen kurabu': short stories to heat up your blood], edited by Katō Ken'ichi. Tokyo: Kodansha, 1969.

Gladstone, W. "Germany, France, and England." *Edinburgh Review*, Oct. 1870, 554–93.

Gilbert, Bentley. "Lloyd George and the Historians." *Albion* 11, no. 1 (1979): 74–86.

———. "Pacifist to Interventionist: David Lloyd George in 1911 and 1914. Was Belgium an Issue?" *Historical Journal* 28, no. 4 (Dec. 1985): 863–85.

Gilbert, Martin. *Winston S. Churchill*, vol. 5, *Prophet of Truth, 1922–1939*. Boston: Houghton Mifflin, 1977.

———. *Winston S. Churchill*, vol. 6, *Their Finest Hour, 1939–1941*. Boston: Houghton Mifflin, 1983.

Glad, Betty. "Charles Evans Hughes." *American National Biography* (1999).

———. *Charles Evans Hughes and Illusions of Innocence: A Study of American Diplomacy*. Urbana: University of Illinois Press, 1966.

Glantz, David. *Barbarossa Derailed: The Battle for Smolensk, 10 July to 10 September 1941*, vol. 1. Solihull, U.K.: Helion & Company Limited, 2012.

Goldman, Emily O. *Sunken Treaties: Naval Arms Control between the Wars*. University Park: Pennsylvania State University Press, 1994.

Goldman, Stuart D. *Nomonhan, 1939: The Red Army's Victory That Shaped World War II*. Annapolis, Md.: Naval Institute Press, 2012.

Goldstein, Erik. "British Peace Aims and the Eastern Question: The Political Intelligence Department and the Eastern Committee, 1918." *Middle Eastern Studies* 23, no. 4 (1987): 419–36.

———. *The First World War Peace Settlements, 1919–1925*. London: Longman, 2002.

Goldstein, Erik, and John Maurer, eds. *The Washington Conference, 1921–22: Naval Rivalry, East Asian Stability and the Road to Pearl Harbor*. New York: Routledge, 1994.

Grew, Joseph C. *Ten Years in Japan*. New York: Simon & Schuster, 1944.

———. *Turbulent Era: A Diplomatic Record of Forty Years, 1904–1945*, 2 vols. Boston: Houghton Mifflin, 1952.

Grigg, John. *Lloyd George: The People's Champion, 1902–1911*. London: Eyre Methuen, 1978.

Gunther, John. *Inside Asia*. New York: Harper, 1939.

Hall, Melanie, and Erik Goldstein. "Writers, the Clergy, and the 'Diplomatization' of Culture: The Sub-Structures of Anglo-American Diplomacy, 1820–1914." In *On the Fringes of Diplomacy*, edited by Antony Best and John Fisher, 127–54. London: Ashgate, 2011.

Harmsen, Peter. *Shanghai 1937: Stalingrad on the Yangtze*. Havertown, Pa.: Casemate, 2013.

Hankey, Maurice. *Diplomacy by Conference*. London: Ernest Benn, 1946.

Harries, Meirion, and Susan Harries. *Soldiers of the Sun: The Rise and Fall of the Imperial Japanese Army*. New York: Random House, 1991.

Harrison, Mark, ed. *The Economics of World War II: Six Great Powers in International Comparison*. Cambridge: Cambridge University Press, 1998.

Heinrichs, Waldo. *American Ambassador: Joseph C. Grew and the Development of the American Diplomatic Tradition*. New York: Oxford University Press, 1986.

———. *Threshold of War: Franklin D. Roosevelt and American Entry into World War II.* New York: Oxford University Press, 1982.

Henretta, James A. "Charles Evans Hughes and the Strange Death of Liberal America." *Law and History Review* 24, no. 1 (Spring 2006): 115–71.

Herman, Arthur. *Freedom's Forge: How American Business Produced Victory in World War II.* New York: Random House, 2013.

Herrick, F. H. "Gladstone and the Concept of the 'English-Speaking Peoples.'" *Journal of British Studies* 12, no. 1 (Nov. 1972): 150–51.

Hill, Alexander. "British Lend Lease Aid and the Soviet War Effort, June 1941–June 1942." *Journal of Military History* 71, no. 3 (July 2007): 773–808.

Hinsley, F. H. *British Intelligence in the Second World War: Its Influence on Strategy and Operations,* vol. 2. Cambridge: Cambridge University Press, 1981.

Hirata Shinsaku. *Kokubō no kiki: nichibei kaigun no taiheiyō sakusen* [National defense crisis: The Japanese-U.S. navies' Pacific strategies]. Tokyo: Seikyōsha, 1930.

———. *Shinsenkan takachiho* [New battleship Takachiho]. Tokyo: Kodansha, 1970.

Honda, Katsuichi, and Frank Gibney. *The Nanjing Massacre: A Japanese Journalist Confronts Japan's National Shame.* Armonk, N.Y.: M. E. Sharpe, 1999.

Horinouchi Saburō. *Gunshuku mondai no shinsō* [The truth of the arms limitation issue]. Tokyo: Kaigun Kyōkai, 1929.

Hosoya Chihiro. "Washinton taisei no tokushitsu to hen'yō" [The Washington system's characteristics and modifications]. In *Washinton taisei to nichibei kankei* [The Washington system and Japanese-U.S. relations], edited by Hosoya Chihiro and Saito Makoto. Tokyo: Tokyo Daigaku Shuppankai, 1978.

Hotta, Eri. *Japan 1941: Countdown to Infamy.* New York: Alfred A. Knopf, 2013.

———. *Pan Asianism and Japan's War 1931–1945.* New York: Palgrave Macmillan, 2007.

Hughes, Charles Evans. *The Autobiographical Notes of Charles Evans Hughes.* Edited by David Danelski and Joseph Tulchin. Cambridge, Mass.: Harvard University Press, 1973.

Huntington, Samuel P. *The Clash of Civilizations and the Remaking of World Order.* New York: Simon & Schuster, 1996.

Ickes, Harold. *The Lowering Cloud: The Secret Diary of Harold L. Ickes.* New York: Simon & Schuster, 1955.

Iguchi, Takeo. *Demystifying Pearl Harbor: A New Perspective from Japan.* Tokyo: International House of Japan, 2010.

Ike, Nobutaka. *Japan's Decision for War: Records of the 1941 Policy Conferences.* Stanford, Calif.: Stanford University Press, 1967.

Ikeda Kiyoshi. *Kaigun to Nihon* [The navy and Japan]. Tokyo: Chūkō Shinsho, 1981.

Inoue Kazutsugu. *Nichibei sensō no shōhai* [Victory and defeat in a Japanese-U.S. war]. Tokyo: Ichigensha, 1932.

International Institute for Strategic Studies. *Military Balance.* London: International Institute for Strategic Studies, 2020.

Iriye, Akira. *After Imperialism: The Search for a New Order in the Far East 1921–1931.* New York: Atheneum, 1969.

———. *Japan and the Wider World: From the Mid-Nineteenth Century to the Present.* London: Longman, 1997.

———. *Origins of the Second World War in Asia and the Pacific.* New York: Routledge, 2013 (1987).

Ishida, Ken. *Japan, Italy and the Road to the Tripartite Alliance.* Cham, Switzerland: Palgrave Macmillan, 2018.

Ishimaru Fujita. *Beikoku yori mitaru nichibei sōhasen* [The U.S. views the Japanese-U.S. struggle for supremacy]. Tokyo: Hakubunkan, 1926.

———. *Nichibei hatashite tatakauka* [Will Japan and the United States fight?]. Tokyo: Shunjūsha, 1931.

Itō Masanori. *Kafu kaigi to sono ato* [The Washington conference and thereafter]. Tokyo: Tōhō Jironsha, 1922.

James, Robert Rhodes, ed. *Churchill Speaks, 1897–1963: Collected Speeches in Peace and War.* New York: Barnes and Noble, 1980.

Jin, Ha. *Nanjing Requiem.* New York: Pantheon Books, 2011.

Kaiser, David. *No End Save Victory: How FDR Led the Nation into War.* New York: Basic Books, 2014.

Kelly, Robert. *The Transatlantic Persuasion: The Liberal Democratic Mind in the Age of Gladstone.* New York: Alfred A. Knopf, 1969.

Kennan, George. *American Diplomacy.* Chicago: University of Chicago Press, 2012 [1951].

Kichisaburo, Nomura. "Japan's Demand for Naval Equality." *Foreign Affairs*, vol. 13 (Jan. 1935).

Kimball, Warren F. *The Juggler: Franklin Roosevelt as Wartime Statesman.* Princeton, N.J.: Princeton University Press, 1991.

King-Hall, Stephen. *Western Civilization and the Far East.* London: Methuen, 1924.

Kiyosawa Kiyoshi. *Amerika wa nihon to tatakawazu* [America will not fight Japan]. Tokyo: Chikura Shobō, 1932.

Klein, David, and Hilary Conroy. "Churchill, Roosevelt and the China Question in Pre-Pearl Harbor Diplomacy." In *Pearl Harbor Reexamined: Prologue to the Pacific War*, edited by Hilary Conroy and Harry Wray. Honolulu: University of Hawaii Press, 1990.

Klein, Ira. "Whitehall, Washington, and the Anglo-Japanese Alliance, 1919–1921." *Pacific Historical Review* 41, no. 4 (Nov. 1972): 460–83.

Knaplund, Paul. *Gladstone's Foreign Policy.* New York: Archon, 1935.

Kobayashi Tatsuo. "The London Naval Treaty, 1930." In *Japan Erupts: The London Naval Conference and the Manchurian Incident, 1928–1932, selected translations from taiheiyō sensō e no michi*, edited by James W. Morley. New York: Columbia University Press, 1984.

Koistenen, Paul A. C. *Arsenal of World War II: The Political Economy of American Warfare, 1940–1945.* Lawrence: University Press of Kansas, 2004.

Komatsu, Keiichiro. *Origins of the Pacific War and the Importance of MAGIC*. New York: St. Martin's, 1999.

Kush, Linda. *The Rice Paddy Navy: U.S. Sailors Undercover in China*. Oxford: Osprey Publishing, 2012.

Lafeber, Walter. *The Clash: A History of U.S.-Japanese Relations*. New York: W. W. Norton, 1997.

Langer, William L., and S. Everett Gleason. *The Undeclared War*. New York: Harper, 1953.

Lary, Diana. *The Chinese People at War: Human Suffering and Social Transformation, 1937–1945*. Cambridge: Cambridge University Press, 2010.

Lauren, Paul Gordon. "Human Rights in History: Diplomacy and Racial Equality at the Paris Peace Conference." *Diplomatic History* 2 (1978): 257–78.

Layne, Christopher. "Coming Storms: The Return of Great-Power War." *Foreign Affairs* (Nov.–Dec. 2020).

———. *The Peace of Illusions: American Grand Strategy from 1940 to the Present*. Ithaca, N.Y.: Cornell University Press, 2006.

Layton, Edwin T. *"And I Was There": Pearl Harbor and Midway—Breaking the Secrets*. New York: William Morrow, 1985.

Lensen, George Alexander. *Strange Neutrality: Soviet-Japanese Relations during the Second World War 1941–1945*. Tallahassee, Fla.: Diplomatic Press, 1972.

Li, Laura Tyson. *Madame Chiang Kai-shek: China's Eternal First Lady*. New York: Grove Press, 2006.

Link, Arthur. *Wilson the Diplomatist*. Baltimore, Md.: Johns Hopkins Press, 1957.

Lloyd George, David. *War Memoirs*, vol. II. London: Odhams Press Limited, 1938.

Lu, David John. *Agony of Choice: Matsuoka Yosuke and the Rise and Fall of the Japanese Empire*. Lanham, Md.: Lexington Books, 2002.

MacKinnon, Stephen R. *Wuhan, 1938: War, Refugees and the Making of Modern China*. Berkeley: University of California Press, 2008.

Maddox, Robert James. *William E. Borah and American Foreign Policy*. Baton Rouge: Louisiana State University Press, 1969.

Mandelbaum, Michael. *The Frugal Superpower: America's Global Leadership in a Cash-Strapped Era*. New York: Public Affairs, 2010.

毛泽东 [Mao Zedong], "论抗日游击战争的基本战术—袭击" [On Basic Tactics in Guerrilla War against Japan—Surprise Attack]. In 毛泽东文选 第二卷 [Collected Works of Mao Zedong, Volume II]. Beijing: People's Press, 2000.

———. *Problems of Strategy in China's Revolutionary War*. In *Selected Military Writings of Mao Tse-tung*. Beijing: Foreign Language Press, 1963.

———. *Problems of Strategy in Guerrilla War against Japan*. In *Selected Military Writings of Mao Tse-tung*. Beijing: Foreign Language Press, 1963.

Marder, Arthur J. *Old Friends New Enemies: The Royal Navy and the Imperial Japanese Navy*, vol. I. Oxford: Clarendon Press, 1981.

Marder, Arthur J., Mark Jacobsen, and John Horsfield. *Old Friends New Enemies: The Royal Navy and the Imperial Japanese Navy*, vol. II. Oxford: Clarendon Press, 1990.

Matsushima, Hajime. "The Logic of Our Naval Claims." *Contemporary Japan*, vol. 3 (December 1934). This is a translation of Kaigunshō Gunji Fukyūbu, ed., *Gunshuku mondai ni tsuite* [About the issue of naval arms limitation]. Tokyo: Kaigunshō Gunji Fukyūbu, 1934.

Mauch, Peter. *Sailor Diplomat: Nomura Kichisaburō and the Japanese-American War.* Cambridge, Mass.: Harvard University Asia Center, 2011.

Maurer, John H. "'Winston has gone mad': Churchill, the British Admiralty, and the Rise of Japanese Naval Power." *Journal of Strategic Studies* 35, no. 6 (Dec. 2012): 775–98.

McDougall, Walter A. *Let the Sea Make a Noise: A History of the North Pacific from Magellan to MacArthur.* New York: Basic Books, 1993.

———. *The Tragedy of U.S. Foreign Policy: How America's Civil Religion Betrayed the National Interest.* New Haven, Conn.: Yale University Press, 2016.

Mearsheimer, John J. *The Tragedy of Great Power Politics*, updated edition. New York: Norton, 2014.

Miles, Milton. *A Different Kind of War.* Garden City, N.Y.: Doubleday and Company, 1967.

Miller, Edward S. *Bankrupting the Enemy: The US Financial Siege of Japan before Pearl Harbor.* Annapolis, Md.: Naval Institute Press, 2007.

Mitter, Rana. *China's Good War: How World War II Is Shaping a New Nationalism.* Cambridge, Mass.: Harvard University Press, 2020.

———. *Forgotten Ally: China's World War II, 1937–1945.* Boston: Houghton Mifflin, 2013.

Mitter, Rana, and A. W. Moore. "China in World War II, 1937–1945: Experience, Memory, Legacy." *Modern Asian Studies*, March 2011.

Mizuno Hironori. *Dakaika hamestuka kōbō no kono issen* [Breakthrough? Or catastrophe? This battle which will decide our rise or fall]. Tokyo: Tōkai Shoin, 1932.

———. *Umi to sora: sensō shōsetsu* [The sea and the sky: A war novel]. Tokyo: Kaiyōsha, 1930.

Morley, James W., ed. *Japan Erupts: The London Naval Conference and the Manchurian Incident, 1928–1932, selected translations from taiheiyō sensō e no michi.* New York: Columbia University Press, 1984.

———. *Japan's Road to the Pacific War: Deterrent Diplomacy.* New York: Columbia University Press, 1976.

———. *Japan's Road to the Pacific War: The Fateful Choice: Japan's Advance into Southeast Asia, 1939–1941.* New York: Columbia University Press, 1980.

Neidpath, James. *The Singapore Naval Base and the Defence of Britain's Eastern Empire, 1919–1941.* Oxford: Clarendon, 1981.

Neilson, Keith. *Britain and the Last Tsar: British Policy and the Last Tsar, 1894–1917.* Oxford: Clarendon Press, 1996.

———. "The Defence Requirements Sub-Committee, British Strategic Foreign Policy, Neville Chamberlain and the Path to Appeasement." *English Historical Review* 118, no. 477 (June 2003): 651–84.

Ness, Leland. *Rikugun: Guide to Japanese Ground Forces 1937–1945*, vol. 1, *Tactical Organization of the Imperial Japanese Army and Navy Ground Forces*. Solihull, U.K.: Helion & Company, Ltd, 2014.

Neumann, William L. "Franklin D. Roosevelt and Japan, 1913–1933." *Pacific Historical Review* 22, no. 2 (1953): 143–53.

Nish, Ian. *Alliance in Decline: A Study in Anglo-Japanese Relations, 1908–23*. London: Athlone Press, 1972.

———. "Japan and Naval Aspects of the Washington Conference." In *Modern Japan: Aspects of History, Literature and Society*, edited by W. G. Beasley, 67–80. London: Allen and Unwin, 1975.

———. *Japanese Foreign Policy, 1869–1942*. London: Routledge and Kegan Paul, 1977.

———. "Lord Curzon." In *British Foreign Secretaries and Japan, 1850–1990*, edited by Antony Best and Hugh Cortazzi. Folkestone: Renaissance Books, 2018.

Offner, Arnold A. *The Origins of the Second World War: American Foreign Policy and World Politics, 1917–1941*. New York: Praeger, 1975.

Ogata, Sadako N. *Defiance in Manchuria: The Making of Japanese Foreign Policy, 1931–1932*. Berkeley: University of California Press, 1964.

Oka, Yoshitake. *Konoe Fumimaro: A Political Biography*. Tokyo: Tokyo University Press, 2015.

Otte, T. G. *The China Question: Great Power Rivalry and British Isolation, 1894–1905*. Oxford: Oxford University Press, 2007.

Paine, S. C. M. *The Wars for Asia, 1911–1949*. New York: Cambridge University Press, 2012.

Pakula, Hannah. *The Last Empress: Madame Chiang Kai-shek and the Birth of Modern China*. New York: Simon & Schuster, 2009.

Peattie, Mark R. *Ishiwara Kanji and Japan's Confrontation with the West*. Princeton, N.J.: Princeton University Press, 1975.

———. *Kaigun: Strategy, Tactics, and Technology in the Imperial Japanese Navy, 1887–1941*. Annapolis, Md.: Naval Institute Press, 1982.

———. *Sunburst: The Rise of Japanese Naval Air Power, 1909–1941*. Annapolis, Md.: Naval Institute Press, 2001.

Peattie, Mark, Edward J. Drea, and Hans van de Ven, eds. *The Battle of China: Essays on the Military History of the Sino-Japanese War 1937–1945*. Stanford, Calif.: Stanford University Press, 2010.

Peden, G. C. *Arms, Economics and British Strategy*. Cambridge: Cambridge University Press, 2007.

Pelz, Stephen E. *Race to Pearl Harbor: The Failure of the Second London Naval Conference and the Onset of World War II*. Cambridge, Mass.: Harvard University Press, 1974.

Peterson, Stephen J. *Gladstone's Influence in America*. New York: Alfred A. Knopf, 2018.

Pomfret, John. *The Beautiful Country and the Middle Kingdom: America, China, 1776 to the Present*. New York: Picador Henry Holt and Company, 2016.

Pusey, Merlo J. *Charles Evans Hughes*. New York: Macmillan, 1951.

Riddell, Lord. *Lord Riddell's Intimate Diary of the Peace Conference and After, 1918–1923*. London: Victor Gollancz, 1933.

Rudd, Kevin. "Beware the Guns of August—in Asia: How to Keep U.S.-Chinese Tensions from Sparking a War." *Foreign Affairs*, Aug. 2, 2020.

Salisbury, Harrison. *The Long March: The Untold Story*. New York: Harper and Row, 1985.

Saito Hirosi. *Japan's Policies and Purposes: Selections from Recent Addresses and Writings*. Boston: Marshall Jones, 1935.

Satō Kiyokatsu. *Teikoku kokubō no kiki* [The Imperial nation's crisis]. Tokyo: Hōseisha, 1931.

Satō Tetsujō. *Kiki 1936-nen to nichi-bei no kaigun: nichi-bei moshi tatakahaba* [The critical 1936 and the Japanese and U.S. navies: What if Japan and the U.S. fight?]. Tokyo: Chishiki to Shūyōkai, 1933.

Schoppa, R. Keith. *In a Sea of Bitterness: Refugees during the Sino-Japanese War*. Cambridge, Mass.: Harvard University Press, 2011.

Sekine Gunpei. *Beikoku kaigun seisaku no kaitei to sono eikyō* [Revisions to U.S. naval policy and its effects]. Tokyo: Kaigunshō Gunji Fukyūbu, 1933.

Sharp, Alan. "From Caxton Hall to Genoa via Fontainebleau and Cannes: David Lloyd George's Vision of Post War Europe." *Diplomacy & Statecraft* 30, no. 2 (2019): 314–35.

Shillony, Ben-Ami. *Revolt in Japan: The Young Officers and the February 26, 1936 Incident*. Princeton, N.J.: Princeton University Press, 1973.

Simms, Brendan. *Hitler: A Global Biography*. New York: Basic Books, 2019.

Simpson, Michael, ed. *Anglo-American Naval Relations, 1919–1939*. Farnham: Ashgate for Naval Records Society, 2010.

Smedley, Agnes. *Daughter of Earth*. New York: G. P. Putnam's Sons, 1929.

———. *The Great Road, the Life and Times of Chu Teh* (Zhu De). New York: Monthly Review Press, 1956.

Smethurst, Richard J. *From Foot Soldier to Finance Minister: Takahashi Korekiyo: Japan's Keynes*. Cambridge, Mass.: Harvard University Asian Center, 2007.

———. *A Social Basis for Prewar Japanese Militarism: The Army and the Rural Community*. Berkeley: University of California Press, 1974.

Snow, Edgar. *Red Star over China*. New York: Random House, 1938.

Spence, Jonathan. Review of Jay Taylor, "The Enigma of Chiang Kai-shek," *New York Review of Books*. October 22, 2009.

Sprout, Harold, and Margaret. *The Rise of American Naval Power, 1776–1918*. Princeton, N.J.: Princeton University Press, 1939.

Stahel, David. *Operation Barbarossa and Germany's Defeat in the East*. Cambridge: Cambridge University Press, 2009.

Stinnett, Robert B. *Day of Deceit: The Truth about FDR and Pearl Harbor*. New York: Free Press, 1999.

Stirling, Fran. *The Nanjing Atrocities: Crimes of War*. Brookline, Mass.: Facing History and Ourselves National Foundation, 2014.

Sugimoto Ken. *Kaigun no shōwashi: teitoku to shimbun kisha* [History of the navy's shōwa period: The admirals and the newspaper reporters]. Tokyo: Bungei Shunjū, 1982.

Taylor, Jay. *The Generalissimo: Chiang Kai-Shek and the Struggle for Modern China.* Cambridge, Mass.: Belknap Press of Harvard University Press, 2011.

———. *The Generalissimo's Son: Chiang Ching-Kuo and the Revolutions in China and Taiwan.* Cambridge, Mass.: Harvard University Press, 2000.

Taylor, W. Cooke. *Life and Times of Sir Robert Peel*, vol. III. London: Peter Jackson, Late Fisher, Son, & Co., 1851.

Theobald, Robert A., Rear Adm. USN (Ret.). *The Final Secret of Pearl Harbor—The Washington Contribution to the Japanese Attack.* New York: Devin-Adair Company, 1954.

Thorne, Christopher. *The Limits of Foreign Policy: The West, the League, and the Far Eastern Crisis of 1931–1933.* New York: Capricorn, 1973.

Tobe, Ryôichi. "The Japanese Eleventh Army in Central China, 1937 to 1941." In *The Battle of China: Essays on the Military History of the Sino-Japanese War 1937–1945*, edited by Mark Peattie, Edward J. Drea, and Hans van de Ven. Stanford, Calif.: Stanford University Press, 2010.

Tombs, Jason. *Balfour and Foreign Policy: The International Thought of a Conservative Statesman.* Cambridge: Cambridge University Press, 1997.

Trachtenberg, Marc. *The Craft of International History.* Princeton, N.J.: Princeton University Press, 2006.

Trotter, Ann. *Britain and East Asia, 1933–1937.* Cambridge: Cambridge University Press, 1975.

Tsunoda, Jun. "The Decision for War." In *Japan's Road to the Pacific War; The Final Confrontation: Japan's Negotiation with the United States 1941*, edited by James Morley. New York: Columbia University Press, 1994.

Tuchman, Barbara W. *Stillwell and the American Experience in China 1911–45.* New York: Macmillan Company, 1971.

Utley, Jonathan G. *Going to War with Japan, 1937–1941.* Knoxville: University of Tennessee Press, 1985.

van de Ven, Hans. *War and Nationalism in China 1925–1945.* London: Routledge Curzon, 2003.

van de Ven, Hans, Diana Lary, and Stephen R. MacKinnon, eds. *Negotiating China's Destiny in World War II.* Stanford, Calif.: Stanford University Press, 2015.

Wang, Zheng. *Never Forget National Humiliation: Historical Memory in Chinese Politics and Foreign Relations.* New York: Columbia University Press, 2014.

Watson, David R. "Clemenceau's Contacts with England." *Diplomacy & Statecraft* 17 (2006): 715–30.

Weinberg, Gerhard. *The World at Arms: A Global History of World War II*, 2nd ed. Cambridge: Cambridge University Press, 2005.

Welles, Benjamin. *Sumner Welles: A Biography.* New York: St. Martin's, 1997.

Wilson, Dick. *The Long March 1935: The Epic of Chinese Communism's Survival*. New York: Penguin Books, 1971.

Wilson, Sandra. *The Manchurian Crisis and Japanese Society, 1931–1933*. London: Routledge, 2002.

Wolff, Michael, ed. *The Collected Essays of Sir Winston Churchill*. London: Library of Imperial History, 1976.

Woodward, David R. "The Origins and Intent of David Lloyd George's January 5 War Aims Speech." *The Historian*. Nov. 1971.

Xiaotong, Fei. *Peasant Life in China: A Field Study of Country Life in the Yangtze Valley*. New York: Dutton, 1939.

Yagami, Kazuo. *Konoe Fumimaro and the Failure of Peace in Japan 1937–1941*. Jefferson, N.C.: McFarland Publishers, 2006.

Yamakawa Tadao. *Rondon kaigun gunshuku kaigi no seika* [The outcome of the London naval arms limitation conference]. Tokyo: Kokusai Renmei Kyōkai, 1930.

Yang, Kuisong. "The Evolution of the Relationship between the Chinese Communist Party and the Comintern during the Sino-Japanese War." In *Negotiating China's Destiny in World War II*, edited by Hans van de Ven, Diana Lary, and Stephen R. MacKinnon. Stanford, Calif.: Stanford University Press, 2015.

Yūshūkai, eds. *Beikoku kaigun no shinsō* [The truth of the U.S. Navy]. Tokyo: Yūshūkai, 1932.

Zakaria, Fareed. *The Post-American World*. New York: Norton, 2008.

INTERNET

Japan Center for Asian Historical Records (JACAR). Digital Archive.

MacKenzie King Diary. www.bac-lac.gc.ca/eng/discover/politics-government/prime ministers/william-lyon-mackenzie-king/pages.

National Diet Library Digital Collections. https://dl.ndl.go.jp/.

"The Washington Naval Conference, 1921–1922." Washington D.C.: U.S. State Department, Office of the Historian, n.d. https://history.state.gov/milestones/1921–1936/naval-conference.

Winston Churchill. "Give Us the Tools." February 9, 1941, broadcast from London, https://winstonchurchill.org/resources/speeches/1941–1945-war-leader/give-us-the-tools/#:~:text=We%20shall%20not%20fail%20or,we%20will%20finish%20the%20job.

Joseph Connor. "Who Leaked FDR's War Plans?" History Net. https://www.historynet.com/who-leaked-fdrs-war-plans.htm.

CONTRIBUTOR BIOGRAPHIES

ABOUT THE EDITORS

John H. Maurer, a Senior Fellow at the Foreign Policy Research Institute, serves as the Alfred Thayer Mahan Distinguished Professor of Sea Power and Grand Strategy at the Naval War College.

Erik Goldstein is professor of international relations and history at Boston University. He is a Fellow of the Royal Historical Society.

ABOUT THE CONTRIBUTORS

Richard B. Frank is internationally recognized as a leading authority on the Asia-Pacific War. His first book, *Guadalcanal*, appeared in 1990. His book *Downfall: The End of the Imperial Japanese Empire* has been called one of the six best books in English about World War II. *Tower of Skulls*, the first volume of his trilogy on the Asia-Pacific War, was published in March 2020.

Walter A. McDougall serves as professor of history, Alloy-Ansin Professor of International Relations at the University of Pennsylvania. He also is the Ginsburg-Satell Chair of the Foreign Policy Research Institute's Center for the Study of America and the West, and he is the cochair of Foreign Policy Research Institute's Madeleine and W. W. Keen Butcher History Institute.

Peter Mauch is a senior lecturer in modern history in the School of Humanities at the University of Western Sydney.

Grant F. Rhode is a senior lecturer at Boston University, adjunct professor at the Naval War College, and associate in research at the Fairbank Center for Chinese Studies at Harvard University.

Toshi Yoshihara is a Senior Fellow at the Center for Strategic and Budgetary Assessments.

INDEX

American-British-Chinese-Dutch
(ABCD) coalition, 135, 136, 140
Anglo-American collaboration:
Anglo-Japanese alliance and, 99–100;
Atlantic Charter, 10, 138; British aspi-
rations for, 21, 24, 107–8; China and,
63–64; Gladstone's influence on, 24;
Hughes plan and, 29–30; against Japanese aggression, 31; Lloyd George and,
15, 26; Navy Ministry on, 54; Washington Conference and, 31, 32
Anglo-American naval arms race, 21, 25,
30, 100
Anglo-American-Japanese relations, 40,
41, 45, 50–51, 52, 57–59
Anglo-Japanese alliance: Anglo-
American collaboration and, 99–100;
British benefits from, 98; British shipbuilding for Japan, 97; Chamberlain
on, 104–5; Four-Power Treaty and, 41,
67; global power balance and, 96–97;
Hughes plan and, 30, 126; as imperial
issue, 25; Japanese benefits from, 97;
parity principle and, 30; radicalization
of Japanese politics and, 101; ratio
scheme and, 30; renewal of, 15, 20–21,
25–26, 57; United States and, 24, 25, 27,
56; U.S.-Japanese relations and, 99
Anti-Comintern Pact, 106, 130, 133
appeasement, 104, 129, 132
arms control agreements: Churchill and,
101; Gladstone on armaments, 17,
23; Hughes' proposal for, 29; Japanese
naval leadership and, 5; Lloyd George
and, 3, 17, 23; Wilson and, 17. *See also*

Five-Power Treaty; fleet ratios; Four-
Power Treaty
arms control regime, 4, 8, 9, 12, 15, 18, 23
Atlantic Charter, 10, 138
Australia, 25–26, 93, 95, 98, 105, 134, 166
Axis alliance, 7–9, 109, 110, 130, 134,
136–37, 138, 146n45, 151. *See also*
Japan; Nazi Germany

Balfour, Arthur, 3, 19, 28, 29, 100
Bell, Christopher, 155, 160n24
Britain: British army, 8; budgetary
restraint, 15, 19, 22–23, 33, 102, 103;
declaration of war on Japan, 63, 76;
defeats in Pacific, 113–17; Four-Power
Treaty and, 126; Indian subcontinent
unrest, 15; interwar era economic
decline, 103–4; Japan as competitor to,
95; Japanese attacks on, 31, 76; Japanese Navy and, 20; lack of resources for
World War II, 8; liberal international
order and, 16, 24, 32; in post–World
War I era, 3, 15; in post-World War I
Asia, 3, 93–95; ratio scheme, 38;
Second Sino-Japanese War and, 6–7;
shipbuilding for Japan, 97; Singapore
naval base, 32; U.S. and 3, 14–15, 18,
107–8, 136; war debts issue, 21; at war
with Nazi Germany, 106–13, 136. *See
also* Anglo-Japanese alliance; British
Royal Navy; Lloyd George government
British Empire. Canada, 26, 155, 160n24;
Egypt, 15; global power of, 93; imperial
coordination, 25; Japan as threat to,
94–95, 98; U.S. surpassing of, 94;